NANNIE HELEN BURROUGHS

Nannie Helen BURROUGHS

A TOWER *of* STRENGTH *in the* LABOR WORLD

DANIELLE PHILLIPS-CUNNINGHAM

GEORGETOWN UNIVERSITY PRESS / WASHINGTON, DC

The publisher is not responsible for third-party websites or their content. URL links were active at time of publication.

Library of Congress Cataloging-in-Publication Data

Names: Phillips-Cunningham, Danielle T., author.
Title: Nannie Helen Burroughs : a tower of strength in the labor world / Danielle Phillips-Cunningham.
Description: Washington, DC : Georgetown University Press, [2025] | Includes bibliographical references and index.
Identifiers: LCCN 2024444117 (print) | LCCN 2024011602 (ebook) | ISBN 9781647125271 (hardcover) | ISBN 9781647125288 (paperback) | ISBN 9781647125295 (ebook)
Subjects: LCSH: Burroughs, Nannie Helen, 1879-1961. | National Trade and Professional School for Women and Girls (Washington, D.C.) | Labor movement—United States—History—20th century. | Women labor leaders—United States—Biography. | African American labor leaders—Biography. | LCGFT: Biographies.
Classification: LCC HD8073.B87 P45 2025 (print) | LCC HD8073.B87 (ebook) | DDC 331.8082—dc23/eng/20240926
LC record available at https://lccn.loc.gov/2024444117
LC ebook record available at https://lccn.loc.gov/2024011602

⊚ This paper meets the requirements of ANSI/NISO Z39.48–1992 (Permanence of Paper).

26 25   9 8 7 6 5 4 3 2 First printing

Printed in the United States of America

Cover design by TG Design
Interior design by Classic City Composition

Thoughts of a greedy and generous woman . . .
I have been doing some tall thinking
I am going to change the day-to-day working lives of Negro women
We have been slaving for white families and the world for centuries
Now, the world will get a *correct estimate* of the Negro woman
No more working long hours for little or no pay
We will claim our God-given right to work for ourselves
Our families
Our communities
Two million of us cannot work outside of domestic service or
    sharecropping.
We need to organize around an expansive vision.
One that is full of *opportunity*.
Just imagine it:
Negro domestic workers as union members
Negro women as barbers, stenographers, print shop owners, actresses,
    waitresses, nurses, beauty culturalists, agriculturalists, seamstresses,
    laundry business owners (whether commercial or in their own
    homes)
Negro women earning a living wage in any field that they desire
Work is about the mind as much as it is about the hands.
Negro women deserve opportunities for upward career mobility
Positions where they make decisions and come up with solutions to
    problems.
A hotel maid becoming the person who checks in people at the front
    desk:
"You say there is a problem with your reservation? I will fix it."
Labor and Leisure are among the great lights of life.
We deserve wages that allow us to enjoy buying holiday gifts for our
    children, friends, and family
Buying new furniture and comfortable homes in any neighborhood we
    choose
Sending our children to the best schools
Trying on the latest clothing, shoes, and cosmetics at any department
    store
Going to plays and jazz band performances at any club of our choice

Going on vacations and staying at nice hotels anywhere in the world
Riding in clean and comfortable train cars
This is a large undertaking.
We must work on this vision from several angles:
Schools
The Church
Labor Unions
Women's Organizations
The Ballot Box
Theaters and Music
Articles, Newspapers, and Books
Businesses
Legislation
It can be done.
Our discontent is righteous and we have a burning zeal to move
    forward.
Hmm . . .
Negro women becoming a tower of strength in the labor world.
Now . . . that would be some kind of achievement.
It would be *the* wholly impossible.

CONTENTS

Introduction

Black Women's Organized Anxiety in Jane Crow America

Nannie Helen Burroughs is both extraordinary and incredibly familiar. When I first came across her papers, she reminded me of the "old-school colored women" who taught and challenged me in the public schools of Atlanta, Georgia, and at Spelman College. These daring and risk-taking teachers resonate throughout Burroughs's records. Like Burroughs, my teachers and professors were free-thinking women whose analyses and frustrations concerning the limitations of society far exceeded the four walls of their classrooms. They developed pedagogies and established women's committees and organizations that challenged the rigid boundaries of dominant ideologies and institutions that kept them, their students, and their communities from accessing and enjoying the fruits of their labors. Generations of Black people came into consciousness of liberatory ideas and have expanded the work opportunities available to them today because of the transgressive pedagogical traditions and labor organizing of Black women educators like Burroughs.

Burroughs's writings radiate with her optimism and impatience for the arrival of a society in which Black women and girls could live and work freely. In addition to the hundreds of articles, essays, pamphlets, and speeches she wrote over the course of her career, the massive collection of Burroughs's papers—which are held today at the Library of Congress—include an extensive archive of the brainstorming notes she wrote on scrap pieces of paper, on the backs of letters and school records, and in the margins of newspaper articles. These notes reveal her eagerness and determination to change the world for Black women and

1

girl wage earners. When George Schuyler, editor of *The Messenger*, the official organ of the Brotherhood of Sleeping Car Porters, asked her to write a piece for the magazine about what she considered the most pressing problem for Black women, Burroughs could not wait to type a formal response. She wrote in pencil at the bottom of his letter that Black women had "enormous economic value," but they were confined to the "limited field" of domestic service, in which they were treated as "household slaves" and did not "have a dime to celebrate [their] physical charm." What Black women needed most, Burroughs wrote, was "to be emancipated from economic slavery" so that they could "further the ideal ends of social life."[1] For Burroughs economic freedom meant Black women and girls living and working under the protections of labor, civil, and women's rights. She believed that organizing for living wages, opportunities for learning and leisure, and expanded career and entrepreneurial possibilities was paramount to Black women's movement of transforming economic, educational, political, and social institutions.

Burroughs dared to bring this holistic vision of economic freedom for Black women and girls into fruition in Jane Crow America. Legal scholar Pauli Murray created the term "Jane Crow" to identify and critique racial and gender discrimination against Black women in laws, institutions, and social movements during the twentieth century.[2] Due to legalized racial and gender discrimination during this period, most Black women and girls were restricted to working in domestic service and sharecropping into the latter half of the twentieth century. In 1909 Burroughs founded the National Training School for Women and Girls (NTS) in Washington, DC, to improve working conditions in domestic service and create new career possibilities for Black women and girls. She was among the first labor leaders to declare that economic justice meant living in a world free of racial violence and gender and class discrimination as much as it meant earning a living wage. Even if paid a living wage, she asked, how could Black women enjoy their citizenship right to liberty when they and their loved ones were always in danger of being raped, incarcerated, or lynched? After a hard day's work, why couldn't Black women spend their earnings where and on whom they wanted? If Black women and girls didn't have access to a well-rounded education, how could they obtain jobs that they wanted? If Black women could not vote, how did they stand a chance at challenging any obstacle that stood in their way? These are questions Burroughs wrestled with and addressed in her organizing for most of her life and career. Her influence in American culture and society has been immense, and it continues to shape American education, labor, and policy today.

Nannie Helen Burroughs tells the story of Burroughs's lifelong commitment to labor justice, and of the steps she took to advance her bold vision for change. This book does not cover all aspects of Burroughs's life and career, but by addressing the evolution of her labor philosophies and projects, it brings into view the scope of Burroughs's influence as a labor leader and demonstrates how Black women organized for labor rights outside of labor unions. During the late nineteenth century and for more than half of the twentieth-century, Black women were excluded from the agendas and leadership positions of most major labor unions. As this book shows, Burroughs's life reveals how late nineteenth-century and early twentieth-century Black women established their own labor movement by organizing for a new political economy and social order through their schools, churches, writings, organizations, businesses, and the performing arts.

The Black Clubwomen's Labor Movement

In 1896, at only seventeen years old, Burroughs became a founding member of the National Association of Colored Women (NACW). Among its many pioneering and important roles, the NACW was the first national Black women's labor organization. Fannie Barrier Williams, cofounder of the NACW, coined the term "organized anxiety" in the dawn of the twentieth century to describe NACW members' fierce determination to create a new world by challenging every form of systemic racism, classism, and sexism through their writings, schools, settlement homes, church organizations, secret trade societies, libraries, clinics, occupational and general education courses, travel aid societies, and employment assistance programs.[3] Transforming the working and living conditions of Black women and girls in Jane Crow America was central to every pedagogy, research report, book and article, and committee that emanated from every institution and organization that Black clubwomen established.

This book situates Burroughs alongside major labor philosophers including Booker T. Washington and W. E. B. Du Bois. While Burroughs and other early NACW members were architects of an unprecedented labor movement, Booker T. Washington and W. E. B. Du Bois are widely remembered as the major representatives of the schools of thought on race and labor.[4] Washington and Du Bois were educators, yet Black clubwomen are remembered through the middle-class and feminized occupational lens as teachers. While establishing several major labor initiatives, Burroughs played a key role in the early development of Washington's National Negro Business League, a majority-men's organization that Washington established in 1900 to unite Black business owners and create economic prosperity in Black communities after emancipation.[5] She was also an executive board member of the National Association for the Advancement of Colored People, an interracial organization that W. E. B. Du Bois cofounded in 1909 and that played a major role in addressing employment discrimination. Du Bois consistently reached out to Burroughs from the late nineteenth century until her later years to speak at the National Association for the Advancement of Colored People labor forums and to offer her ideas on Black women's labor issues that he integrated into his articles for *The Crisis*.[6] Unlike Washington and Du Bois, Burroughs did not have time to write books, a form of scholarship that is commonly used to identify leading thinkers. Maintaining a school for Black women and girls in the face of patriarchy, racism, and limited funding sources was an everyday battle that left no time for Burroughs to complete her book projects. Burroughs, however, produced a large body of writings and founded a school and several organizations that are a testament to her impactful scholarship and labor leadership.

Nannie Helen Burroughs establishes Burroughs and her NACW co-organizers as labor scholars and strategists and centralizes the work they did to remedy America's racial, gender, and class inequalities that were at the heart of its labor problem. Burroughs and her NACW comrades saw labor rights as inextricable from civil rights and women's suffrage. The NACW's expansive theorizing and organizing against inequalities made their work to address the labor problem more comprehensive in scope and thereby even more beneficial to workers in the United States and beyond.

Furthermore, the book focuses on the NTS to inspire more conversation about histories of labor resistance embedded in Spelman College, Bennett College, and other women's schools where Black clubwomen were teachers. As women who had been enslaved or whose parents had labored under slavery, Black clubwomen prioritized confronting labor exploitation and employment discrimination. They proudly declared it their responsibility as women with intimate knowledge about slavery to make the country and world anew. Burroughs was born circa May 2, 1879, in Orange, Virginia, to Jennie and John Burroughs. Like many children of formerly enslaved parents, different birth years are associated with Burroughs. Birth records in Virginia from January 1853 to December 1896 are unavailable, and Burroughs herself recorded possible birth years ranging from 1870 to 1880. The most consistent birth date that has been documented is 1879.[7] Despite the different recordings of her birth year, Burroughs was always clear that she was the proud descendant of enslaved people. She considered it her responsibility to fix a country that had subjected Black people to centuries of oppression. Burroughs also charged younger generations of Black people to take on the same mission. As she told young members of the National Association for the Advancement of Colored People at a church meeting in Washington, DC, "You, the third generation from slavery, have no right to sit here tonight and enjoy the blessings from the sacrifices of other generations, unless you, too, are willing to shoulder the burdens and responsibilities facing your race, and carry on!"[8]

Growing up, Burroughs had deep respect and admiration for her grandmother, who maintained her sense of pride while enduring the brutality of slavery, and for her mother, Jennie, who labored long hours as a domestic worker after emancipation to provide a quality education for Burroughs. Although most clubwomen like Burroughs received a formal education, they worked as underpaid teachers, and sometimes in lower-wage jobs, due to racial and gender discrimination that limited their occupational choices to teaching and domestic service. On average, no matter where they lived or how many students they taught, Black teachers' salaries were lower than those of white teachers. Like Black women who had not received a formal education, when clubwomen labored as domestic workers, their salaries were lower than those of immigrant and US-born white domestic workers.

Whether born free or enslaved, all early National Association of Colored Women members were angered by the failed economic and political promises of Reconstruction and vowed to take matters into their own hands by organizing to expand the career possibilities and improve the working conditions of Black women and girls. Clubwomen saw education as inextricable from their fight to end the labor exploitation of Black people. The politicization and violent targeting of contemporary classrooms makes clear that education remains a deeply historic battleground for Black communities.

As education historian James Anderson has argued, formal education has been used since slavery as a tool to control the labor of Black people and deny them full citizenship rights. During slavery Southern state governments enacted legislation that made it illegal to teach enslaved people how to read and write, while they established a public education system for white laborers. Enslaved Black people could be lynched or physically assaulted if they attempted to learn how to read and write. After emancipation and the short-lived progress of Reconstruction, state governments passed laws that severely limited formal education opportunities for formerly enslaved people and their descendants. Judges and lawmakers also refused to incarcerate Ku Klux Klan members and other whites who set Black schools on fire to deter Black people from pursuing an education. Black people's restricted access to formal education, along with voter suppression laws, curtailed their occupational choices.[9]

In this repressive political and economic system, Black people's pursuit of formal education and their establishment of schools and educational programs for their communities were radical acts. Education was so important to Black people and their freedom struggle that sharecroppers included an educational clause in their labor contracts that granted them time to attend school. Although Black people faced threats of violence when they pursued educational opportunities, by 1866, only three years after emancipation, Black people had established approximately five hundred schools throughout the South without help from the Freedmen's Bureau or white philanthropists. As historian Jarvis Givens has argued, when Black teachers entered their classrooms, they did not simply reproduce the status quo. They developed subversive pedagogies that challenged the foundation of oppressive political and education systems and beliefs.[10]

Clubwomen used education as a tool for resistance in their movement for labor rights. They worked inside and beyond the immediate boundaries of their schools turning newspapers, church pulpits, theater stages, and women's organizations into public classrooms to educate US presidents, legislators, labor unions, and Black, white, and immigrant communities about intersecting inequalities in the economy. They urged everyone to join their movement by taking action against the labor exploitation of Black women and girls.

Burroughs, who came of age after Reconstruction and witnessed the glaring racial, class, and gender inequalities that pursued, was keenly aware of the tall barriers Black women and girls faced to make a decent living. At the dawn of the twentieth century, less than fifty years after emancipation and with racial segregation laws in place across much of the country, Black girls and women faced a harsh career landscape. Compared with their white women and girl counterparts, Black women and girls had the highest participation in the labor force across age and marital status and worked in the lowest-wage occupations.[11] The overrepresentation of Black girls as young as ten years old in the labor force is especially striking given that native-born white girls outnumbered Black girls in the total US population.[12]

Domestic service and sharecropping—which were unregulated and the lowest-paying fields of work for women in the US economy—were the primary options available to them to make a living. And they dominated household employment: in 1909, across the nation, 81.4 percent of all domestic service jobs were held by Black women and girls.[13] With no labor protections, Black women and girls in these positions were regularly subjected to dangerous working conditions. Obtaining jobs with better working conditions was a literal matter of life and death. Black women and their children often experienced poverty, malnutrition, sexual assault, and imprisonment while laboring under the harsh dictates of white landowners and domestic service employers.

Burroughs was especially sensitive to the needs of Black girls who had been deemed wayward and were in the custody of state welfare agencies and training schools that were pipelines to prisons. Burroughs once told Booker T. Washington she accepted girls into her school that were not considered respectable enough to attend Howard University. Knowing the grim reality Black girls faced at welfare agencies, Burroughs some-times took it upon herself to call state departments and convince them to release girls into her care.[14] As historian Sarah Haley has documented, Black women and girls in the South were imprisoned for the smallest infractions and contracted out to work as domestic servant parolees in white people's homes. NACW leaders Mary Church Terrell and Selena Sloan Butler were at the forefront of challenging state lawmakers to out-law convict leasing, the precursor to the prison labor that occurs in what is now known as mass incarceration, a system that disproportionately impacts Black women and men. Considering the high stakes for Black people during the late nineteenth and early twentieth centuries, it is no wonder why Burroughs and her NACW co-organizers moved with ur-gency to establish a labor movement in defense of Black women and girls, and Black people more broadly.

The NACW saw labor rights as a nonnegotiable condition of their work for Black political and social progress. Their strong emphasis on labor was reflected in the names they chose for themselves and their institutions, such as Burroughs's National Training School for Women and Girls, and local clubs such as the Detroit Willing Workers, Provi-dence Working Woman's League, and the Jacksonville Woman's Chris-tian Industrial and Protective Union.[15] NACW members often addressed each other in correspondence as "My Dear Co-worker," and Burroughs encapsulated the significance of women's labor in her aptly titled peri-odical *The Worker*. Burroughs and her NACW colleagues authored and delivered speeches condemning elitist attitudes toward working-class women. Burroughs boasted during her speech in front of the National Negro Business League that she was a "friend of the working woman" in domestic service.[16] Burroughs was not alone in her advocacy for domes-tic workers. In an article for the Hampton Institute's *Southern Work-man*, NACW leader Fannie Barrier Williams criticized Black people who looked down on domestic service as having "foolish notions" and that they needed to help Black women hold onto a profession that was "ours almost by birthright" and was being taken away by European immi-grant women in northern cities. Williams also declared that Black peo-ple should respect the women and girls who enter domestic service out of "either preference or necessity."[17] Across their diverse regional identities and philosophies, Black clubwomen shared the belief that the entire Black community could not advance politically or economically if bread-winning Black women and girls could not make a living wage. They drew from their families' histories of enslavement, along with the quantitative and qualitative data that they collected about Black labor and housing conditions, to intervene in the race and labor problem they and their sisters faced after emancipation.

As part of their labor movement, NACW members planned conventions and conducted in-depth research about Black women's working conditions in domestic service, sharecropping, schools, and prisons. During the 1920s, while directing the Business Department of the NACW, Burroughs co-organized NACW conferences about child labor, the health conditions of prison workers, employment discrimination, and the unequal wage scales between Black and white teachers. Burroughs presented NACW findings at US Department of Labor meetings and to lawmakers, US presidents, and white labor organizations, demanding that they advocate for legislation against the labor exploitation of Black women and girls.[18] Burroughs worked closely with her NACW colleague and sociologist Elizabeth Ross Haynes to use data about domestic service that Haynes produced when she worked for the US Department of Labor to assert the dire need for a domestic workers' union.[19] While collecting data and publishing studies about the systemic labor exploitation of Black women, Black clubwomen put into national practice their philosophy that wage-earning Black women and girls deserved a right to a comprehensive education to give themselves the best chances of making a living wage and pursuing multiple career pathways. The clubs and organizations they created consistently focused on these intersecting objectives. In New York City, for example, Victoria Earle Matthews created the White Rose Mission Home. The White Rose Mission Home not only shielded migrant Black women from the dangers of employment agencies but also provided Black literary and domestic science courses. As far south as Florida, Mary McLeod Bethune started the Daytona Educational and Industrial Training School for Girls in 1904 with just five students and $1.50 to her name. Concerned about the job prospects of Black girls, Bethune explained that she was eager to begin the school because "the greatest hope for the development of my race lies in training our women thoroughly and practically."[20]

Black women educators shared a special bond as they weathered the difficulties of keeping their schools afloat in the face of racist and misogynist hostility toward Black women who dared to think, write, and organize against racial and gender disparities. As Audrey McCluskey has documented, Burroughs visited the schools of and exchanged pedagogical ideas with her sister circle of NACW educators.[21] They shared and advanced through their schools their fundamental belief that a blended academic and trade education was critical to Black women's and girls' survival as wage earners and would give them access to a wider array of occupations. As wage earners who had intimate and studied knowledge of the deeply ingrained labor problem, Burroughs and her NACW colleagues created transgressive curricula, literature, conferences, businesses, and intersectional labor studies to dismantle the hurdles that they themselves encountered in the labor market and that they knew awaited their students after graduation. They also carried their subversive strategies and philosophies into their church meeting rooms and association headquarters to effect change in a world for Black workers who would never have a chance to sit in their classrooms.

A Labor Leader of Many Firsts

No one in the NACW championed domestic workers more loudly or persistently than Burroughs. As a labor philosopher and daughter of a domestic worker, she found layered meanings of importance in domestic service. She believed that Black women's household work was not exclusively about cleaning and cooking for white families. Rather, Burroughs saw domestic workers as race leaders. In her eyes, domestic workers were best positioned to lead Black people and the country writ large into a future of racial equality. As she declared in her 1915 article "The Negro Woman's Opportunity," "The efficient service and superior conduct of 900,000 [Black] women who come in closer personal contact with the white people of this country than any other race group, can do more to create an atmosphere of respect and to change the mental attitude of the world toward their race than all the self-appointed leaders and orators at the platform."[22]

Burroughs also knew that Black people could not wait for white people to change their perceptions of them. She believed domestic workers were essential to the survival of Black people. They had constituted the economic base of most Black communities as the breadwinners of their families since emancipation. Domestic workers also held significant roles in churches, schools, and social organizations—institutions that stabilized and helped Black communities flourish during racial segregation. What angered Burroughs to no end was the preference of domestic service employers in northern cities for hiring European immigrant women as domestic workers and paying them higher wages than they would Black women. She believed that it was Black women's and girls' birthright to have preferable treatment in a field of work that they had been doing since slavery. With employment preference, living wages, and better working conditions, according to Burroughs, Black domestic workers could transform society and empower Black communities.

She committed her entire career to dispelling negative stereotypes about domestic workers and advocating for better working conditions in domestic service. Along the way, she established several historic labor initiatives. Her National Training School for Women and Girls (NTS) was the only school in Washington, DC, dedicated to training domestic workers as race leaders while charting new career pathways for Black women and girls in occupations dominated by men and white women. NTS students became the firsts and leaders in a range of fields, from the arts to entrepreneurship to education. In 1921 Burroughs established the National Association of Wage Earners, the first national Black women's labor organization dedicated to reforming household employment. Shortly after launching that historic organization, she declared that Black women could, through collective bargaining, become "a tower of strength in the labor world."[23]

Burroughs also understood that not all Black women would work as domestics. As a "friend of the working woman," she advocated for living wages and fair employment practices for all Black women wage earners. In 1912 she launched *The Worker*, the first international labor periodical produced by a Black woman at a Black women's school. In 1919 she cofounded the Woman Wage Earners' Association, the first labor organization in DC headed by Black clubwomen to study all labor matters concerning Black women. In 1922 she cofounded the International Council of Women of the Darker Races, the first international Black women's organization committed to improving Black women's and Asian women's working and living conditions. In the 1920s, Burroughs urged President Herbert Hoover to commission the first federal study about housing discrimination and the exploitation of Black child labor, and in 1931 Hoover moved on Burroughs's recommendation at last and appointed her director of a research team to study the housing crisis in Black communities. Under Burroughs's leadership, the committee went beyond Hoover's directive and produced the first federal study of unequal wage scales along the lines of race, class, and gender that subjected Black people and youth to poor living conditions. As if Burroughs had not done enough to advance the Black clubwomen's labor movement, in 1934 she established Cooperative Industries, Incorporated, the first cooperative at a Black women's school in Washington, DC.

Burroughs considered not only schools and organizations but also churches as fertile ground for organizing in the economic interests of Black women. She harnessed her early NACW training to challenge patriarchy and the devaluation of Black women's work in the church. In 1900 she led the establishment of the Woman's Convention of the National Baptist Convention. Under her leadership as corresponding secretary and eventually president, the Woman's Convention became a decision-making body that controlled the money Baptist women fundraised for the NTS and other civil and labor rights initiatives. It was Burroughs's idea to establish a Woman's Day to promote women's leadership in churches and honor women's fundraising work, which had been foundational to the survival and expansion of Black churches since their inception. Woman's Day is celebrated as Women's Day in many Baptist and non-Baptist churches across the country today to recognize women's contributions to organized religion and larger society. More women have stepped into pulpits, traditionally a forbidden space for women in churches across denominations, to acknowledge their work and express their political views about the world than they would have if Burroughs had not established Woman's Day.

Burroughs was humiliated, angered, and disappointed by women and clergymen who deeply resented her audacity to defy gender norms through her advocacy for women's autonomy in the church and establishment of an all-women's school. She also developed lifelong working relationships and intimate friendships with women and men who stood shoulder to shoulder with her as she protected and grew the NTS and labor initiatives that emanated from the mission of her school. While Burroughs was well connected with several leaders in overlapping civil, women's, and labor rights movements, she had the most intimate and enduring friendships with southern NACW women and her Delta Sigma Theta Sorority sisters who were institution builders and who came from working-class backgrounds like herself. Burroughs had two close men allies who were by her side during some of the most pivotal moments of her life and career.

Her social and political life was anything but dull. As a music director of the Woman's Convention admitted, Burroughs could be difficult to work with, and she ruffled several people's feathers. As the saying goes, she was not everyone's cup of tea, but she had to hold her own to advance her agenda among women and men leaders with huge egos. She was a blunt person who did not hesitate telling people "straight up and down" to their face or in writing what she thought.[24] Burroughs had no problem calling out Black people who she felt held the Black race from progress, "Uncle Toms." She also did not spare white people from criticism. In a manifesto, she outlined twelve things they *must* stop doing to Black people.[25] For much of Burroughs's career, she defended herself and her school against women and men who wanted to remove her from leadership positions for a variety of reasons that ranged from sexism, jealousy, and their dislike of her bold personality. Burroughs was also a brilliant, hardworking, and determined person who gained immense rewards and loyal friends across generations. While she had a tough exterior, she cared deeply for the most disadvantaged and she was emotionally vulnerable with her confidants. She achieved the wholly impossible in the labor world because of her demanding, truth-telling, and compassionate personality and because of her hard work and fierce circle of friends.

A Note on Intimacy

As I conversed with people about this book, several questioned if Burroughs was queer. As an unmarried woman, Burroughs, and her friends, likely heard rumors about her sexuality in church and organizational circles. She might have shared details about her personal life with Mary McLeod Bethune, Margaret M. Washington, Maggie Lena Walker, and other close friends, but she did not reveal much about a romantic life in her writings. She briefly mentioned in an informal interview about her life that she had experienced two romantic relationships. Both were with men, an artist and a popular pastor, but when they proposed to her, she told them that she was not interested in marriage and she ended those relationships. Burroughs was not homophobic in the strict sense of the word. She and Mary McLeod Bethune were close friends with bisexual Harlem Renaissance writer Alice Dunbar-Nelson. Burroughs did not have children, but she had an informally adopted daughter named Alice Smith. Smith was a student at the NTS, worked closely with Burroughs, and made the school a permanent home, eventually becoming a lifelong staff member.

Burroughs's overall silence about romance and her close-knit women's circle have led people to question if she was queer. As scholars Ruby Sales and Jackie Blount have argued, teaching was a profession that primarily employed women. In the early twentieth century, women teachers often lived and developed loving partnerships with each other that were sexual and nonsexual.[26] While we might not ever know how Burroughs defined her sexuality, she certainly had emotionally intimate relationships with women, as did many Black and white women educators of her time. She was also a respected member of her family and had close relationships with her mother and several family members. Out of respect for her decision not to publicly reveal details about her romantic or sexual relationships, this book adopts intimacy as a more generative framework for exploring Burroughs's personal life and how her close relationships impacted her work.

As this book takes up Burroughs's innovative vision for social change, it also seeks to humanize the woman behind these daring ideas. While working to improve Black women's and girls' lives, Burroughs worked tirelessly to help her own family. She was a revered breadwinner in her family, and that social status came with familial expectations and responsibilities. Burroughs took care of her mother, aunts, and cousins, and they helped her maintain her school in return. She was an audacious leader who leaned on women and men in her circle to wrestle with feelings of joy, anger, optimism, and doubt. She was also a complex human being who could be judgmental of both Black people and white people and a progressive, tireless, and effective advocate for women and the Black working class.

Nannie Helen Burroughs interweaves these parts of her into the story of the NTS and other labor initiatives that she established. Her range of emotions and intimate relationships speaks to the enormity of what she set out to do and the obstacles to enacting her vision. In this sense, her feelings reveal as much about her as they do about the radical aspects of her organizing work. She had an intensely driven personality. Her ideas and organizing methods shifted sometimes within a few months and other times across years. She experimented with what she thought were the best ways to eradicate the hurdles to Black economic freedom. People commonly grapple with the dynamic ideas of men civil rights and labor leaders to think through issues we face today. It is crucial to also seriously engage Burroughs's ideologies to widen the historical terrain when confronting similar issues of workers' rights, racial justice, and women's rights that continue to loom.

Burroughs's Intimate Organizing Circle

As NACW leaders who were not born into elite Black circles and whose mothers worked in service occupations, Maggie Lena Walker and Burroughs's Delta Sigma Theta Sorority sisters Mary McLeod Bethune and Margaret Murray Washington respected and understood Burroughs's passion for reforming household employment. They were loyal friends and confidants who remained at Burroughs's side and defended her at some of the most crucial times in her career. Burroughs found them just as inspiring as they did her. Brief mentions of Burroughs's visits with them in her letters suggest that they shared their innermost thoughts and feelings with each other much more in person than they did in their letters.

Burroughs had an intimate relationship with Walker, fifteen years Burroughs's senior, that would prove beneficial to her worker organizing through education and labor organizations in years to come. Walker was the first woman of any race to charter and serve as president of a

US bank. As founder of the St. Luke Penny Savings Bank, Walker created hundreds of jobs for Black women through her banking institution. She believed especially in investing in working-class Black women to give them a fighting chance in a labor market that severely restricted their career options. As historian Shennette Garrett-Scott has explained, "Black women stood at the center of Walker's vision for St. Luke Bank. Girls and working-class women—washerwomen, tobacco factory laborers, sharecroppers, and domestics—would be more than just the bank's target customers."[27] Burroughs met Walker through the Baptist church when she was a teenager. When Burroughs's own mother could not see her vision, Burroughs turned to Walker for support. Walker began as Burroughs's mentor, providing her with personal and critical financial support during her teenage and young adult years to navigate the Jane Crow job market. Forever believing in Burroughs's dreams, Walker supported not only the NTS but the National Association of Wage Earners, Cooperative Industries of Washington, DC, and Burroughs's other national labor initiatives for decades.

Born into slavery in Mississippi, Margaret Murray Washington, daughter of a laundress and the third wife of Booker T. Washington, did not establish her own institution, but she played a significant role in developing the history and women's industrial training curricula at Tuskegee Institute, known today as Tuskegee University. As historian Jacqueline Anne Rouse has asserted, Margaret was an institution builder. She wrote some of Booker T. Washington's speeches, and she helped expand Tuskegee during and beyond Booker T.'s tenure as president of the institution.[28] As an institution builder, Margaret believed in Burroughs's vision when her husband Booker T. Washington, one of the most powerful Black education and business leaders in the country, undermined Burroughs's plans to establish the NTS. Although Burroughs's senior by fourteen years, Margaret quickly developed an intimate friendship with Burroughs, each supporting the other's curricula and national and international political agendas to improve the working and living conditions of Black women and girls in the US and abroad. They also worked closely together on the same NACW committees.

Mary McLeod Bethune, founder of Bethune-Cookman University, which is still in operation today in Daytona Beach, Florida, was also one of Burroughs's ride-or-die friends. She was four years Burroughs's ju-nior, but they worked as equals supporting the expansion of each oth-er's institutions. Burroughs worked with Bethune and Margaret Mur-ray Washington to establish the International Council of Women of the Darker Races of the World to improve the working and living conditions of Asian women and of Black women in the United States, Caribbean, and Africa. As one of Burroughs's Baptist confidants, Bethune provided a line of defense for Burroughs when patriarchal leaders of the National Baptist Convention attempted to destroy Burroughs's career and take over her school.

While Burroughs had a sometimes contentious relationship with Mary Church Terrell, civil and women's rights leader, first president of the National Association of Colored Women, and Burroughs's teacher, their shared politics as labor strategists outweighed their differences. Terrell influenced Burroughs's early life, and together they cofounded historic organizations that advocated for wage-earning Black women, in-cluding the Woman Wage Earners' Association, the National League of Republican Colored Women, and the International Council of Women of the Darker Races. As honorary members of Delta Sigma Theta Soror-ity, Incorporated, Burroughs and Terrell also worked together on Black women's suffrage projects organized by the sorority.[29]

Nannie Helen Burroughs also highlights Burroughs's male allies. Men were either drawn to or were intimidated by an unmarried, assertive, and smart woman with a rare ability to command attention in a room. The most confident and intellectually curious men endorsed Burroughs's school and her other labor initiatives. Most notably, she gained the re-spect and support of Reverend Walter H. Brooks and Dr. Carter G. Wood-son, who began as her mentors and over time became her equals as con-fidants and organizing comrades. Brooks was supportive of the National Association of Colored Women, and Woodson, as historian Pero Dag-bovie has argued, had progressive gender views and worked with Black women to build his Association for the Study of Negro Life and His-tory.[30] Reverend Walter H. Brooks was Burroughs's pastor at Nineteenth Street Baptist Church, where he baptized and mentored her when she was a child and teenager. He supported her rise to leadership in labor politics, education, and the National Baptist Convention. While working alongside Burroughs to establish and expand the National Training School for Women and Girls, Reverend Brooks leveraged his stature in Baptist circles to defend Burroughs against efforts in the National Baptist Convention to silence her and take over her school.

Dr. Carter G. Woodson, renowned scholar and father of Black History Month, was so close to Burroughs that she was one of a select few who could call him by his first name.[31] They shared a love for Black history and the belief that Black history should be integrated into all school curricula. She respected his research on Black history and used his books as textbooks at her school. The books she chose as instructional materials included Woodson's detailed analysis of Black labor history during slavery and Reconstruction. Woodson initiated Burroughs's relationship with Shiloh Baptist Church, an organizing site for her National Association of Wage Earners. As Burroughs developed into a serious researcher, she and Woodson became research partners, with Burroughs counseling Woodson on his research about Black women's history. His personal archival collection contained books and rare artifacts that Burroughs gifted to him from the archive at her school. Burroughs joined his Association for the Study of Negro Life and History, now known as the Association for the Study of African American Life and History, after spending decades paying her lifetime membership fee in installments and organizing fundraising conferences for the association.

Burroughs worked with other male leaders who she was not as close to as Woodson and Brooks but who supported her labor initiatives at important moments in her life. During the early part of her career she worked closely with Reverend Lewis Garnett Jordan, historian and senior secretary of the National Baptist Convention and corresponding secretary of its Foreign Mission Board. As a formerly enslaved and self-named man who earned a doctor of divinity degree, founded a periodical, and ascended to a highly influential position in the National Baptist Convention, Jordan respected Burroughs's enormous drive to bring her big ideas into fruition. Jordan shared her zeal for education, religion, and entrepreneurship.[32] Burroughs's first steady job after high school was working with Jordan as an editorial secretary for the Foreign Mission Board of the National Baptist Convention in Philadelphia. As Burroughs told it, she did her own and most of Jordan's jobs. They continued working together when the headquarters of the Foreign Mission Board moved to Louisville, Kentucky.

In Louisville, Burroughs and Jordan cofounded the Douglass Improvement Company. The company, Burroughs's first national business venture, produced calendars and postcards for Black businesses. Jordan supported Burroughs's establishment of the Woman's Industrial Club. The club, which was housed in the same building as the Foreign Mission Board, operated like a school and was a precursor to the National Training School for Women and Girls. While Burroughs respected and worked with W. E. B. Du Bois on several labor and civil rights initiatives, she had no problem critiquing some of his philosophies publicly. She also called him out when he did not ensure equal representation of women and men in his organizing initiatives. Du Bois respected her. He made a point of promoting Burroughs's school, creative writings, community work, and labor organizations from when she was in her early twenties until she passed into history. He also sought her collaboration on his Pan-African and anticolonial projects.

Expanding the Canon of Labor Philosophers and Organizers

Burroughs engaged in multilevel organizing with her allies and close friends to transform the US economy. With the NTS as her organizing base, Burroughs integrated into her fight for labor rights organizing for voting rights, antilynching laws, and access to quality education, healthcare, food, and safe and affordable housing. The expansive strategies that Burroughs employed to address these issues illuminate how she understood labor resistance as the imaginative, discursive, and physical work of organizing against intersecting inequities across institutions to improve workers' lives.

Nannie Helen Burroughs embraces Burroughs's inclusive conceptualization of labor resistance and expands the canon of leading labor philosophers and strategists to include Burroughs and other Black women educators with whom she organized. As Bettye Collier-Thomas notes, Burroughs was "adored by the masses" for "her willingness to champion issues and causes most important to the poor and working-classes" in her multiple leadership roles.[33] By detailing her organizing work, this book establishes her as one of the most influential labor philosophers and leaders in the twentieth-century United States and reveals the powerful lessons her work and ideas still offer for US workers and social justice activists today.

The fact that Burroughs and the NTS are largely unknown to the general public is in no way due to a lack of writings about her and her historic school. She was such a dynamic leader that even in the 1920s her peers began publishing articles, books, and pamphlets to preserve her legacies in education and the church. There is also a holiday and a major street named after her in Washington, DC. This book adds to the collective efforts of scholars, journalists, community leaders, independent researchers, and students to ensure Burroughs's and the NTS's formidable work are not lost to the annals of history. As early as 1921, William Pickens, field secretary of the National Association for the Advancement of Colored People and employee of the US Department of Treasury, wrote *Nannie Helen Burroughs and the School of the 3 B's* to document Burroughs's herculean efforts in establishing the NTS and to defend her historic institution against naysayers and efforts to shut it down.[34] The following year, in 1922, social reformer and southern Methodist church leader Lily Hardy Hammond featured a chapter about Burroughs and the NTS in her book *In the Vanguard of a Race*.[35]

At the insistence of Carter G. Woodson, educator Sadie Iola Daniel devoted a chapter to Burroughs in her work *Women Builders*, first published in 1931.[36] In the mid-1930s, while coediting *The Worker* with Burroughs, Woman's Missionary Union leader Una Lawrence began working with Burroughs to write a biography about her. While the book was never published, Lawrence left behind interview notes detailing Burroughs's childhood and her rise to leadership in the Baptist world. Reverend Earl Harrison of Shiloh Baptist Church wrote *The Dream and the Dreamer* in 1956 to capture as much about her life and leadership in the church as he could, drawing on his organizing and conversations with Burroughs who was, when they spoke, quite elderly.[37] In an effort to preserve her public memory, in 1975, Mayor Walter Washington declared May 10 Nannie Helen Burroughs Day in Washington, DC.[38] That same year the city renamed part of Minnesota Avenue Nannie Helen Burroughs Avenue.[39]

Evelyn Brooks Higginbotham's classic *Righteous Discontent: The Wom-*

en's Movement in the Black Baptist Church 1880–1920, published by Harvard University Press in 1993, and her groundbreaking article "Religion, Politics, and Gender: The Leadership of Nannie Helen Burroughs," which she published in 1988, put Burroughs on the intellectual map of religious and African American history.[40] Higginbotham's scholarship laid the foundation for other scholars who, inspired to address the overall lack of attention to and study of Burroughs, produced a number of other important works. These included Opal V. Easter's book *Nannie Helen Burroughs*, published in 1995, and Sharon Harley's 1996 article "Nannie Helen Burroughs: 'The Black Goddess of Liberty.'"[41]

Another round of publications followed in the twenty-first century, including Bettye Collier-Thomas's *Jesus, Jobs, and Justice: African American Women and Religion* in 2010. In 2014, Audrey McCluskey published *A Forgotten Sisterhood: Pioneering Black Women Educators and Activists in the Jim Crow South*, and other scholars published several book chapters and articles.[42] In 2019 Kelisha Graves published *Nannie Helen Burroughs: A Documentary Portrait of an Early Civil Rights Pioneer, 1900–1959*, a timely edited volume of Burroughs's speeches and writings that rightly places her in the canon of the greatest US philosophers.[43] James Wyatt, an independent researcher, has also made key contributions by bringing Burroughs's philosophies and community activism to people beyond the boundaries of academia through his Nannie Helen Burroughs Project.[44]

Despite this important writing by scholars and community and organizational leaders on Burroughs, her position as a labor leader is not widely documented, and her work is not part of labor studies curricula. *Nannie Helen Burroughs* fills this gap. While detailing Burroughs as one of the foremost doers and thinkers on domestic workers, this book adds to the rich historiographical timeline of domestic worker organizing, as documented by Tera Hunter's *To 'Joy My Freedom: Southern Black Women's Lives and Labors after the Civil War* and Premilla Nadasen's *Household Workers Unite: The Untold Story of African American Women Who Built a Movement*. Burroughs's National Association of Wage Earners was a hallmark in the long history of domestic worker organizing, from the late nineteenth-century washerwomen's strikes to Dorothy Bolden's 1968 National Domestic Workers Union of America.

It is not enough to simply marvel at Burroughs's accomplishments; progress is never linear. The same progress she fought for must be continually fought for. In an era of threats to voting rights, women's rights, and labor organizing, awareness of Burroughs's work is especially needed. US courts and lawmakers today are gutting the very rights that Burroughs and other Black women fought for decades to enshrine in our workplaces, schools, and legislation. Her organizing against the Jane Crow economy remains a key guide for people navigating the same hurdles in the country today.

Until Burroughs passed into history, she never stopped organizing through education, public speaking, civil rights and women's organizing, and using her rolodex of colleagues and friends to advance the Black labor movement. While she did not live to see the establishment of the National Domestic Workers Alliance and its We Dream in Black Chapter and the passage of affirmative action legislation, the Civil Rights Act of 1964, the Voting Rights Act of 1965, and the inclusion of domestic workers in the Fair Labor Standards Act and various state protective laws, Burroughs's school and organizations played a tremendous role in laying the foundation for these historic acts and organization that pushed society closer toward her vision of a world full of opportunity for Black women and girls.

Organization of the Book

This book takes a chronological and thematic approach to telling Burroughs's labor history. After charting the earlier influences of her life, the chapters are organized thematically to capture how she worked feverishly on multiple fronts in overlapping time periods to improve the working and living conditions of Black women and girls. Burroughs rarely talked about herself and her family, and as a southern Black woman, I was particularly motivated to disrupt this loud silence about the early and important influences on her life. While I was growing up between Atlanta, Chattanooga, and southern migrant Detroit, elders would often ask me, "Who are your people?" "Who did you say are your kin, again?" As southern Black wisdom goes, knowing someone's family can tell you important things about people and the trajectory of their lives.

When I began studying Burroughs's papers and her work in the archives, I approached this research with my southern Black sensibilities and experiences as I sought to locate information about her early life. While delving into Burroughs's extraordinary work in several archives spread across a number of libraries, I kept asking myself, who were her people? Surely she must have been influenced by family members and mentors who helped make her unprecedented work possible. Burroughs was the visionary behind the NTS and its labor mission; the NTS story cannot be told apart from the story of her labor philosophies and life history. That story is anchored in a much larger history of collaboration with other people—a network of sharing, debate, solidarity, and support.

Chapters 1 and 2 are organized chronologically to capture the origins of Burroughs's ideas and broader life's work. The chapters highlight key influences in her early life, including her parents and aunts from Orange, Virginia, as well as the teachers and extensive network of professionals who supported her on her path to becoming one of the great labor leaders and visionaries of the twentieth century. Chapter 1, "Burroughs's Burgeoning Labor Consciousness: A Precursor to the National Training School, 1879–1896," draws from an unpublished interview with Burroughs and census and organizational records to trace how the NTS's labor agenda emerged from views Burroughs developed in her early life and career. The chapter places her labor philosophies within the life histories of her family members and the larger socioeconomic and political context of the South and Washington, DC, two geographical areas whose cultures influenced her thinking. I argue that Burroughs's groundbreaking philosophy that domestic workers and Black women laborers were central to the Black freedom struggle was reflected in her family members' life histories, the scholarly and community work of her teachers and mentors, and the Black intellectual, social, and political scenes of Louisville, Kentucky, and Washington, DC. These overlapping contexts were integral to her initial thoughts of starting a school and the emphasis on racial pride and redefining Black women's work that she would later integrate into her curriculum at the NTS.

While navigating a string of disappointing work experiences after graduating from high school with honors in domestic science in Washington, DC, Burroughs made up her mind that she would establish a school to transform education and the US economy so that no Black women and girls would have to encounter the hardships she had experienced. She was also determined to elevate Black women's work in the Black Baptist church to national and international levels of recognition and importance. As she later recalled, she was a young woman "dying to be and to do."[45] Chapter 2, "'Dying to Be and to Do': Burroughs as a Working-Class Laborer and Rising Leader, 1896–1909," details who Burroughs was as a worker and how she implemented the skills and experiences she learned from nearly a decade of precarious employment to begin challenging disparities that impacted Black women's working and living conditions. In the Black business district of Louisville, Burroughs created the Woman's Industrial Club, a small school with an explicit mission of raising wages for teachers and expanding employment opportunities for Black women. She also cofounded a domestic science institute in Philadelphia with the mission of improving working conditions for Black women in household employment. This chapter also traces how she workshopped her vision for channeling Black women's labors toward asserting themselves as church leaders and establishing financial and decision-making autonomy by cofounding the Women's Convention of the National Baptist Convention and establishing Woman's Day. Burroughs's early work in education, community organizing, and the church enabled her to create the organizational and intellectual foundation that she would build on to establish the NTS.

After ten years in Louisville, she would return to Washington, DC, where at only thirty years old, Burroughs would establish a national trade and academic school for daughters of the African diaspora, built and governed by Black women. In a country where most schools for Black students were run by men or white missionaries, a school managed by Black women was radically significant. The second part of the book begins with chapter 3, "'The National Training School for Women and Girls Will Materialize': A Timeline of Patriarchy, Land, and Ambition," which brings to the forefront the intense battles and debates that Burroughs had with patriarchal leaders to establish the NTS and a domestic-worker-centered movement. To illustrate the enormity of her struggles and ambitions, this chapter features Burroughs's exchanges with Booker T. Washington and John D. Rockefeller.

Chapter 4, "'To Command Respect and Good Living': Curriculum Building to Organize Women of the Race, 1909–1961," examines how Burroughs's multilayered agenda for achieving labor rights for Black women and girls influenced her very design of the NTS campus. Every building on campus reflected her belief that Black history, Black women's leadership, spirituality, and leisure activities, and redefining the racial and gendered definitions of work were essential to holistic labor justice. This chapter also maps the overarching labor agenda of the NTS and its distinct history. The classrooms of the school were sites of labor resistance with an underlying mission to prepare students to demand living wages in household employment and dismantle racial and gender barriers in occupations reserved for American and immigrant white women and men. This chapter shows the NTS's powerful influence on Black women's and girls' survival, employment, and ambitions during the Great Migration.

I argue that Burroughs's centering of household employment in the NTS curriculum led to the development of unprecedented labor organizing initiatives that emerged from the founding mission of the school. The chapters in the third section of the book trace Burroughs's organizing through the arts, politics, writing, and her attempt to unionize Black domestic workers. Chapter 5, "'Show the World What Negro Women Can Do in a Labor Movement': Black Women's Organizing against Jane Crow Unionism, 1917–1928," maps Burroughs's labor organizing during what I call the Jane Crow unionism era, or the period when labor unions were unwilling to integrate Black women's labor needs and interests into their agendas. Black women's systemic exclusion from legal protections and political representation was similar to the extensive obstacles they faced within US labor movements and organizations—an exclusion the term "Jane Crow" unionism captures. This chapter details Burroughs's establishment of the National Association of Wage Earners, the first national labor organization of the early twentieth century of women and men across occupations dedicated to improving the working conditions of Black domestic workers. It also places her labor organizing strategies and philosophies alongside other leaders, including A. Philip Randolph, W. E. B. Du Bois, and Amy Jacques Garvey. Chapter 5 also documents how Burroughs's vision for Black women's economic empowerment lived beyond the active years of the National Association of Wage Earners through several labor and entrepreneurial projects housed at the National Association of Wage Earners headquarters.

While presiding over the NTS and National Association of Wage Earners, Burroughs became more involved in labor politics to end pay disparities, the housing crisis, lynchings, and voter suppression. Chapter 6, "'We Are in Politics to Stay': Securing Labor Protections and Legislation, 1913–1955," maps the extension of her political vision for the NTS and National Association of Wage Earners into her Pan-Africanist organization, 1932 federal housing study, and the national and international women's organizations she cofounded and led during this time. This chapter also documents how she extended her political work and legacies by mentoring younger activists, including Martin Luther King Jr., Paul Robeson Sr., and Thurgood Marshall.

Burroughs had time to focus more intently on her creative writing and developing innovative organizing strategies during the Depression. Enrollment in the NTS sharply declined, leaving her with no choice but to shut down the school during the winter months for a few years. Never one to rest, Burroughs saw this difficult period as the prime opportunity to keep organizing, but in new and more audacious ways. Chapter 7, "'Interested in Making a Life': Beginning Anew through the Arts and Entrepreneurship, 1929–1940," maps how Burroughs expanded her organizing for racial justice and women's and workers' rights as a playwright of the Black Little Theater Movement and the president and co-owner of Cooperative Industries, Incorporated, a cooperative laundry, farm, store, and medical clinic at the NTS.

Of everything Burroughs did during her lifetime, she loved reading and writing the most. She believed in the power of literature to inspire people to work toward change. If she could have made a living as a full-time writer, she probably would have made that transition at some point in her life. Chapter 8, "*The Worker*: A Literary Vehicle for Change, 1912–1961," details the publication and evolution of *The Worker*, one of Burroughs's most enduring legacies and contributions to the Black women's labor movement. She grew her religious magazine into a national and international periodical for Black women in a variety of occupations, including domestic service, professional writing, missionary work, and teaching. Due to funding challenges and the Great Depression, she had few options but to stop publishing *The Worker* from roughly the mid-1920s to the early 1930s. She was able to revive the paper by establishing a partnership with Una Lawrence, a writer for the Woman's Missionary Union of the Southern Baptist Convention. Chapter 8 documents her writings from rare and early editions of the paper until editions published closer to when Burroughs passed into history. The epilogue, "Black Clubwomen in Labor History," reflects on memories of Burroughs from people who knew her and on the implications of her story for the study of labor history and for organizing today.

Notes

Epigraph. Mona Phillips uses the term "greedy and generous women" to describe intellectually curious women teachers. They challenged their students to think critically. They were teachers in the broader sense. They may have taught students in the first grade, twelfth grade, or at universities. Nannie Helen Burroughs was part of a cohort of women who used their classrooms to effect change for all Black women and girls during the women's suffrage and racial segregation eras. This epigraph is a tribute to not only Burroughs but the tradition of Black/Negro women teachers. Burroughs's writings, school records, and notes represent her insatiable vision and drive to create a world for Black women and girl wage-earners. LeConté et al., "Learning, Teaching, Re-membering," 124–26.

1. George Schuyler to NHB, Box 27, Folder 3, Nannie Helen Burroughs Papers, Manuscript Division, Library of Congress (hereafter NHB Papers).

2. See Murray, "Jane Crow," 232–56.

3. Williams, "The Club Movement among Colored Women," 384.

4. See "The Debate between W. E. B. Du Bois and Booker T. Washington," PBS, https://www.pbs.org/wgbh/frontline/article/debate-w-e-b-du-bois-and-booker-t-washington/; "Structured Academic Debate: Booker T. Washington and W. E. B. Du Bois," Blackpast, https://www.Blackpast.org/structured-academic-debate-booker-t-washington-and-w-e-b-dubois/; Aiello, *The Battle for the Souls of Black Folks.*

5. Excerpt taken from Burroughs's speech at the sixteenth annual convention of the Negro Business League. See National Negro Business League, *Annual Report of the Sixteenth Session*, 165–66.

6. Gray and Musgrove, *The NAACP in Washington, DC*, 56.

7. People have documented May 2, 1875, May 2, 1878, or May 2, 1879, as Burroughs's birth date. Burroughs reported to the US Census that she was born in

1880 and 1870. The most consistent birth date I have come across is May 2, 1879. I also saw this date on Burroughs's grave when I visited the Lincoln Memorial Cemetery in Maryland. See Orange County, Virginia, June 19, 1880, in US Bureau of the Census, *Tenth Census of the United States, 1880*; Philadelphia City, Pennsylvania, April 15–16, 1910, in US Bureau of the Census, *Thirteenth Census of the United States, 1910*; Washington City, District of Columbia, April 13, 1930, in US Bureau of the Census, *Fifteenth Census of the United States, 1930*; Bratton, "'Chloroform Your Uncle Toms,'"; "Nannie Helen Burroughs," Find a Grave Index, https://www.findagrave.com/memorial/45139307/nannie-helen -burroughs; Easter, *Nannie Helen Burroughs*, 25; Graves, *Nannie Helen Burroughs*, xviii; Washington, *Story of Nannie Helen Burroughs*, 13.

8. "School Head Applauds District NAACP for Its Persistence: 3rd Generation Must Sacrifice," *Afro-American*, December 29, 1934.

9. Anderson, *Education of Blacks in the South*, 2.

10. Anderson, *Education of Blacks in the South*, 6–7, 21; Givens, *Fugitive Pedagogy*, 4.

11. Banks, "Black Women's Labor Market History."

12. See table 5, "Native White Persons of Native Parentage 10 Years of Age and Over Engaged, 1900," 22; table 8, "Colored Persons 10 Years of Age and Over Engaged in Each," 32; and table 13, "Foreign White Persons 10 to 15 Years of Age Engaged in Each of 140 Groups of Occupations, Classified by Sex and Year of Age: 1900," 46, all in US Bureau of the Census, General Tables, *Twelfth Census of the United States, 1900*, Women's Bureau Records, Washington, DC.

13. Table 2, "Gainful Workers 10 years old and over, by color, nativity, sex, and General Divisions of Occupations, for the United States: 1930, 1920, 1910," in US Bureau of the Census, *Fifteenth Census of the United States, 1930*, 74. It was difficult reporting exact numbers of women in domestic service due to the private nature of the occupation.

14. Booker T. Washington to NHB, September 2, 1912, Box 36, Reels 32–33, Booker T. Washington Papers, Manuscript Division, Library of Congress; "Reminiscences of Dr. Nannie Helen Burroughs by a Number of People Who Know Her in a Variety of Capacities," September 23, 1976, Rack Number LWO 9171, Carrier Number 1957640-3-1 and 1957640-3-2, Recorded Sound Research Center, Library of Congress.

15. Fannie Barrier Williams, educator and cofounder of the NACW, wrote an extraordinary section of Booker T. Washington's *A New Negro for a New Century* that was the first comprehensive report of the organizing agenda and activities of all the NACW clubs across the country. See Williams, "The Club Movement among Colored Women," 378–428.

16. National Negro Business League, *Report of the Tenth Annual Convention*, 177.

17. Williams, "The Problem of Employment," 432–37.

18. See *National Notes: Official Organ of the National Association of Colored Women* 30, nos. 6–7 (February–March 1928): 4; National Association of Colored Women, *Minutes of the Fourteenth Biennial Session Held at Chicago, Illinois, August 3–8, 1924*; *National Notes: Official Organ of the National Association of Colored Women* 28, no. 12 (September–October 1926): 4. *National Notes: Official Organ of the National Association of Colored Women* 28, no. 5 (February 1926): 3, 8, 9, 10, 23; National Association of Colored Women, *Minutes of the National Association of Colored Women, Incorporated, Held at Chicago, Illinois, July 21–28, 1933*, 22, 42. Also see chapters 5–6 and 8 for discussion about Burroughs's labor research and presentations.

19. See chapters 5 and 6 for further discussion about the collaborative work between Haynes and Burroughs.

20. Mary Bethune, Letter to the Editor, *New York Times*, April 16, 1920.

21. McCluskey, *A Forgotten Sisterhood*, 2. See chapter 4 for a discussion of Burroughs's work with Bethune, Lucy Craft Laney, and Charlotte Hawkins Brown. Together, they are known as the Fab Four of education.

22. NHB, "The Negro Woman's Opportunity," *Washington Post*, May 9, 1915.

23. NHB, "Colored Women to Organize Domestic Workers."

24. See "Reminiscences of Dr. Nannie Helen Burroughs."

25. Graves, *Nannie Helen Burroughs*, 86–88, 169–72.

26. Blount, "Spinsters, Bachelors, and Other Gender Transgressors," 83, 87; Faderman, "Surpassing the Love of Men Revisited," 26.

27. Garrett-Scott, *Banking on Freedom*, 44, 74.

28. Rouse, "Out of the Shadow of Tuskegee," 31.

29. Giddings, *In Search of Sisterhood*, 43.

30. Dagbovie, "Black Women, Carter G. Woodson, and the Association," 22. The Association of Negro Life and History is now known as the Association for the Study of African American Life and History.

31. Givens, *Fugitive Pedagogy*, 167.

32. Jordan was enslaved near Meridian, Mississippi. After emancipation, he changed his birth name to Lewis Garnett Jordan. Richardson, "Lewis Garnett Jordan," 239.

33. Collier-Thomas, *Jesus, Jobs, and Justice*, 132–33.

34. Pickens, *Nannie Helen Burroughs and the School of the 3 B's*, 6.

35. Hammond, *In the Vanguard of a Race*, 47–62.

36. Daniel, *Women Builders*; Carter G. Woodson to NHB, August 15, 1930, Box 32, Folder 19, NHB Papers.

37. Harrison, *The Dream and the Dreamer*.

38. Murphy, Melton, and Ward, *Encyclopedia of African American Religions*, 135.

39. McCluskey, *A Forgotten Sisterhood*, 163.

40. Higginbotham, *Righteous Discontent*; Brooks, "Religion, Politics, and Gender," 7–23.

41. Easter, *Nannie Helen Burroughs*; Harley, "Nannie Helen Burroughs," 62–71.

42. McCluskey, *A Forgotten Sisterhood*; Collier-Thomas, *Jesus, Jobs, and Justice*. Some other twenty-first-century publications include Danielle Phillips-Cunningham, "Nannie Helen Burroughs, Trailblazing Black Teacher and Labor Organizer," *Washington Post*, September 5, 2022; Phillips-Cunningham and Popp, "Labor Organizer Nannie Helen Burroughs," 9–40; Popp and Phillips-Cunningham, "Justice for All"; Bratton, "'Chloroform Your Uncle Toms,'" 7–12; Murray, *The Development of the Alternative Black Curriculum*; Brown and Taylor, "Nannie Helen Burroughs (1883–1961)"; Taylor, "'Womanhood Glorified,'" 390–402; Bair, "Educating Black Girls in the Early 20th Century," 9–35; Hornsby-Gutting, "'Woman's Work.'"

43. Graves, *Nannie Helen Burroughs*.

44. James Wyatt, director of the Nannie Helen Burroughs Project, has been researching and delivering public talks about Burroughs in a variety of community venues and media outlets for more than ten years. His website can be accessed at http://www.nburroughsinfo.org/.

45. Pickens, *Nannie Helen Burroughs and the School of the 3 B's*, 27.

AN EMERGING LABOR LEADER

Yes, honey, I was in slavery, but I wasn't no slave. I was just in it, that's all. They never made me hold my head down and there was a whole parcel of Negroes just like me; we just couldn't be broke. . . . We ain't no hung[-] down-head race; we are poor, but proud.

—Marie Poindexter, Burroughs's grandmother,
as quoted in "From a Woman's Point of View,"
Pittsburgh Courier, September 27, 1930

CHAPTER I

Burroughs's Burgeoning Labor Consciousness

A Precursor to the National Training School, 1879–1896

The National Training School for Women and Girls was the brainchild of a southern Black woman with an intersectional labor consciousness. The familial, regional, and political contexts in which Nannie Helen Burroughs came of age, coupled with her own sharp intelligence, shaped her keen awareness of and her lifelong fight against systemic racial, class, and gender inequalities in the US economy. Earl L. Harrison, a friend of Burroughs and pastor of Shiloh Baptist Church in DC, recalled that Burroughs rarely revealed details about her early life. As he put it, "She never talks about herself spontaneously. For facts about herself one must prod her with direct questions. . . . There is ever so much in front of her that she has little time to spend with what is behind."[1]

Fortunately, Una Roberts Lawrence, a leader of the Woman's Missionary Union of the Southern Baptist Convention, prodded Burroughs for details about her childhood and rise to prominence.[2] Lawrence was eager to write a book about Burroughs but had only a few sources about her—a chapter about Burroughs in *Women Builders*, a book by educator Sadie Iola Daniel, and brief statements from Burroughs's friends.[3] Lawrence urged Burroughs to open up about her life. As Lawrence told her, "Please give me all I should know to do the job right."[4] After temporarily shortening the academic year at the NTS during the Great Depression to save on the school's operating costs, Burroughs had a small window of downtime to share with Lawrence her thoughts about the major influences and turning points in her life.[5] In this chapter and the next, I immerse Burroughs's and her friends' recollections of her early life in the

Figure 1.1. Burroughs circa 1909. Nannie Helen Burroughs Papers, Prints and Photographs Division, Library of Congress.

familial, political, and regional contexts that influenced her organizing and labor philosophies.

Very little has been written about Burroughs's family, but she was close to her mother and a respected member of her family. Burroughs was born into a family of parents, grandparents, and aunts who valued education, worker autonomy, and property ownership. While there are claims that her family lived in abject poverty, Burroughs did not describe her family and her early life in Virginia in that way.[6] This could have been because her parents and grandparents guarded her from the harsh realities of financial struggles. It is also possible that she remembered her family accurately and recalled the accuracy of her family's oral histories that are not captured in Virginia state archives. Whether living in poverty or relative comfort, Burroughs's family members' beliefs in Black independence and racial pride resonated with her throughout her life.

Burroughs learned the most intimate lessons about the significance of racial pride and Black women's household work to Black political and economic progress—her primary philosophical commitments—from her grandmother Marie Poindexter and her mother, Jennie Poindexter Burroughs (also known as Virginia Burroughs).[7] Although Jennie was close to Burroughs, and lived for a period of time at the NTS, little has been written about her. Burroughs's father, Reverend John Burroughs, has been described as a shiftless preacher who was largely absent from Burroughs's life.[8] While Burroughs was raised by her mother, she learned her first lessons about the significance of religion from her father, which influenced her future career as a religious leader. This chapter brings Jennie, John, and Burroughs's other family members out of obscurity to make visible their significant influences on Burroughs's philosophies and trajectory.

In the 1880s, Burroughs's mother migrated from Orange to Richmond, Virginia, and then to Washington, DC, to give Burroughs and her younger sister Maggie access to some of the best schools in the country. Joining the many other Black girls whose mothers made journeys northward during the early years of the Great Migration, Burroughs would undergo formal study, become a young adult, and first aspire to become a major figure in worker organizing and education in Washington, DC. She attended M Street School (later renamed Paul Laurence Dunbar High School)—

the first public high school for Black students in the United States. While attending this prestigious school, Burroughs was mentored and taught by labor scholars who were leading organizing efforts to improve Black women's working conditions on a national scale through their writings, research, and their organizing in the National Association of Colored Women's Clubs. Burroughs and her mother lived a few blocks down the street from Nineteenth Street Baptist Church, another lasting influence on her life's work, and where she found a lifetime mentor, friend, and colleague in Reverend Walter Brooks. Learning from family, labor scholars, and a Baptist church leader was inspiring for Burroughs, and her experiences would play a significant role in her decision to commit her life to organizing against racial, gender, and labor disparities.

Born into a Family and Region of Black Labor Resistance in the Post–Civil War Era

Burroughs was born into a family of manual laborers in Orange, Virginia, circa May 2, 1879. As formerly enslaved laborers, her grandparents and parents had established varying degrees of independence from white landowners and employers. Burroughs's maternal and paternal grandfathers were part of the entrepreneurial class of freed people who leveraged their skills to establish some economic independence from white people.[9] Her maternal grandfather, Elija Poindexter, known as "Lizah, the Slave Carpenter," purchased his freedom and a sizable plot of land on which he earned a living as a farmer before the Civil War. Burroughs recalled pleasant memories of her early childhood in Orange, Virginia, due to her grandfather's independence. According to her, what she enjoyed most as a young girl was playing with her younger sister Maggie and two white girl neighbors on a "beautiful, picturesque" plantation where Elija had built a small farmhouse. Burroughs's paternal grandfather, Sam Burroughs, also purchased his own freedom and labored as a skilled carpenter and farmer on a parcel of land that he bought and where he raised her father, John Burroughs.[10]

While Burroughs did not speak about her paternal grandmother, Mary Burroughs (born Mary Mansfield in 1835), she spoke proudly of her maternal grandmother, Marie Poindexter (born Marie or Maria

Taliaferro in 1827).[11] According to Orange County census records, Marie was a housekeeper. Although Marie had not received a formal education, Burroughs described her as a seamstress and philosopher to emphasize her skills and intellect.[12] It was Marie who taught Burroughs the importance of racial pride and Black people defining themselves. Refusing to work as a domestic worker or a sharecropper after emancipation, Marie insisted on "keeping house," or performing the everyday maintenance of her family's home and rearing of her own children.[13] During slavery, Marie proudly referred to herself as an "F.F.V. slave" and would say, "Yes, honey, I was in slavery, but I wasn't no slave. I was just in it, that's all. They never made me hold my head down and there was a whole parcel of Negroes just like me; we just couldn't be broke. . . . We ain't no hung[-] down-head race; we are poor, but proud."[14] FFV stood for First Families of Virginia and refers to socially prominent and wealthy white people in the state. By referring to herself as an "F.F.V. slave," Marie challenged the notion that white people were superior to enslaved Black people. She was just as, if not more, important than those considered part of the FFV.

Burroughs's parents John Burroughs and Jennie Poindexter married on November 19, 1875, and continued the labor resistance tradition of their parents by valuing education and migrating for desired work opportunities.[15] Burroughs described her paternal grandparents as "good livers" who insisted that their children obtain an education. Like many formerly enslaved Black people, Burroughs's grandparents viewed education as a pathway to freedom and full citizenship. As education scholar John Langston explained, "It was apparent that although African Americans had been emancipated, they were still not 'free and equal' and somehow education was to be a means of reaching this goal."[16] They also believed that education would protect them and their children from slavery-like working conditions.

Burroughs's paternal grandparents sent John and his sister Jennie Holmes to elementary school in Richmond to receive better educational opportunities than those available to Black children in their rural hometown of Louisa County, Virginia.[17] In the 1870 and 1880 census, John, his parents, and four of his siblings were listed as literate.[18] John insisted on continuing his education well into his adult years, even if it cost him personal financial stability and the ability to help Burroughs's mother, Jennie, take care of their two daughters. He was an itinerant Baptist preacher and lived in between Jennie's family household and his own parents' home while attending Richmond Institute (later renamed Richmond Theological Seminary in 1886 and Virginia Union University in 1899). The seminary was a school founded by the American Baptist Home Mission Society, with funding from the Freedmen's Bureau, to provide educational opportunities for formerly enslaved Black men.[19] Jennie did not become literate until later in her life, which was not uncommon for most Black women, who had to prioritize working to support their families, leaving them with fewer opportunities than men for pursuing a formal education.[20] Jennie's determination to eventually migrate to Richmond and then to DC for higher-paying jobs for herself and quality schools for Burroughs and Maggie and Jennie's insistence on learning how to read and write at fifty-seven years old reflected her strong belief in accessing the work and educational opportunities denied to her when she was enslaved.[21]

Early in life Burroughs became critical of patriarchy and of her paternal aunts, who supported her father's decision to put his desires before the needs of his wife and children. According to Burroughs, John was never the breadwinner of their family because his parents and sisters believed he was too smart to do "ordinary" work for wages. Burroughs's aunts opted to send money to her mother to make up for what her father did not provide. In Burroughs's words, John was a spoiled child who was tall and stern, yet a likable, well-dressed, bright, and attractive preacher. After completing the Richmond Theological Seminary, John became a traveling evangelist who referred to himself as "another [Apostle] Paul." Never staying at home for long with Jennie, Maggie, and Burroughs, he preached at churches in Virginia, Maryland, and Washington, DC, where he received gifts and lots of compliments on his sermons, but he never took charge of a church. He was a mechanic, yet he never held a steady job in his trade. Burroughs never understood why a man as bright and as gifted as John never worked much nor took care of his family responsibilities.[22] Henceforth, she disliked people who did not see the value in wage labor, and she would teach her future students the importance of hard work and establishing financial independence from men as a security measure in life.

The prevailing narrative has been that John disappeared from Burroughs's life before Jennie migrated to DC. According to the Washington, District of Columbia, City Directories, however, John lived with Burroughs and Jennie in 1892.[23] By 1900 he had moved back to Orange County, Virginia, where he lived the rest of his life with his sister Mollie B. Frye on the land where they were raised in Louisa County.[24] While John was not an everyday presence in Burroughs's life, he was in her life long enough to teach her lessons about religion and ethics, which Burroughs admitted made an impact on her life and philosophies. She recalled that while John had strict rules for her and her sister Maggie, his teachings were effective because he was never punitive. He taught them to never steal, always tell the truth, and do everything to the best of their abilities. She remembered cutting the shoelaces from his "Sunday go-to-meeting" shoes and placing them in her shoes because she thought men's shoelaces were sturdier and thereby more aesthetically pleasing in girl's shoes. After learning that Burroughs was the culprit, John sewed the laces back together, instructed Burroughs to put them back into his shoes, and said, "As long as you live, always ask for what you want."[25]

Although John was initially angry at his precocious daughter about the shoelaces, he admired her defiance and determination. He directed Burroughs's energies into a spiritual direction by insisting that she learn the Lord's prayer by heart.[26] His three-hour one-on-one Bible study lessons with her and his stern rules greatly influenced her decision to commit to the Christian faith and her belief that truth-telling, spirituality, and discipline were necessary to effect change in society. Burroughs was not close to John when she became an adult, but she had close relationships with his sisters, and she knew about his general whereabouts until he passed away in Orange, Virginia, in 1923.[27]

Burroughs's mother and aunts taught her the importance of Black women wage earners to the everyday survival of their families. She was always grateful for her mother, Jennie, who Burroughs witnessed struggle to provide for her with the low wages of domestic service and without financial support from John. Domestic work was considered the antithesis of skilled labor in the nineteenth century, yet Burroughs always described her mother as a skilled worker. According to her, Jennie was "independent, proud, sweet, industrious, and a marvelous cook." In addition to her mother, Burroughs felt that she "owed much" to her aunts for providing her with the necessary support and inspiration to face life's challenges as a Black girl and young adult. She admired her paternal aunt Virginia "Jennie" Holmes, who she described as the cofounder of an independent Black town in Virginia. Burroughs looked up to Holmes as a model for Black entrepreneurship and landownership.[28] By 1900 Holmes left her domestic service job in Virginia and migrated to DC with her husband where he worked as an elevator operator and she labored as a seamstress and housewife.[29] While critical of Holmes for supporting what she thought was John Burroughs's carefree lifestyle, Burroughs appreciated when she sacrificed to send money to her mother to make up for her father's lack of financial support. When Burroughs became an adult, Holmes thought highly of her and was proud of what she had accomplished. Holmes visited Burroughs often at the NTS and trusted Burroughs with her most confidential business affairs.[30]

Burroughs's maternal aunt Cordelia Mercer (née Taliaferro) was also an important source of support for Burroughs during her key development years. Mercer made it possible for Burroughs's mother to provide her with an education and overall better life in DC, a city that became the origin and anchor of Burroughs's adult career.[31] Similar to many Black women in the post-Reconstruction South, Jennie migrated from a rural town to various cities in search of higher-wage domestic service jobs and better educational opportunities.[32] Shortly after moving from Orange to Richmond, Virginia, Jennie learned from her biracial step-sister Cordelia, who had settled in Washington years earlier, about the even greater opportunities that awaited Jennie and her daughters in the nation's capital.[33] Cordelia more than likely told Jennie that life was going well for her in DC. She had met and in 1882 married a man named Cyrus Mercer, who worked as a waiter and earned a living wage that made it possible for Cordelia to work at home as a housewife.[34] Around 1884 Jennie left her domestic service job in Richmond and moved in with Cordelia and Cyrus in DC, where, as Burroughs described, "work was more plentiful and schools were better for Negro children."[35] With a five-year-old Nannie and infant Maggie to care for, Jennie took advantage of the unique opportunities for Black people in Washington, DC. Jennie's move to the District was significant. She exercised independence from domestic service employers and the men in her own family by settling in

DC to create her own life for herself and her children. While Burroughs left Virginia at an early age, her grandparents', parents', and aunts' assertions of autonomy over their working lives would carry on through her life's work decades later.

Coming of Age in Black Washington, DC

When Jennie migrated to Washington, DC, in the late nineteenth century, she and her children became part of the early phase of the Great Migration of Black women and girls from southern cities to northern cities. According to historian Elizabeth Clark-Lewis, this early migration of Black women "contributed to the near doubling of the African American population in the District of Columbia from 1900 to 1910," making it the city with the largest Black urban population in the nation.[36] The federal census for DC in 1860 reported that the Black female population totaled 8,402; ten years later, it had risen by nearly 300 percent, to 24,207. In 1890 the Black female population numbered 41,581, and forty years later, in 1930, it had increased to 69,843.[37] By 1900 the nation's capital had more Black residents than other popular destinations during the Great Migration, including Chicago, Detroit, and New York City.

As historian Treva Lindsay argues, Washington was where Black women imagined "New Negro" possibilities for themselves during the Jane Crow era.[38] Washington was a popular destination for pursuing careers in the arts and entrepreneurship and for seeking higher-paying teaching, nursing, and domestic service jobs than those in the South. Jennie could have been drawn to the possibility of working in the homes of government officials, who could pay higher wages than private white employers. Some domestic service jobs in Washington paid three times more than household employment in the South.[39] Black people could also enjoy themselves outside of work in DC's thriving social scene. Burroughs would eventually develop a curriculum at her school that was responsive to these varied goals and desires of Black women and girls.

Southern Black women like Jennie were especially attracted to the symbolism of Washington as the center of American freedom and citizenship.[40] There were fewer Jim Crow laws and restrictions in Washington than in most southern towns. There was mandated racial segregation in public schools and recreation facilities, but Blacks and whites could study in the same sections of the public libraries and sit next to each other in public streetcars. While racism certainly existed in DC, Jennie probably considered it a safer place to live and raise her children. She wanted her children to take advantage of the unique formal educational opportunities that Washington had to offer Black girls. Washington was home to M Street, Howard University, the Miner Normal School for Colored Girls, and the Armstrong Manual Training School. Each of these schools had national reputations as among the first and best schools for Black students in the country.

While the nation's capital was a place where some Black people could reach new heights socially and economically, it was also a city where working-poor Black women struggled to make a living. In 1900, 54 percent of Black women in Washington labored as domestic workers.[41] On average, domestic service employers in DC paid higher wages than their counterparts in the South, and some domestic workers, like Jennie, worked in the homes of well-to-do families, but they were not always paid wages that matched the long hours and arduous tasks they were expected to perform or that covered the higher cost of living.[42] Some domestic workers and their families could only afford to live in alleys that were home to mostly poor Black migrant communities in Washington.[43]

Rather than create policies to remedy low wages, housing discrimination, and other systemic inequalities that led to the emergence of alleyway neighborhoods, government officials and researchers blamed alley residents for their impoverished living conditions. Employing racial tropes that had been used to justify the oppression of Black people since slavery, lawmakers and researchers often described alley residents as inherently lazy, immoral, dirty, sexually promiscuous, and thereby undeserving of resources and policy interventions that could better their living conditions. Black people across socioeconomic classes experienced racial discrimination when buying homes, staying at hotels, and searching for jobs. Black women could shop at white-owned department stores, but they were banned from trying on cosmetic products, clothes, and shoes.[44] Jane Crow in the nation's capital made Black people—native born and migrants—across socioeconomic class even more determined to transform Washington into a place that truly reflected its democratic ideals. In the words of Paula C. Austin, the ideals were a "call to action" for elite and working-class African Americans alike.[45]

While navigating this promising and challenging landscape, Jennie and Burroughs encountered personal challenges and triumphs. Not long after they arrived in the city, Maggie, Burroughs's infant sister, died. Mourning this loss, while at the same time adjusting to a new city, would have only deepened the challenges Jennie might have faced in her life in Washington. Shortly after arriving in DC, Burroughs contracted typhoid fever and had to stay out of school for four years.[46] Caring for Nannie without an extended family network in DC and while working full-time must have been difficult for Jennie. Jennie was determined, however, to nurse Burroughs back to health, probably with the help of her sister Cordelia, who worked from home, and to enroll Burroughs in the best school in Washington, with teachers who were deeply engaged in community and scholar-activism. Doing so set her surviving daughter on a path to organize against the very institutions and inequalities that could make life difficult for many working-class Black women like herself.

Burroughs was a fiercely determined young pupil and made up two grades a year after she recovered from typhoid fever, ultimately allowing her to enter M Street School (later renamed Dunbar High School) in 1892 at the typical high school age.[47] While Burroughs was certainly a smart and diligent student, her mother. her aunt Cordelia, and others must have provided her with the informal educational support that Burroughs needed to excel in school after a four-year absence. While matriculating at M Street, Burroughs developed a deep level of respect for Black women teachers and profound appreciation for the teaching profession.[48] Teachers at M Street modeled how Burroughs could put her family's values in racial pride and education into action. Burroughs learned from and developed lifelong friendships and working relationships with M Street faculty, labor scholars who had taken on the challenge of transforming the District and the entire country into a true democracy.

Nineteenth Street Baptist Church became another critical learning site for Burroughs to develop the knowledge and skills she would use as a labor leader. She learned from and developed a lifelong friendship with its pastor, Reverend Walter Brooks, who provided crucial support for Burroughs well into her adult years.[49] The church also provided an important source of support for both Jennie and Burroughs after their closest family member in DC, Cordelia, passed away in 1895.[50] Earl Harrison, pastor of Shiloh Baptist Church, a trusted ally, and a staunch advocate of Burroughs's school, attributed Burroughs's commitment to the church to the influence of Jennie, who had been a devoted church member in Washington and had worked as a Sunday school teacher in Virginia.[51] When Jennie got on her feet and left her sister Cordelia's home, she moved to a home at 1016 Nineteenth Street, only one block down from Nineteenth Street Baptist Church, the first and oldest Black Baptist congregation in Washington, DC. Burroughs and Jennie became active members in the church, which figured prominently in the social and political fabric of the Black community in DC, and Burroughs remained a member there for the rest of her life.[52] As Burroughs later recalled, Nineteenth Street was a church attended by the "Talented Tenth" of the DC Black community. Although she came from a working-class background, Nineteenth Street became a second home for her.

Educated by Feminist Labor Scholars

Faculty at M Street included some of the world's leading intellectuals, such as Mary Church Terrell, Anna Julia Cooper, Edward Franklin Frazier, and Carter G. Woodson. Woodson did not join the M Street faculty until after Burroughs graduated, yet their paths crossed in other circles, and they developed a strong friendship that would prove beneficial to their shared projects.[53] Due to the political commitments and pedagogies of M Street teachers, Black history was emphasized in their lessons. Students performed so well academically across the schools designated for them that not all Blacks in Washington supported racial integration in schools because they thought that underperforming white students would hinder the success of Black youth. Students at M Street surpassed white high school students in the local area on standardized tests, and often with fewer resources. The excellent school system for Black youth contributed to a sharp decline in illiteracy rates—from 80 to 20 percent—and the expansion of the Black middle class in Washington between 1870 and 1910.[54]

As Burroughs declared, her experiences at M Street fueled her desire and determination to become an educator. Crucially, at M Street Burroughs was exposed to educators who advocated for labor protections for Black women through their writings, speeches, and community work. She was taught by Julia Mason Layton, a towering activist in the District and a leader in the National Association of Colored Women and the Baptist church who advocated for the poor and Black working-class while directing women's clubs and civil rights organizations. Layton's and Burroughs's paths also crossed at Nineteenth Street Baptist Church, where they were both members. Layton was a role model for Burroughs on how to combine education, spiritual beliefs, and community activism to fight for labor rights. Layton would later advocate for the NTS when it was just an idea for Burroughs. Layton was so supportive of Burroughs's idea of establishing the NTS that Burroughs listed her on the school's property title, and Layton served on the NTS board of trustees from its inception until she passed into history.[55] Mary Church Terrell and Anna Julia Cooper also made strong impressions on Burroughs's career trajectory. Terrell and Cooper were outspoken about the exploitation of Black women and girl workers. Burroughs looked up to them, and her future career and vision paralleled their scholar-activism.[56]

Burroughs had deep admiration for Cooper, describing her as the "most dignified person she had ever seen."[57] She credited Cooper for seeing promise in her entrepreneurial interests and abilities at an early age. Burroughs recalled that Cooper smiled at her encouragingly and urged her to concentrate in business courses at M Street. Burroughs took her advice and majored in business in addition to domestic science. The training she received in the business courses set a strong foundation for her entrepreneurial plans more than a decade later. Cooper's encouragement to pursue entrepreneurial opportunities inspired Burroughs to open a dry goods store with six of her peers the year before graduating from M Street. Although the store never opened, Burroughs never gave up on the idea and started several women's businesses throughout her adult career.[58] Cooper was impressed with Burroughs's overall performance at M Street and wrote supportive letters of recommendation on her behalf for future jobs.[59] Burroughs did not volunteer complimentary remarks about Terrell. This could have been for a host of reasons; they might have had conflicting personalities. But Burroughs bonded most

Figure 1.2. Drawing of Layton in the DC newspaper *The Colored American*, April 25, 1903.

strongly with other Black women from working-class backgrounds, and Terrell came from an affluent background, whereas Cooper's mother was a domestic worker like Burroughs's. Despite their differences, Burroughs and Terrell shared similar philosophies and politics, and they worked closely together in organizations when Burroughs became an adult.

Burroughs would develop Cooper's and Terrell's pedagogical philosophy that Black women and girls should have a combined vocational and liberal arts education. As education scholar Karen Johnson has argued, Terrell and Cooper cared deeply about the futures of their students, and they believed this blended curriculum would minimize their students' chances of being subjected to exploitative jobs and maximize their opportunities for pursuit of higher learning and careers that interested

Figure 1.3. Labor organizer, educator, suffragist, and civil rights activist Mary Church Terrell, circa 1880–1900, around the time she taught Burroughs at M Street High School. Prints and Photographs Division, Library of Congress.

Figure 1.4. Labor philosopher, educator, suffragist, and civil rights activist Anna Julia Cooper, circa 1903–1904. Prints and Photographs Division, Library of Congress.

them most.[60] When Burroughs became an educator herself, she designed a blended academic and trade curriculum for her school, and she harnessed the spirit of labor resistance similar to what Terrell and Cooper had espoused through their teaching, community organizing, and institution building.

The same year Burroughs entered M Street, Cooper published *A Voice of the South by a Black Woman from the South*. While this classic is known today as a foundational text for Black feminist thought, it was also among the first intersectional studies of labor exploitation in the South. Burroughs was mentored by this scholar with strong labor politics and who had produced a groundbreaking book asserting the importance of Black women's labor. Cooper condemned white landowners who exploited Black sharecropping men:

> there are tenants holding leases on farms who toil sixteen hours to the day and work every chick and child in their possession, not even sparing the drudging wife—to find at the end of the harvesting season and the squaring up of accounts that their accumulations have been like gathering water in a sieve. Do you ask the cause of their persistent poverty? It is not found in the explanation often vouchsafed by the white landlord—that the Negro is indolent, improvident and vicious.[61]

Cooper also advocated for better working conditions for Black laundresses. She was especially angered by the racial privileges of white immigrant women in the North, who could easily find jobs in stores, while Black women in the South were "bending over wash-tubs and ironing boards... lugging home weekly great baskets of clothes for families who pay them for a month's laundry barely enough to purchase a substantial pair of shoes." She declared that this glaring inequality demonstrated that the labor interests of Black people "in this country are as yet dumb and limp."[62] When she became an educator and writer herself, Burroughs advanced Cooper's advocacy for Black laundresses through her curriculum and writings.[63]

Cooper was an excellent model for the research methods Burroughs would later use to show the unequal wage scales between Black women and white workers.[64] In *A Voice from the South*, Cooper discussed the importance of research methods that challenged racial biases in quantitative data to illuminate Black workers' immense "billions of wealth given by them to enrich another race" in contrast to the wages they received or were never paid. As she put it,

> One would like to be able to give reliable statistics of the agricultural and mechanical products of the colored laborer, but so far I have not been able to obtain them. . . . Our efficient and capable census enumerators never draw the color line on labor products. You have no trouble in turning the page that shows exactly what percentage of colored people are illiterate, or just how many have been condemned by the courts. . . . Crime statistics and illiteracy statistics must be accurately detailed—and colored.[65]

Cooper used feminist methodologies to estimate just how much prison laborers, domestic workers, and sharecroppers contributed to the wealth of the nation to advocate for worker protections and living wages. She would later preside over Frelinghuysen University and establish the Hannah Stanley Opportunity School to provide accessible educational opportunities to working-class Black people and people with disabilities. Similar to Cooper's missions for Frelinghuysen University and the Hannah Stanley Opportunity School, Burroughs would also establish a school that was accessible to disabled and working-class Black students.[66]

Burroughs aspired to become a public figure like Mary Church Terrell. She led M Street's literary society and volunteered to participate in all school debates to sharpen her public speaking skills. While Burroughs and Terrell did not always see eye-to-eye personally, they would become collaborators in several organizations after Burroughs became an adult because of their shared labor, women's, and civil rights politics. Mary Church Terrell provided an example for Burroughs of how to integrate labor research and resistance into women's organizations. While serving as the first president of the National Association of Colored Women, Terrell leveraged the organization's resources to launch the first national campaign against convict leasing and chain gangs.[67] Terrell supported her NACW colleague Selena Sloan Butler's groundbreaking research about the exploitation of Black prisoners in Milledgeville, Georgia, and helped organize Margaret Murray Washington's public reading of Butler's study at the 1896 NACW Convention in Nashville, Tennessee.[68] After learning about prison conditions from Butler's research, Terrell became much more involved in the prison reform movement. Mapping the historical context of prison labor, Terrell later declared in her own speech "Peonage in the United States" that southern governments enacted "vagrant or peonage laws" to "reduce the newly emancipated slaves to a bondage almost as cruel, if not quite as cruel, as that from which they had just been delivered."[69] Nineteenth Street Baptist Church also had a major impact on Burroughs's life that inspired her to become a community organizer and public speaker. It was at this historic church that she learned how to combine her labor politics with religion.

Learning to Put Faith to Work

As a teenager, Burroughs was so serious about becoming a public leader that she wanted to take public speaking courses at Emerson, a private high school in DC, but she could not afford the course fees.[70] She received the training she needed and more at Nineteenth Street, where Reverend Walter H. Brooks impressed upon her the importance of "getting some religion." Burroughs recalled that Reverend Brooks was wise, handsome, and nice to everyone in the congregation. Brooks baptized Burroughs, and she was drawn to how he taught biblical lessons to the children of the church.[71] She learned from his visits to church members' homes how to connect with community members and she would later adopt his interpersonal communication style as a young adult community organizer. She had lots of fun as a member of his church, and she was inspired to join every church group associated with young people.[72] Burroughs practiced developing her public speaking skills by constantly asking Reverend Brooks to list her as a speaker on church programs.[73] Practice made perfect: Burroughs became known for her unmatched oratory skills early in her career.

Nineteenth Street was a church where people could seamlessly integrate their spiritual faith, community work, and public speaking against structural inequalities and where people could meet like-minded social activist leaders.[74] Reverend Brooks was a strong advocate for Black women's organizations, and he hosted the founding meeting of the National Association of Colored Women at his church. Expressing his optimism and support of the NACW at this historic meeting, Burroughs's pastor

Figure 1.5. Reverend Walter H. Brooks, pastor of Nineteenth Street Baptist Church. Nannie Helen Burroughs Papers, Prints and Photographs Division, Library of Congress.

told attendees that the meeting was a "happy indication of the dawning of a better and brighter day, when the best women of the land unite in one mighty company."[75] In 1896, at only seventeen years old, Burroughs attended the founding meeting of the NACW. It must have been inspiring to see her mentors Mary Church Terrell and Anna Julia Cooper as NACW leaders and other powerful women leaders such as Harriet Tubman at the meeting. The association's motto, Lifting as We Climb, communicated its members' central mission of helping others in their communities as they helped themselves. The NACW membership consisted of Black women educators, healthcare workers, domestic workers, philanthropists, journalists, creative writers, and artists who banded together to fight against intersecting racial and gender inequalities in the US economy and abroad. Burroughs would work within the NACW to launch her labor initiatives.

Until then, she continued learning organizing skills from Reverend Brooks. He was a sounding board for her early career ideas, and she later thanked him for "his noble example" and "constant advice" regarding her life's work.[76] As Burroughs claimed, attending M Street and Nineteenth Street Baptist Church made such an enormous impact on the trajectory of her life that she decided while a student that she would eventually start her own school in DC. She imagined herself in the position of her M Street teachers, who were pleased to see "girls with many books and happy faces going up and down the broad stairway at school," girls who were "really going somewhere" in life. Burroughs also desired to see "girls going up" by changing their working conditions through education.[77]

After graduating from M Street, Burroughs encountered a string of disappointing experiences that left her precariously employed for nearly ten years and made her even more determined to make a mark in education. She moved back and forth between DC and Philadelphia to acquire stable employment. Afterward, she moved to Louisville, Kentucky, where she would experiment with her ideas on education, domestic science, and challenging institutions and ideologies that impacted Black women's working and living conditions. While this was not the path she had dreamed for herself, she took what she learned from these experiences to position herself as a rising labor leader in education and the church.

Notes

1. Harrison, *The Dream and the Dreamer*, 8.

2. The Woman's Missionary Union was an auxiliary group of the predominantly white Southern Baptist Convention. For Burroughs's responses to her interview questions, see Box 1, Folder 23, Una Lawrence Collection, Southern Baptist Convention Historical Library and Archives.

3. See Daniel, "Nannie Helen Burroughs: Youth in the Quest of Opportunity," in Daniel, *Women Builders*.

4. Una Lawrence, notes from interview with NHB, Box 1, Folder 23, Una Lawrence Collection.

5. NHB, "Plan to Close Training School," 1933, Box 46, Folder 24, NHB Papers.

6. See Bratton, "'Chloroform Your Uncle Toms,'" 8; Perkins, "Nannie Helen Burroughs," 231.

7. Jennie's last name became Bell after she divorced John and married her second husband. See Nannie Helen Burroughs's obituary, "A Faith That Has Overcome," Box 195–3, Folder 12, Andrew Lee Gill Papers, Moorland-Springarn Research Center, Howard University.

8. The spelling of Burroughs's paternal family name varies between Burrus, Burruss, and Burroughs in census, death, and marriage records. The most con-

sistent names used in Orange County, Virginia, records were Burruss and Burrus, and at times, Burroughs on death certificates. Burroughs was the only spelling of Jennie's, John's, and Nannie's last names in Washington, DC, records. See Orange County, Virginia, June 16, 1870, June 23, 1880, and June 20, 1900, in US Bureau of the Census, *Ninth Census of the United States, 1870*; John Burroughs, May 4, 1923, Certificate of Death, Bureau of Vital Records, Virginia Department of Health; John Burruss and Jennie Poindexter, December 31, 1875, Orange County, Virginia, Register of Marriages.

9. Hammond, *In the Vanguard of a Race*, 47–48.

10. Una Lawrence, Interview with NHB, n.d., Box 1, Folder 32, Una Lawrence Collection.

11. See Orange County, Virginia, July 14, 1870, in US Bureau of the Census, *Tenth Census of the United States, 1880*.

12. Her name appears as either Marie or Maria in US federal census records. I use Marie throughout the chapter because it is the name that Burroughs used to refer to her grandmother.

13. Bratton, "'Chloroform Your Uncle Toms,'" 8.

14. NHB, "From a Woman's Point of View," *Pittsburgh Courier*, September 27, 1930, 6.

15. John Burruss and Jennie Poindexter, December 31, 1875, Orange County, Virginia, Register of Marriages.

16. King-Calnek, "John Mercer Langston," 35.

17. John had one older brother, Albert Burruss. See Orange County, Virginia, June 16, 1870, in US Bureau of the Census, *Ninth Census of the United States, 1870*.

18. See Orange County, Virginia, in US Bureau of the Census, *Ninth Census of the United States, 1870*; Bratton, "'Chloroform Your Uncle Toms,'" 8.

19. Corey, *A History of the Richmond Theological Seminary*, 88.

20. Clark-Lewis, *Living In, Living Out*, 41.

21. According to the Pennsylvania census, Jennie had learned to read and write by 1910. See Bratton, "'Chloroform Your Uncle Toms,'" 9.

22. Lawrence, notes from interview with NHB.

23. They were living together at 1022 Twentieth Street Northwest; U.S. City Directories, 1822–1995: Washington, District of Columbia, City Directory, 1892.

24. See Virginia, in US Bureau of the Census, *Twelfth Census of the United States, 1900*; population, Orange County, Virginia, in US Bureau of the Census, *Thirteenth Census of the United States, 1910*.

25. Lawrence, notes from interview with NHB.

26. Lawrence, notes from interview with NHB.

27. Certificate of Death 16175, May 2, 1923, Bureau of Vital Records, Virginia Department of Health.

28. Lawrence, notes from interview with NHB.

29. See Washington City, in US Bureau of the Census, *Twelfth Census of the United States, 1900*; U.S. City Directories, 1822–1995: Washington, District of Columbia, City Directory, 1928.

30. Lawrence, notes from interview with NHB.

31. Lawrence, interview with NHB.

32. Jennie's, John's, and Nannie's last name was spelled Burroughs after they migrated to Washington, DC. See U.S. City Directories, 1822–1995: Washington, District of Columbia, City Directory, 1892.

33. Cordelia was Marie Poindexter's daughter with an unidentified white man. Marie gave Cordelia her maiden name (Taliaferro). Before migrating to DC, Cordelia lived in a home next to Marie and the rest of the Poindexter family in Orange County. See Orange County Virginia, June 14, 1870, in US Bureau of the Census, *Ninth Census of the United States, 1870*.

34. See U.S. City Directories, 1822–1995: Washington, District of Columbia, City Directory, 1886, 291.

35. Lawrence, interview with NHB.

36. Clark-Lewis, *Living In, Living Out*, 68.

37. Harley, "Beyond the Classroom," 254.

38. Lindsay, *Colored No More*, 9.

39. McCluskey, *A Forgotten Sisterhood*, 47.

40. McCluskey, 47.

41. Higginbotham, *Righteous Discontent*, 217.

42. Clark-Lewis, *Living In, Living Out*, 68–69.

43. Borchert's *Alley Life in Washington* was one of the first studies about alley communities in DC.

44. Austin, *Coming of Age in Jim Crow DC*, 42–43, 44–45.

45. For a history of how working-poor Blacks resisted the racial and class boundaries of legal segregation in DC, see Austin's *Coming of Age in Jim Crow DC*. For a study of how Mary Church Terrell led the fight to end Jim Crow in DC, see McCluskey, "Setting the Standard," 47.

46. McCluskey, *A Forgotten Sisterhood*, 104.

47. McCluskey, 104.

48. Burroughs named several M Street teachers who influenced her future trajectory. See Lawrence, notes from interview with NHB.

49. Lawrence, interview with NHB.

50. Cordelia died at forty years old and was buried in Columbian Harmony Cemetery, the same cemetery as Burroughs's paternal aunt Jennie Holmes. See Cordelia Mercer, District of Columbia Select Deaths and Burials Index, 1769–1960, Reference ID: 105534.

51. Graves, *Nannie Helen Burroughs*, xxi.

52. Lawrence, interview with NHB. See Burroughs's funeral program, May 25, 1961, Box 195–3, Folder 12, Andrew Lee Gill Papers.

53. Woodson became a faculty member at M Street in 1911. Givens, *Fugitive Pedagogy*, 57. See chapters 4, 5, and 6 of this book for further discussion about Burroughs's work with Woodson.

54. Ruble, *Washington's U Street*, 67–68.

55. Robinson, "Julia Mason Layton, 1859–1926," 16–17; Minutes, in National Baptist Convention, *Journal of the Thirty-Sixth Session*, 58.

56. Lawrence, notes from interview with NHB.

57. Lawrence, notes from interview with NHB.

58. Hammond, *In the Vanguard of a Race*, 12.

59. Lawrence, notes from interview with NHB.

60. Johnson, "On Classical versus Vocational Training," 47–68.

61. Quoted from Cooper, *A Voice from the South*, 253.

62. Cooper, *A Voice from the South*, 255.

63. See chapter 8 for discussion of Burroughs's advocacy for laundresses.

64. See chapter 6 for discussion about Burroughs's 1931 federal housing study.

65. Cooper, *A Voice from the South*, 268.

66. See Vivian M. May's discussion about Frelinghuysen University and the Hannah Stanley Opportunity School in *Anna Julia Cooper, Visionary Black Feminist*, 35–36, 68.

67. Haley, *No Mercy Here*, 123.

68. Butler, *The Chain-Gang System*.

69. Mary Church Terrell, "Peonage in the United States," August 1907, Mary Church Terrell Papers, Library of Congress (hereafter LOC).

70. Lawrence, notes from interview with NHB.

71. Lawrence, notes from interview with NHB.

72. For more information about the activist history of Nineteenth Street, see Moore, *Leading the Race*, 70–85.

73. Lawrence, notes from interview with NHB.

74. Lewis and Taylor, *Unsung Legacies of Educators and Events*, 10.

75. Leslie, *The History of the National Association of Colored Women's Clubs*, 43.

76. Johnson, *Uplifting the Women and the Race*, 148.

77. Lawrence, notes from interview with NHB.

CHAPTER 2

"Dying to Be and to Do"

Burroughs as a Working-Class Laborer and Rising Leader, 1896–1909

In 1896 Burroughs completed her high school education at M Street. She graduated with honors, a concentration in business and domestic science, and extensive coursework in literature, economics, and social science.[1] After graduation, she hoped to earn a comfortable salary and live out her dreams with the comprehensive education she had received from a premier school. In Burroughs's words, she was a young woman with big plans, "dying to be and to do."[2] Little did she know there would be many obstacles to confront along the way. Her initial plan was to save up money working as an assistant domestic science teacher for a few years to support her mother, enroll in the Boston School of Oratory and become a full-time literary writer and elocutionist, and live a comfortable life.[3] Instead, after graduation, she faced a nearly ten-year period of unemployment and underemployment, navigating the hurdles of race, class, and gender discrimination.[4]

Burroughs had been counting on a domestic science teacher she knew to put in a good word for her in the DC public school system. But either the teacher did not keep her promise or did not advocate strongly for Burroughs. Burroughs resented the teacher for several years afterward, attributing the school's rejection of her for a position to her dark skin and working-class background.[5] While skin tone could have contributed to Burroughs's experience, the District's Board of Education also turned on her former teacher and mentor Anna Julia Cooper in a vicious way when she became principal of M Street. Cooper's social status as a fair-skinned Black woman and scholar did not protect her from the board painting her as incompetent, too sympathetic toward "weak pupils," and involved in a romantic relationship with her foster son. Although Cooper's accusers could not produce any substantial evidence to support their claims, the board voted to remove her from her position in 1906.[6] Like Cooper, Burroughs was outspoken, unmarried, and came from a working-class background.

Unable to find a job as a teacher in DC—despite the fact that teaching in Black schools was one of the few jobs formally educated Black women could access in the late nineteenth and early twentieth centuries— Burroughs encountered challenges obtaining a job outside the District as well. She courageously asked Booker T. Washington, president of Tuskegee Institute and the most powerful Black leader in education, for help in obtaining a position in stenography at any school in the country. Hoping to impress Washington, she indicated in her letter that she could furnish strong recommendation letters from her teachers Anna Julia Cooper and Julia Layton and mentor Reverend Walter Brooks.[7] Washington replied that he could not help her. His dismissive response must have been disappointing to her, especially considering his towering influence in education. She had admired Washington's institution-building work at Tuskegee Institute and his philosophies about the importance of entrepreneurship and manual labor to Black people's economic progress.[8]

Burroughs was devastated. She had graduated with honors from a prestigious school and could not obtain gainful employment in fields she had mastered. As Burroughs recalled, "It broke me up at first. I had my life all planned out, to settle down in Washington with my mother, do that pleasant work, draw a good salary and be comfortable for the rest of my life." Her postgraduation experiences ultimately inspired her to open a school that "would give all sorts of girls a chance," irrespective of class status and religious affiliation.[9] As Burroughs told her friend Pastor Earl Harrison,

> somehow, an idea was struck out of the suffering of that disappointment— that I would someday have a school here in Washington that politics had nothing to do with, and that would give all sorts of girls a fair chance and help them overcome whatever handicaps they might have. It came to me like a flash of light, and I knew I was to do that thing when the time came.

But I couldn't do it yet, so I just put the idea away in the back of my head and left it there.[10]

While planning to open her own school, she worked for the National Baptist Convention, the largest organization of Black Baptists in the country, in Philadelphia and Louisville. She acquired significant experiences and skills and established a national reputation that prepared and positioned her to eventually lead a groundbreaking school. In keeping with Burroughs's advocacy for recognizing the value of Black women's work that was often ignored, this chapter documents who Burroughs was as a worker and the labors of Baptist women and members of the National Association of Colored Women who helped her along the way to her rise in national leadership.

Burroughs's Career Start in Philly

Similar to Black women who migrated to various cities in search of secure employment during the late nineteenth century, Burroughs left the District for Philadelphia in the 1890s. Reverend Brooks had put in a good word for her to work there as an associate editor for the *Christian Banner*, a weekly Baptist paper that the National Baptist Convention later adopted as its official organ. Initially, Burroughs was not thrilled about working as an editor, and she did not see it as useful for her future plans. But since it was the only job available to her at the time, she focused on honing what skills she could learn there and growing from the experience. As her employer said, "We have never had her equal. She is a dynamo in an office."[11] It is altogether possible that Burroughs was not only an efficient editor but that she grew to like some aspects of her job in Philadelphia. As a newspaper editor for the *Christian Banner*, she had opportunities to write about racial injustices and religious issues of interest to her, yet editing was laborious work.[12] It required long hours of careful detailing and reading, writing editorials herself, communicating consistently with the managing editor, and soliciting and editing stories from Baptist associations and churches across the country to include in the newspaper.

While working for the paper, Burroughs was approached by a well-known domestic science expert to teach at a domestic science institute in Philly. After work hours, she took advanced courses with the teacher and ultimately decided to decline her domestic science institute job offer because she came to see her job for the *Christian Banner* as a unique opportunity for her to change the economic circumstances of Black women and girls.[13] Despite the benefits of her editing position, she still wanted to earn a higher wage and live in DC. After a short time in Philadelphia, Burroughs returned home with hopes of securing higher-wage employment as a government clerk.

Between the 1880s and 1910s, Black women and men increasingly held government jobs in Washington that paid middle-class wages. A clerk position would have provided a plethora of work opportunities for the young Burroughs, who was eager to create a life for herself without barriers. As a clerk, Burroughs would have made a middle-class salary, and she would have been able to work as a typist, stenographer, transcriber, statistician, assistant librarian, indexer, or cataloger.[14] Her desire to attain a government job, one of the most secure types of employment for a woman of any race to have at the time, might have also been informed by her need for a salary that would have allowed her to take care of herself and her mother. Women clerks who worked for the government earned wages that allowed them to not only meet their daily living costs but also accumulate savings and purchase land and property.[15]

Going after a clerk job was a bold decision for Burroughs to make, especially considering that it was primarily white, US-born, middle-class women—who were *also* the daughters, wives, or widows of men who worked as lawyers, doctors, ministers, and government clerks—who were hired for this type of position. While federal jobs were more available to Black people than in the following years, during President Woodrow Wilson's administration, racism was still ever present during this era of opportunity for women.[16] Burroughs's mother, Jennie, wanted to shield her from further disappointment. She recommended to Burroughs that she apply for domestic service positions. Jennie must have told her employer about Burroughs's hardships as well as her plans to apply for a clerical position. As Jennie told Burroughs, her employer had told her that Black women were hardly ever employed in the clerical fields. In Burroughs's words, Jennie wanted to protect her from the embarrassment of "going on a wild goose chase" by advising her to pursue domestic service positions that she knew she could obtain.[17] Undeterred by Jennie's advice, Burroughs studied for and passed the civil service exam with high marks. When she applied for clerical jobs, however, employers told her that they were not hiring "colored clerks."[18]

After Burroughs was denied clerk positions, she worked as a janitor and a bookkeeper in a small office firm in DC with hopes again of acquiring a comfortable teaching position. Although she worked for a small business, she performed arduous work. If her duties as a janitor were consistent with those of most janitors, she would have had cleaning and organizational responsibilities such as sweeping, mopping, scrubbing floors, cleaning windows and mirrors, sanitizing sinks and toilets, supplying restrooms with soap and toilet paper, replenishing and organizing cleaning supplies, and maintaining a daily record and count of supplies, equipment, and the work that she had completed. Office cleaning work remains underpaid, and while it takes a lot of time, energy, and concentration to perform it today, it probably took Burroughs even more effort to complete her routine with less advanced cleaning resources in the late nineteenth century and while tending to her other office responsibilities.

Adding to Burroughs's work description, her duties as a bookkeeper would have included recording the financial transactions of the board in journals and ledgers manually or by typewriter, documenting employees' wages, balancing the company accounts, and overseeing the company's management system.[19] This was a responsibility that required a lot of attention to detail, including meticulous and perfect financial management and documentation skills. Working for a small company would have also meant more work for Burroughs than for bookkeepers at large companies where the bookkeeping duties were often divided among multiple employees. Burroughs likely made less than her white counterparts in bookkeeping. On average, women made less than men in office jobs, especially as bookkeeping became a women-dominated occupation in the late 1800s and early 1900s. Black women bookkeepers made even less than white women in the same occupation.[20]

Eager to leave her job in DC, Burroughs decided to take a job in Philadelphia as a bookkeeper and editorial secretary for Reverend Lewis G.

Figure 2.1. Maggie Lena Walker posing in a studio in Brooklyn, New York, circa 1900–1910. US National Park Service Photo Collection, Maggie L. Walker National Historic Site, Richmond, Virginia.

Jordan. Jordan was the historian and senior secretary of the National Baptist Convention, corresponding secretary of its Foreign Mission Board, and founder of the convention's *Afro-American Mission Herald*. Burroughs was eager to get to her new job, but there was just one problem. She did not have the funds to get to the City of Brotherly Love.[21] Burroughs's mentor and friend Maggie Lena Walker loaned four hundred dollars to "a woman unknown to that world" but who "she dearly loved" to get to Philadelphia, financial support that would prove crucial in Burroughs's longer life journey.[22] Walker's support must have meant the world to Burroughs, especially considering Jennie's doubts about her daughter's future.

Due to Walker's belief in Burroughs, by 1898 Burroughs was again living in Philadelphia, where she would transform her work with Jordan into a promising career pathway that eventually led to the creation of the National Training School for Women and Girls.[23] While working with Jordan, Burroughs was never shy about documenting her work. According to her, she practically ran the office in Philadelphia because Jordan was a "globe trotter" who was too busy to clean, organize, and run the office himself. Burroughs also claimed to have written Jordan's book *Up the Ladder in Foreign Missions* without any formal recognition, and she often officiated religious ceremonies such as funerals that he was expected to perform.[24] Even given the laborious tasks, Burroughs had more defined working hours than had she followed her mother's advice and sought household employment. In Jordan's relative absence from the office, Burroughs was also able to put into practice the business training that she acquired at M Street and in-

REV. L. G. JORDAN, D.D., LOUISVILLE, KY., COR. SEC. FOREIGN MISSION BOARD NAT. BAPT. CONVENTION, AND MEMBER BOARD OF DIRECTORS N. Y. P. C. AND ED. CONGRESS.

Figure 2.2. Reverend Lewis G. Jordan. Originally published in Penn and Bowen, *The United Negro*, 48.

tegrate her passion for reading, writing, and editing into her community organizing and religious work on national and international levels. While managing the affairs of the Foreign Mission Board, she learned about the global reach and influence of the National Baptist Convention and strategized on how to make it an ideal base for Black women's organizing in the United States and beyond.

Making Ends Meet as a Student, Community Organizer, and Entrepreneur

At twenty-one years old, and after toiling for three years across multiple jobs, Burroughs moved closer toward her vision of improving Black women's working conditions through women's organizing in the church and in education. In the process, she began her rise to leadership in the NACW and National Baptist Convention. In 1900 the headquarters of the National Baptist Convention's Foreign Mission Board moved to Louisville, Kentucky. Burroughs and Jordan left Philadelphia and moved to Louisville, where they continued working together for the Foreign Mission Board. As in Philadelphia, Burroughs ran the office in Louisville.

She explained that she "did everything from scrubbing the floors, making fire, to answering the mail, and writing for the [*Afro-American*] *Mission Herald*." She conducted research for the *Afro-American Mission Herald* articles and printed its editions. Burroughs also managed the printing of the *Christian Banner*.[25]

In addition to her cleaning, secretarial, and editorial duties, Burroughs kept in touch with missionaries in Africa and at home on furlough—keeping meticulous records of their travels and expenses. When they passed away, she was responsible for calculating and distributing life insurance payments to their spouses. Expected to also take on a maternal role, she was responsible for looking after African students brought to the United States by the Foreign Mission Board and placed in her care at the office. There was so much work to do in the office that Jordan occasionally hired assistants to help Burroughs sort mail and business accounts and help clergymen pack for their mission trips. While Burroughs did a lion's share of work for the Foreign Mission Board, she was paid less than Jordan and other clergymen. From 1900 to 1901, she made anywhere from $1.50 to $74 per month as a full-time worker in the office. Jordan, on the other hand, made between $50 and $231.50 per month and male missionaries earned between $79 and $100 per month.[26]

With Reverend Jordan's influence, the National Baptist Convention moved the board's office from an inconspicuous street in Louisville to a home on Walnut Street, a major Black business thoroughfare in the city.[27] As a former Walnut Street resident fondly remembered, "This was the hub of the Black community. I will never get Walnut Street out of my blood. Growing up there was just phenomenal for me." Walnut Street consisted of Black homes, shops, banks, barber shops, salons, insurance companies, clubs, medical offices, newspaper companies, and restaurants.[28] This booming Black district was a good fit for Burroughs's educational and entrepreneurial aspirations. With networks and organizing experiences under her belt, Burroughs emerged from her behind-the-scenes role as Reverend Jordan's assistant and began experimenting with her vision of opening a school and community business for Black women. She negotiated with Jordan to become part owner of the new building.[29] Her insistence on co-ownership was significant considering that only married women were legally allowed to own property in Kentucky in the early 1900s.[30] As part owner, in 1900 Burroughs established the Woman's Industrial Club of Louisville in the same building. By opening the club on Walnut Street, Burroughs inserted wage-earning Black women's interests into the main artery of Black economic and social life in Louisville.[31]

The word "club" does not capture the range of services and resources that the Woman's Industrial Club offered to the community. Similar to her National Association of Colored Women colleagues across the nation who created clubs for Black women, Burroughs had a firm belief that clubs were educational sites that should be beneficial to the larger Black community. Leaders of local women's clubs inserted themselves into local, national, and international politics and established themselves as experts on the labor problem. They operated their clubs like schools that offered intellectual stimulation, job training, and employment assistance. Historian Charles H. Wesley, founding president of Central State University in Ohio, witnessed firsthand the power of Burroughs's leadership in Louisville. His mother worked at the Woman's Industrial Club with Burroughs, and he attended one of Burroughs's community lectures there. He recalled, "She was talking about the treatment of the Negro people and their failure to emphasize the good things of life. . . . It really was a sort of a flag of direction for me as I sat listening to her. She was eloquent. She was humorous and she was able to drive home a point with action which a man would demonstrate in the pulpit as a minister. I was attracted to her."[32]

Employing her expertise in domestic science, business, and secretarial work, Burroughs taught the first business class for Black women in the state of Kentucky at the club. She also taught classes on sanitation, hygiene, childcare, sewing, cooking, millinery, and laundry work to prepare Black women for a variety of occupations and offered continuing education courses for local teachers who needed to advance their stenography training. She taught the courses in the evening to ensure they were accessible to Black women who worked during the day.[33] Sensitive to the challenges of working-class women, Burroughs set affordable fees for the courses. Women who took the courses at the club paid ten cents a week to help cover the expenses for maintaining the school. Her Woman's Industrial Club provided community lectures, low-cost lunches, cakes, pies, and bread rolls every day at 6 p.m. to support low-wage workers in the business district, create a revenue stream for the club, and provide practical entrepreneurial learning experiences for club members.[34] Burroughs covered what was left of the expenses and operated the school for nine years with the small salary she received from working for the National Baptist Convention.

Her club grew exponentially over the course of those nine years. When the club expanded, Burroughs dedicated some of the rooms for lodging to women who had migrated to Louisville for work opportunities and needed a temporary place to stay until they got on their feet. She also created job opportunities for local women by hiring teachers to manage the courses while she supervised the operations of the entire club.[35] Local bankers admired the combination of Burroughs's entrepreneurial skills and racial politics that she exhibited through the club, and they expressed their respect for her by nicknaming her the "Booker T. Washington of Louisville."[36] Burroughs herself saw her work as aligned with Washington's philosophies about the value of manual labor and entrepreneurship to Black economic progress.

Proud of her own achievements in Louisville, she invited Washington to speak at a graduation ceremony for the students of the Woman's Industrial Club. In 1902 she wrote to him:

> This is the first commencement of typewriters and stenographers in this city. I have a class and some of them will finish. The work ought to be in schools and steps are being taken I think to put it in. No Negroes are prepared to take up the teaching. I have gotten these public school teachers ready should it be done. This is a very great favor I am asking since "silver and gold" have I none but you can do the people here "untold" good. Your presence will help inspire them. Do say yes. Make even a sacrifice for the work sake and say yes. Wire me at my own expense. *Please, please, please say yes.*[37]

Washington did not respond. Burroughs sent a follow-up letter: "I write to extend to you an invitation to come to this city under the auspices of the Woman's Industrial Club to speak again to the people of Louisville. Great is the demand for you here and I have been begged to have you. The club is able to do by you what your position on the platform demands and I hope you will see your way to say yes."[38] Washington did not respond to her letter.

Figure 2.3. Burroughs (*far right*) and Louisville Public School system student teachers in her stenography class at the industrial club in Louisville, Kentucky, circa 1909. Reverend Augustus Jones (*far left*) later became pastor of Fifth Street Baptist Church (now known as Walnut Street Baptist Church) in Louisville, Kentucky. Nannie Helen Burroughs Papers, Prints and Photographs Division, Library of Congress.

Burroughs persisted with growing the club. It was such a success that it became the most popular women's club in Louisville, Kentucky, and caught the attention of local newspapers and national Black leaders. She achieved this even though she was not making a living wage herself—a notable irony considering her club was particularly heralded for helping empower women economically. To make ends meet, while establishing the club, she taught in the theological department of Louisville's State University (the segregated part of the University of Louisville).[39] W. E. B. Du Bois featured a story about the club in his Atlanta University study about Black political and social organizing across the country. He detailed the growth of Burroughs's club and its impact on the working lives of Black women in Louisville. As he wrote, "The Woman's Industrial Club of Louisville, Kentucky is a business, charitable and industrial club, quartered in a well-equipped twenty-room building on one of the most popular thoroughfares of the city. Various industries are carried on under its roof, and it has given impetus to the business life of the city of Louisville. From the millinery department have gone out scores of young women who are doing high-class work."[40]

Local Kentucky newspapers also praised the club and its founder. The *Louisville Courier-Journal* reported: "Probably no woman's organization in Louisville or, for that matter, elsewhere is doing as much practical, far-reaching good [as the organization founded by] this remarkable young colored woman, Miss Burroughs."[41] Burroughs had also developed a reputation in Louisville as a domestic science expert. She accepted an invitation to write the preface to a cookbook authored by Kentucky native Atholene Peyton. Making history yet again, Burroughs had a hand in bringing to light the first domestic science book published by a Black woman in the state of Kentucky.[42] The book was a significant publication considering that Black women were considered incapable of learning and exhibiting the socially prescribed virtues of domesticity.

While directing the club, Burroughs organized and managed nine industrial clubs in other cities, but the exact details of all these organizations are unknown.[43] She must have regarded the Pennsylvania Institute of Domestic Science in Philadelphia one of the most important schools that she established outside of Louisville, considering that she invited Booker T. Washington to speak at the opening ceremony.[44] Burroughs cofounded the institute with L. G. Jordan, who served as president, and she as corresponding secretary, while several clergymen of the National Baptist Convention served on the board of directors. Their aim was to provide Black women in Philadelphia with a range of trade courses in nursing, housekeeping, millinery, shorthand, typewriting, cookery, and laundry work. Burroughs's connections and work history in Philadelphia and the similarity between the institute's curriculum and the courses at the Woman's Club in Louisville strongly suggest that Burroughs was the brains behind the institute. Establishing domestic science schools across the country elevated Burroughs's national profile as a domestic science expert.

As an ever-evolving and intellectually curious thinker, Burroughs furthered her studies in business while teaching students in Philadelphia and Louisville. She enrolled in Eckstein Norton University, an African American industrial school in Cane Springs, Kentucky, where she was later granted an honorary master of arts degree in 1907. She developed a strong and enduring working relationship with her teacher and national Baptist leader Mary Virginia Cook Parrish. Parrish was a champion of women's rights and she was married to Charles H. Parrish, president of Eckstein Norton University, and president of the executive board of the General Association of Negro Baptists in Kentucky. The Parrishes opened the doors of their home for Burroughs to live with their family because she could not afford a place of her own. While living with the Parrishes and managing the Woman's Industrial Club and the Foreign Mission Board, Burroughs joined the Kentucky Association of Colored Women's Clubs and cofounded new clubs in the state that were associated with the National Association of Colored Women.[45]

As an educator, institution builder, professional writer, and rising leader in the NACW and Baptist church, Burroughs had finally hit a stride in doing work that she considered meaningful and transformative. According to her, she enjoyed her work so much that she chose it over two opportunities to get married. While living in Louisville, she had two serious relationships—one with an artist and another with a popular pastor—but both men strongly objected to her having a "globe-trotting life."[46] Burroughs enjoyed traveling and community organizing and refused to give it all up for their limited perceptions of what a wife should do and be. While making the choice to defy patriarchal dictates in her romantic life, she also challenged patriarchal culture in the church, which set her on the path to becoming one of the most renowned leaders in the Baptist world.

Redefining and Elevating Women's Work in the Church

Burroughs insisted on the right for women of the church to own the fruits of their own labors by developing their own decision-making body. On the morning of September 13, 1900, she delivered her most renowned speech, "How Their Sisters in the Land of Light May Help Them," otherwise and popularly known as "How the Sisters Are Hindered from Helping," at the National Baptist Convention's meeting in Richmond,

Virginia.[47] During this large gathering she boldly critiqued the male leadership of the National Baptist Convention for not valuing women's labor in the church. She also declared that the women of the National Baptist Convention should create their own Woman's Convention, without the oversight of the National Baptist Convention's male leaders. Burroughs asserted the business acumen of women organizers by rolling out her plan for how the Woman's Convention could contribute to the national and global fundraising goals of the National Baptist Convention: "10 woman's conventions to give $25.00 each; 20 woman's associations and district conventions to give $5.00; 1,000 missionary societies to give $2.00 each; 2,000 women to give $1.00; 300 children's bands to give 50 cents each; 15,000 pastors to pray for a great uplift in woman's work at home and abroad."[48]

Burroughs argued that men needed to support women in their organizing work because their fundraising and recruitment benefited the entire organization. As she put it, "Will you as a pastor and friend of missions help by not hindering these women when they come among you to speak and to enlist the women of your church?" Burroughs's confidence and her assertion that women's organizing was not just socially but also economically advantageous to the church ruffled the feathers of some men in the audience. An audience member interrupted her by shouting, "Who's that young girl? Why don't she sit down? She's always talking. She's just an upstart." Burroughs heard him and replied, "I might be an upstart, but I am just starting up."[49] Burroughs continued with her daring speech, underscoring the tremendous power and influence women's organizing had on the existence and expansion of the National Baptist Convention. Many Black women could not draw from inherited wealth to make contributions to the church. They did the work of fundraising, which entailed countless hours of planning events, letter and speech writing, speaking at churches and women's organizations, and traveling long distances across the United States and Europe (by ship, train, and horse and carriage) to convince people to join and donate to the National Baptist Convention.

Burroughs's early involvement in the NACW likely influenced her push for women's self-determination and ownership of the finances that they contributed to the National Baptist Convention.[50] According to the

NACW, the late nineteenth and early twentieth centuries constituted the Women's Era, or the period in which women asserted their rightful places in social and political leadership positions to transform society for the better. Whereas the NACW emerged as a critique of Black patriarchy and white clubwomen's racism, the Woman's Convention of the National Baptist Convention was established as a response to Black clergymen's refusal to grant Black women of the church seats at the decision-making table.

According to Burroughs, the gendered division of labor in the Baptist church was illogical, unnatural, and thereby not what God intended. How could Baptist churches accomplish the massive goals that God put them on this earth to achieve, if women, a significant portion of the membership, were expected to sit idly and let time pass by simply because they were women? As she put it, "the work is too great and laborers too few for us to stand by while like Trojans the brethren at the head of the work under the convention toil unceasingly. We come now to the rescue. We unfurl our banner upon which is inscribed this motto, 'The World for Christ. Woman, Arise, He calleth for Thee.'"[51] While Burroughs's "How the Sisters Are Hindered from Helping" was considered a radical speech and angered some clergymen in the audience, her argument that women could contribute their labors to the church was modest, considering that Black women were always fully active members of churches. Women had always done most of the share in the physical, mental, and social work essential to missionary work and growing churches.

At the Richmond meeting, and soon after Burroughs's impactful speech, Reverend L. G. Jordan convinced the National Baptist Convention to respond to Burroughs's call for a women's decision-making body by approving the creation of the Woman's Convention.[52] The National Baptist Convention approved the measure. Burroughs celebrated the historic decision and noted that it was long overdue. As she put it, "For a number of years, the faithful women and loyal men have prayed that the day would come when like the women of other denominations the godly women would be organized into a national body."[53] The Woman's Convention was a groundbreaking organization that would challenge gender hierarchies in the church and create the foundation for Burroughs's future work as a pioneering educator, labor scholar, and community orga-

Figure 2.4. Woman's Convention of the National Baptist Convention. Date unknown. Burroughs stands on the top step, with Sarah Layten at the front and Mary Cook Parrish behind her. Nannie Helen Burroughs Papers, Prints and Photographs Division, Library of Congress.

nizer. Under Burroughs's leadership, the Woman's Convention took on projects that it could have never done under the complete control of the National Baptist Convention.

Burroughs and her co-organizers wasted no time in setting up the infrastructure of the Woman's Convention and asserting their voices into the main arteries of the National Baptist Convention and beyond. Soon after the National Baptist Convention's approval vote, the newly formed Woman's Convention elected officers before the end of the Richmond meeting. They elected Sarah W. Layten of Philadelphia, Pennsylvania, as president and Nannie Helen Burroughs as corresponding secretary. There were twenty-six state vice presidents who represented various states and places without statehood, including Washington, DC, and Native American territories in Oklahoma.[54] Throughout Layten's and Burroughs's tenures as president and corresponding secretary, respectively, they would butt heads over the agendas and trajectories of the organization. Unlike Burroughs, Layten was not up for the hard task of confronting clergymen to grow the convention's autonomy. Burroughs was never shy about letting Layten know what she thought about her passive approach to running the organization. Considering Burroughs's outspoken and assertive personality, Layten must have at times felt disrespected by Burroughs and jealous of what she had accomplished. There was no denying the successful outcomes of Burroughs's unrelenting drive to promote women's leadership in the church, education, and beyond.

As she had done in the earlier part of her career, during the founding years of the Woman's Convention, Burroughs documented the extensive work she had done as corresponding secretary to grow the new organization.[55] As she noted, during her first year in office, she had "labored 365 days, traveled 22,125 miles, delivered 215 speeches, organized 12 societies, written 9,235 letters, and received 4,820 letters."[56] She often read and handwrote responses to the majority of people who sent letters to her, which took additional work and time. Due to her organizing work and that of other Woman's Convention members, in 1903 Burroughs enthusiastically reported that the Woman's Convention represented approximately one million Black Baptist women.[57] Burroughs and other Woman's Convention organizers never received wages that compensated them adequately for the community organizing work they had done to recruit members to the Woman's Convention, which added to the overall membership of the National Baptist Convention. Their work, however, paid off: by 1906 the Woman's Convention's membership had reached 1.7 million people, making it the largest Black women's religious organization in the country.[58]

As a leader of the Woman's Convention, Burroughs promoted missionary work in Africa. It would be simplistic, however, to describe her as an imperialist. She believed that Black people across the world should become Christian, yet she saw missionary work in Africa as parallel to the work she and other Black clubwomen were doing in the United States. She wanted to build institutions and resources that were largely inaccessible to African women and children because of colonialism. She worked

OBJECTS:

1. To engage in World Wide Missions, by praying, giving and working.
2. To stimulate and enlist the Women of all Missionary Baptist Churches in Mission and Educational work at home and abroad.
3. To labor for the highest development of Christian womanhood.

We want every woman to get up a club of 10 readers of the Mission Herald, the organ of our work, at 15 cents each and send the $1.50 to the Corresponding Secretary, Louisville, Ky.

We meet with the National Baptist Convention, Birmingham, Ala., September, 1902.

The WORLD for CHRIST
WOMEN ARISE HE CALLETH TO

WOMAN'S CONVENTION Auxiliary to the National Baptist Convention.

Mrs. S. W. Layten, Pres., Penn.

Miss S. C. V. Foster, Treas., Montgomery, Ala.

Miss N. H. Burroughs, Corresponding Secretary, 718 West Walnut St.

Figure 2.5. Woman's Convention letterhead. Booker T. Washington Papers, Box 36, Reels 32–33, Manuscript Division, Library of Congress.

with primarily West African Baptist teachers and Woman's Convention members to establish schools, libraries, health clinics, and farms on the continent, and she saw these sorts of institutions in both the United States and Africa as education and employment opportunities for African and African American women. According to Burroughs, it was important for African and African American women to work together to address the needs of their communities. As she once told Woman's Convention members, they (Africans) are the "bones of our [African Americans'] bones and the flesh of our flesh."[59] The logo of the Woman's Convention's letterhead illustrated Burroughs's belief in this shared kinship and work between African and African American women. It featured a drawing of two presumably African American women sitting next to a globe that centered Africa. Under Burroughs's leadership, the Woman's Convention would develop into a religious organization that was active in Black schools in Africa and Black women's suffrage, civil rights, and public health movements in the United States.

Due in no small part to Burroughs's influence, the Woman's Convention also made its mark in the publishing world. The convention established a column in the Foreign Mission Board's bi-monthly *Afro-American Mission Herald* to express members' religious views and report on their organizing work. The Woman's Convention also declared as its headquarters the Louisville building that housed the Foreign Mission Board and Burroughs's Woman's Industrial Club.[60] With a leadership title and an in-house periodical, Burroughs had more freedom to write short stories that highlighted the significance of working-class women to the church. She sold these stories to raise money for the Woman's Convention and create a positive sentiment in the church toward wage-earning women. In the early 1900s, she authored a four-page pamphlet entitled "How a Negro Girl Servant Educated a Heathen White Girl," in which a "Negro servant girl was the heroine." It was a short story about the financial sacrifices that a domestic worker named Louisa Osborne made to fund the construction of a church in Sri Lanka. To illustrate her lesson about the significance of working-class Black women to religious institutions, Burroughs portrayed Louisa as a loyal Christian in contrast to her "heathen" white employer who had more money than Louisa but did not contribute to the building of the church in Sri Lanka.[61] Burroughs's Woman's Convention pamphlet was one of her first publications that championed domestic workers, a conviction she would live by throughout her career.

Promoting women's work through the Woman's Convention would not come without a continuous fight against sexism. While Burroughs and her co-organizers made historic progress at the Richmond convention, not all men leaders of the National Baptist Convention were on board with the establishment of an autonomous women's organization. They believed that women's rightful place was in the background behind the men.[62] Shortly after the Woman's Convention was established, the male-controlled National Baptist Convention attempted to downgrade the organization to a Women's Home and Foreign Mission Board under the direct supervision of the National Baptist Convention. Burroughs invited Booker T. Washington to speak at a Woman's Convention meeting to help convey the importance of the organization during this hostile period.[63] Washington, however, did not see the value in speaking only to the Woman's Convention. He told Burroughs that he preferred to speak at a joint meeting.[64] Burroughs complied with his wish but wrote, "There may be an effort later on by our brethren to secure you but I beg that you bear in mind that the Baptist women gave the first invitation, even before they thought of it."[65] Due in large part to Burroughs's refusal to back down to male leaders, the Woman's Convention prevailed in asserting a degree of autonomy from the National Baptist Convention.

While co-directing the Woman's Convention with Sarah Layten, Burroughs asserted her labor philosophies and agenda on national and global stages. Beginning in 1901, Burroughs expanded her local vision for the Women's Industrial Club by using her influential position as corresponding secretary of the Woman's Convention to advocate for the establishment of a trade school for Black women and girls. She wanted the school placed in the nation's capital, nondenominational, and welcoming of all daughters of the African diaspora, irrespective of skin color and class and ethnic backgrounds. She spent the next eight years doing the laborious work of bringing her dream school into fruition. Burroughs traveled to various churches and organizations drumming up national support for what would become the National Training School for Women and Girls in Washington, DC.

Burroughs continued to assiduously document the scope of her work in the records she sent to the National Baptist Convention. In the 1902 Woman's Convention financial statement, for example, she noted that she had traveled 32,350 miles, labored 365 days, delivered 350 lectures, formed 156 organizations, and received 8,723 letters in response to the 12,890 letters that she sent to women about the importance of Christian education and a national trade school.[66] Burroughs gained influence during her crusade for building the NTS. By 1907, when she finally convinced the Woman's Convention to support the construction of the NTS, the Woman's Convention had raised a total of $47,903.27. While some Woman's Convention and National Baptist Convention members criticized her idea of starting a school, Burroughs's demonstration that she could raise such a large amount of money at the time made it harder for her critics to ignore her arguments for establishing a school. She was such an outspoken advocate for the NTS that Woman's Convention and National Baptist Convention members often referred to the NTS as Nannie Burroughs's school before and long after it was created.[67]

Although Reverend L. G. Jordan, Reverend Walter H. Brooks, and a few other men supported Burroughs's idea, there was much resistance from other men in the National Baptist Convention who believed that the school would disrupt "natural" gender roles. According to them, teaching women and girls academic subjects and a range of trades would take women out of the domestic sphere. They would become too independent and displace men as the breadwinners.[68] Of course, this argument ignored the fact that most Black women were already the primary wage earners of their families. Resistant National Baptist Convention leaders also argued that a school with multiple trade and academic programs would detract girls from missionary training, which should be their sole focus. Woman's Convention's president Sarah Layten, who often did not challenge male convention leaders, also expressed doubts about Burroughs's push for a trade school. Burroughs would eventually achieve her goal with her convincing speeches, writings, and fundraising work for a school that would break barriers in American education.

Creating a Foundation for the NTS

Burroughs's primary aim for establishing the NTS was to improve working conditions for Black women in household employment while creating new pathways for Black women and girls within and outside service occupations. She worked at maximizing the fruitful possibilities of the Woman's Convention's large membership and expansive national and global networks to garner widespread support for the school. While the convention was her organizing base, she stressed the importance of welcoming students into the school from any religious affiliation. As she told the Woman's Convention, "It must be national, not Baptist—something all colored women can do for all colored girls."[69] Relying on the oratory and writing skills she had developed in Philadelphia and Louisville, Burroughs also positioned herself as an educational and religious leader, an expert on women's work, and a staunch advocate for domestic workers who was more than prepared to establish a trade school for Black women and girls.

She first publicly introduced the idea of building a school for all daughters of the African diaspora at the 1901 Woman's Convention meeting in Virginia. In an effort to convince her colleagues of the importance of establishing a school to improve the working conditions of domestic workers, Burroughs declared:

We would call your attention to the fact that the majority of our women make their living at service, and the demand is for trained servants. Unless we prepare ourselves, we will find within the next few years that our women will be pushed out of their places, filled by white foreigners who are alive to the demands and are taking advantage of the instructions now being given in schools of domestic science far and near. Since we must serve, let us serve well, and retain the places we have long held in the best homes in the land.[70]

Burroughs continued pressuring the Woman's Convention to support her idea a year later at the 1902 conference: "We are anxious for our girls to learn to think, but it is indispensable that they learn how to work. They may not have it to do, but to know how for themselves is far better than trusting it to someone to know for them. *We come again appealing louder than we did last year for a National Training School* where we may teach women how to live and how to labor all the way from earth to glory."[71]

The next year, Burroughs took her message nationwide. In 1902 she delivered one of her first and most direct speeches about addressing the needs of Black domestic workers at the Negro Young People's Christian and Educational Congress in Atlanta, Georgia. Burroughs was the only woman board member of the congress, and she served on the board at the same time as Booker T. Washington.[72] Although she had made waves with her speech "How the Sisters Are Hindered from Helping," she almost did not deliver her crowd-rousing speech "The Colored Woman and Her Relation to the Domestic Problem" at the conference. Ironically, the conference organizers thought Burroughs was too young and inexperienced to speak in front of such a large audience and at such a prominent gathering. They told Burroughs, "You are new and young and no one knows you. The audience would break." After she convinced them that she could hold her own, the bishop of Big Bethel AME Church, where she was scheduled to speak, asked her, "All this world of young people. How do you feel about it? Will you read?"[73] Burroughs replied, "I feel alright. No, I will not read. I shall speak." And she did not disappoint. As one card that she received afterward read, "My heartiest congratulations. Finest, best thing I have ever heard."[74]

During her speech, Burroughs urged the young audience to stand up against employers who hired European immigrant women instead of Black women for domestic and laundry work. She sounded the alarm during the rise of European immigration from Western Europe in the early 1900s that community leaders needed to intervene in the "supplanting of Negro servants by Irish, [Italians], and English" who uprooted Black women "from the places we have held for over two centuries."[75] She offered domestic science education programs as a solution to the problem. According to her, this form of education would "dignify labor" so that "our services may become indispensable on the one hand and Negro sentiment will cease to array itself against the 'working girls' on the other hand."[76] Understanding that few other occupations were available to Black women, Burroughs believed that domestic science education would provide Black women with the certification necessary for stable employment in domestic service or related service occupations until they pushed their way into other occupations, if they so desired. After all, she had taken a similar route herself.

In her effort to ignite the interests of a religious audience, Burroughs argued that centering the needs of domestic workers in school curricula and community organizing initiatives was morally and economically critical for the survival and advancement of the Black race. She warned the audience that industrialization was moving full steam ahead and leaving Black workers behind. Burroughs asserted, "If we lose sight of the demands of the hour we blight our hope for progress. The subject of domestic science has crowded itself upon us, and unless we receive it, master it and be wise, the next ten years will so revolutionize things that we will find our women without the wherewith[al] to support themselves." To shrug one's shoulders about this possible outcome, Burroughs argued, did not benefit the race. She continued, "We are not less honorable if we are servants. . . . Again, if we scorn women who have character and are honest enough to work to preserve it . . . are we making the race any more moral?"[77] As Burroughs pushed for Black women to advance in multiple sectors of employment through a blended education, she had a two-pronged approach to solving the race and labor problem.

As she promoted her vision for the trade school, Burroughs also stressed the importance—and the right—for the Black laboring class to access a combined classical and industrial education. She argued that white people had greater access to educational opportunities that enabled them to pursue jobs with higher wages, whereas Black students were primarily relegated to narrowly focused industrial curricula that limited their occupational and overall life outcomes. According to Burroughs, a blended curriculum in Black schools was the only approach to addressing the race and labor problem in America. In 1904 Burroughs wrote in the *Colored American Magazine*:

> The Negro Problem is a problem of color, and of fitness. Industrial education is not a skin changer, and could not, therefore, solve a problem that is but skin deep. By industrial education I take it that you mean the development of that part of the mental and physical that will respond to all or some special phase of manual labor. . . . The Negro must have all phases of the problem solved in order to secure the key to the situation.[78]

Challenging scientific racist claims that resurfaced after emancipation to justify the exclusion of Black people from non–manual labor jobs, Burroughs pointed out that there was no sound scientific evidence that Black people were only fit for low-wage work. As she put it, "Those who outline a specific course of study and attempt to confine him to one field of labor must remember that his capacity, his ability, his ambition is as varied as to quality and quantity and capacity and the ability of each individual of any other race." Burroughs concluded that Black people should be able to follow any pursuits that they enjoy and are good at doing from "the bootblack to the college chair" or "from the coal cart to congress halls."[79]

Her argument extended to women, though she used masculine pronouns throughout most of her article. She asserted that women also had varied interests and skills. Working within the gendered confines of work at the time, she proclaimed that women should have the option of making a good living by "cooking, washing, ironing, sewing, and working on a farm" or as "first-class clerks, stenographers, book-keepers, musicians, and teachers."[80] As Burroughs became a more well-known writer and speaker, she gained support from some of the people who had once doubted her vision. In 1904, the same year the *Colored American Magazine* published Burroughs's article about industrial education, Woman's

Figure 2.6. A twenty-six-year-old Burroughs delivering her first international speech, "Women's Work," in front of a large crowd at the 1905 World Baptist Alliance's conference in London, England. Courtesy of the People's Archive, Martin Luther King Jr. Memorial Library, Washington, DC.

Convention president Sarah Layten formally endorsed Burroughs's proposal to start the NTS.

As she gained more support for building the NTS, Burroughs brought greater visibility to the significance of Black women's labor in the church. As the keynote speaker at the 1905 World Baptist Alliance's conference in London, she delivered a speech in Hyde Park she entitled "Women's Work." The speech, very well received by the audience, was Burroughs's detailed historical timeline of women's missionary work around the world demonstrating why women were just as important as men to the social and economic value of the Baptist denomination.[81]

A number of British press outlets covered Burroughs's "Woman's Work" speech at the World Baptist Alliance conference. As one journalist wrote,

"It is useless to telegraph to Heaven for shiploads of blessings and then not to be on the wharf to unload the vessel when they arrive." This was one of the many quaint expressions which fell from the lips of Miss Burroughs, a Negress, in a witty address delivered by her in an open-air service held in Hyde Park yesterday. . . . Miss Burroughs voice is far-reaching and well pitched and her manner of speech suggested a delightful mixture of Negro and American peculiarities which was greatly enjoyed by the large audience.[82]

Another journalist wrote, "She has great oratorical gifts, and her justification of the claim that women have a great place in missionary achievement was as eloquent as it was convincing." This journalist, however, could not help himself from commenting on her skin color. According to him, "her pleasant features are those of a typical Negress, though she is many shades removed from Black."[83] His comments confirmed Burroughs's perspectives that colorism influenced people's perceptions of her. The British journalist needed to lighten Burroughs's skin tone to see her as a brilliant orator. Nevertheless, Burroughs was excited that her first international speech went over well. She knew at that point that she was a rising leader. Eager to impress and receive praise from her former teacher, she sent a postcard to Mary Church Terrell from London to inform her about her recent successes. She wrote, "Greeting[s]. Spoke at Exeter Hall and received an ovation. By special request at Hyde Park demonstration to 5,000 and again at Arthur St. Church to one of the most enthusiastic audiences I have ever faced. My color is a help. The world is here [at] this meeting. I have made friends for life."[84] Burroughs's experience in London left a lasting impression on her. As historian Angela Hornsby-Gutting has astutely argued, Burroughs's participation in the conference and in the subsequently formed Women's Committee of the Baptist World Alliance would later influence her Pan-African approach to building her school and its curriculum.[85]

Figure 2.7. A postcard Burroughs sent to Mary Church Terrell in 1905. Mary Church Terrell Papers: Correspondence, 1904–1905, Manuscript Division, Library of Congress.

Not too long after Burroughs delivered her riveting speeches in London, she proposed harnessing the power of women's work and organizing in the Baptist church.

In 1906 she proposed Woman's Day (now celebrated as Women's Day in Baptist and other denominational churches) at the National Baptist Convention meeting in Memphis, Tennessee.[86] Challenging clergymen who opposed women's leadership, she declared that all local Baptist women's organizations dedicate the fourth Sunday of July to raising money for foreign missions and supporting women's public speaking. On Woman's Day, Burroughs encouraged women to deliver speeches in the pulpit, which had been considered an exclusively male space, and she directed Woman's Convention members to allocate profits from their fundraising toward creating educational opportunities for women and girls in Africa and the Caribbean. On the first Woman's Day, the Woman's Convention created a scholarship for a student in Cape Town, South Africa, to attend Burroughs's school, which was close to coming to fruition.[87]

In 1906 Burroughs also made important steps toward establishing structural support for the NTS. Layten and male leaders of the National Baptist Convention authorized the formation of the National Training School Committee. The committee consisted of eighty members, including Burroughs, Reverend Jordan, Layten, and National Baptist Convention president Reverend Elias Camp Morris.[88] Some members of the committee proposed that the school be placed in Indianapolis, Indiana, and others pushed for it to be located in Louisville, Kentucky, where they could easily purchase large plots of land. Burroughs insisted that these ideas were shortsighted. She was adamant about establishing the NTS in Washington, DC. As she argued, the nation's capital was considered the mecca of employment, and it was a gateway city for Black women who migrated to northern US cities to find better jobs and educational opportunities. Black women had a better chance of accessing quality schools and getting higher-paying domestic service jobs in the homes of congressmen and other government officials in the nation's capital. She eventually convinced the committee that DC was the place for the NTS.[89]

Community Organizing to Establish the NTS

In the final consequential years leading up to the actual construction of the NTS, Burroughs and the Woman's Convention worked tirelessly raising money to purchase land for the school. Of the convention members, no one worked harder or was as committed to establishing the NTS as Ella Eugene Whitfield. Whitfield left her position as the matron of a girls school in Seguin, Texas, to become a missionary field worker. In the Baptist community, Whitfield was heralded as a "unique and richly gifted worker" with an "executive ability to transform theories into practice" that "crowned her labors with remarkable success."[90] She was a savvy and confident leader with a commanding presence and an authoritative voice that enabled her to convince audiences to support her causes. Burroughs had deep respect for Whitfield, describing her as "God's special agent for this work." Their collaborative work and close friendship was essential to the launch and expansion of the NTS.[91]

The NTS might not have opened as soon as it did had it not been for Whitfield's long hours traveling across the country, writing articles, delivering speeches, organizing fundraisers, and creating thousands of promotional materials to distribute at church services to create public demand for a Black women's school.[92] For over three decades Whitfield traveled to cities across the world, from San Francisco, California, to Charleston, South Carolina, and from Nova Scotia, Canada, to Juneau, Alaska, to raise money for the NTS and recruit students to the school. In one year alone, Whitfield "delivered 491 addresses; visited 823 homes; 312 churches; and collected over $2,009" to garner support and raise money for the NTS and Woman's Convention.[93] It took fortitude, extensive strategizing, and impeccable communication skills to travel thousands of miles a year by train, boat, and horse buggy and deliver moving speeches to church congregations and women's organizations about the great promises of a school for Black girls and women that would be managed by Black women. As early as 1905, Whitfield had traveled to Seattle, San Francisco, Boston, and Denver, as well as Galveston, Texas, and Charleston, South Carolina, asking for small donations from working-class communities that, in the words of Earl Harrison, "turned to loaves of bread, and the scraps to hams and sides of bacon" for the school.[94] Whitfield's work generated substantial seed money for building the NTS and she continued raising funds and recruiting students to the NTS from Africa, Canada, and the United States for thirty years after the school opened.

Figure 2.8. Ella Eugene Whitfield. Date unknown. Nannie Helen Burroughs Papers, Prints and Photographs Division, Library of Congress.

Along with the crucial initial funds raised by Whitfield, Reverend Walter Brooks garnered support for the NTS. He used his prominence in the National Baptist Convention to defend Burroughs's efforts to establish a school in conversations and meetings with clergymen. As Burroughs recalled, he often said to her, "Go ahead, if you think you can do it." Brooks hated to see Burroughs in contentious struggles with convention leaders, but he always supported her in public and behind closed doors.[95]

By 1907 Burroughs had gained enough support from the National Baptist Convention to secure a charter and purchase six acres of rugged and hilly land in the northeastern section of Washington, DC. On this plot of land, she and her colleagues would build a campus out of the original eight-room dilapidated building.[96] Burroughs insisted that the convention would not have sole ownership rights to or power over the institution. Burroughs wanted to make sure that the school would survive internal fissures within the National Baptist Convention and that Black women would hold the majority of decision-making power over the school. Making a power move, Burroughs, L. G. Jordan, and

Sarah Layten procured the articles of incorporation from the District for the NTS.[97] The charter required eighty trustees and that the majority must be Black women and only the board of trustees would have the power to replace vacancies.[98] The property was held in trust, and if the corporation dissolved, the National Baptist Convention and Woman's Convention would have the power to use the trust funds for educational purposes.

Burroughs continued fundraising with Ella Whitfield to purchase what she believed was the perfect place for her school. She found a plot of land on a hill in Lincoln Heights, a section in the rural and historic Black neighborhood of Deanwood in northeast Washington, DC. She dubbed the land on which enslaved Black people labored and that was owned by slaveholders "Holy Hill." Burroughs believed that God had chosen this location for her to build her historic labor school. As she explained, "I prayed about this thing for a long time. . . . Somehow I felt the school had to be set on a hill. It was all red gullies up here and a site to see, with a dilapidated eight-room house atop of it all; but there were six acres of land and this beautiful view." Burroughs described the site as where the "wholly impossible" would occur to overcome the tremendous odds of Black women building and maintaining a school for Black women and girls in a country where there were no federal resources or protections for them. The land needed a lot of work and the larger Deanwood neighborhood itself lacked basic infrastructure, but Burroughs had already received more than 150 applications from prospective students. The NTS committee needed to secure enough funding to develop the land and construct multiple buildings to accommodate the large and prospective student population.[99]

Burroughs was stressed about fundraising for the NTS, and she let out her frustrations on anyone who did not move with the same level of urgency to secure what she considered to be enough funds to open the school. When her former teacher Mary Church Terrell initially refused to send her money for the NTS, Burroughs wrote to her,

It is a bit distasteful to be called a perpetual beggar. I am almost ashamed to write this letter. . . . I am not begging for myself, but for a cause that is as dear to your heart as to mine. . . . I think the best thing for you to do is to read this letter and get right up and go out and solicit the money today and send it to us. There are a number of white friends whom you could reach.[100]

A month after receiving Burroughs's letter, Terrell sent a donation to the NTS committee, and she continued sending money to Burroughs for the NTS for several decades afterward.[101]

Although Burroughs had been a fierce champion of the NTS, she became overwhelmed when her idea came closer to becoming a reality. In 1909 she tried to delay the opening by arguing at a National Baptist Convention meeting that she needed more money to fully accommodate the first class of students. In a rare expression of disagreement with Burroughs, her allies Ella Whitfield and L. G. Jordan immediately opposed her recommendation. L. G. Jordan declared, "Other schools began in cabins and you women now have a better start than most any school operated by Negroes. Put up a frame boarding hall and begin [the] work." Whitfield concurred with Jordan. She added that they could not raise significant amounts of money before opening the school. As she explained, someone was willing to give her a one-hundred-dollar donation, but the person withdrew their offer after she told the potential donor that the school had not yet opened.[102] The majority of National Baptist Convention and Woman's Convention members agreed with Jordan and Whitfield that the NTS needed to open that year. But hurdles ensued as Burroughs pursued this audacious effort to create opportunity for Black women and girls at a school governed by Black women.

Notes

1. Easter, *Nannie Helen Burroughs*, 26.
2. Lawrence, notes from interview with NHB.
3. Pickens, *Nannie Helen Burroughs and the School of the 3 B's*, 27.
4. Harrison, *The Dream and the Dreamer*, 9.
5. Lawrence, notes from interview with NHB.
6. Johnson, *Uplifting the Women and the Race*, 86.
7. NHB to Booker T. Washington, February 18, 1896, Box 36, Reels 32–33, Booker T. Washington Papers.
8. Lawrence, notes from interview with NHB.
9. Harrison, *The Dream and the Dreamer*, 9, 10.

10. Hammond, *In the Vanguard of a Race*, 48–49.

11. Pickens, *Nannie Helen Burroughs and the School of the 3 B's*, 16.

12. McCluskey, *A Forgotten Sisterhood*, 104.

13. Lawrence, notes from interview with NHB.

14. Yellin, *Racism in the Nation's Service*, 13.

15. Aron, "'To Barter Their Souls for Gold,'" 842.

16. Aron, 837, 835.

17. Lawrence, notes from interview with NHB.

18. Autobiographical notes, Box 1, Folder 23, Una Lawrence Collection.

19. Bookkeepers more commonly used typewriters by the late nineteenth century. See Wooten and Kemmerer, "The Changing Genderization of Bookkeeping," 552.

20. See Wooten and Kemmerer, 557.

21. Easter, *Nannie Helen Burroughs*, 27.

22. Adam Clayton Powell Sr. was pastor of Abyssinian Baptist Church in Harlem. For his recollections about Burroughs's early career, see Lawrence, notes from interview with NHB.

23. For a history of Walker, see Garrett-Scott, *Banking on Freedom*.

24. Reverend Jordan published the book in 1939. For the latest reprint edition, see Jordan, *Up the Ladder in Foreign Missions*; autobiography notes, Box 1, Folder 23, Una Lawrence Collection.

25. Lawrence, notes from interview with NHB.

26. National Baptist Convention Foreign Mission Board Accounts, 1900–1901, Box 12, folder 14, NHB Papers.

27. Harrison, *The Dream and the Dreamer*, 10.

28. In 1978 Walnut Street was renamed Muhammad Ali Boulevard. For more recollections about Walnut Street, see Gil Corsey, "Once a Booming Strip of Black Business, Walnut Street Faded from Louisville's Memory for Failed Urban Renewal," WDRB, February 27, 2020, https://www.wdrb.com/in-depth/once-a-booming-strip-of-Black-business-walnut-street-faded-from-louisvilles-memory-for-failed/article_fc600e82-580f-11ea-9ea5-638cf333c542.html.

29. John T. Baty to Lizzie F. Boyce, February 9, 1910, Una Lawrence Collection.

30. Roberts, "Property Rights of Married Women," 1–4.

31. In 2021 the city of Louisville placed a historical marker at the location where Burroughs's club was located. See "New Historical Marker in West Louisville Honors Leader for Gender, Racial Equality," WLKY, May 12, 2021, https://www.wlky.com/article/new-historical-marker-in-west-louisville-honors-leader-for-gender-racial-equality/36414260.

32. "Reminiscences of Dr. Nannie Helen Burroughs."

33. See Hammond, *In the Vanguard of a Race*, 51.

34. Lawrence, notes from interview with NHB.

35. Harrison, *The Dream and the Dreamer*, 50–51.

36. John T. Baty to Lizzie F. Boyce, February 9, 1910, Una Lawrence Collection.

37. NHB to Booker T. Washington, May 18, 1902, Box 36, Reels 32–33, Booker T. Washington Papers.

38. NHB to Booker T. Washington, October 6, 1902, Box 36, Reels 32–33, Booker T. Washington Papers.

39. Lawrence, notes from interview with NHB.

40. See Du Bois, *Efforts for Social Betterment*, 62.

41. Hammond, *In the Vanguard of a Race*, 54.

42. NHB, preface, in Peyton, *The Peytonia Cookbook*, 1–4.

43. Harrison, *The Dream and the Dreamer*, 33.

44. NHB to Booker T. Washington, November 5, 1902, Box 36, Reels 32–33, Booker T. Washington Papers.

45. Lawrence, notes from interview with NHB.

46. Lawrence, notes from interview with NHB.

47. Both paper titles are listed in the minutes; National Baptist Convention, *Journal of the Twentieth Annual Session*, 14, 68.

48. NHB, "How the Sisters Are Hindered from Helping," 196–97.

49. NHB, 196–97.

50. For a history of Black women's activism in churches, see Collier-Thomas's *Jesus, Jobs, and Justice*. Black women religious figures had also been asserting feminist analyses of labor since the early 1800s. See Maria Miller Stewart's untitled speech at the Franklin Hall in Boston, Massachusetts, in 1832 in Guy-Sheftall, *Words of Fire*, 30–33.

51. NHB, "How the Sisters Are Hindered from Helping," 192.

52. National Baptist Convention, *Journal of the Twentieth Annual Session*, 195.

53. NHB, "Two Great Agencies: The Woman's National Baptist Convention," in National Baptist Convention, *Journal of the Twentieth Annual Session*, 195.

54. Brooks, "Religion, Politics, and Gender," 9.

55. See National Baptist Convention, *Journal of the Twentieth Annual Session*, 195.

56. Figures quoted from Burroughs's handwritten notes in the archive, Box 23, NHB Papers.

57. Brooks, "Religion, Politics, and Gender," 12.

58. National Baptist Convention, *Journal*, 1901, 19–21.

59. Lawrence, notes from interview with NHB.

60. National Baptist Convention, *Journal of the Twentieth Annual Session*, 195.

61. NHB, "How a Negro Girl Servant Educated a Heathen White Girl," Box 36, Reels 32–33, Booker T. Washington Papers.

62. Harrison, *The Dream and the Dreamer*, 15.

63. NHB to Booker T. Washington, May 14, 1908, Box 36, Reels 32–33, Booker T. Washington Papers.

64. NHB to Booker T. Washington, September 10, 1902, Box 36, Reels 32–33, Booker T. Washington Papers.

65. NHB to Booker T. Washington, January 24, 1902, Box 36, Reels 32–33, Booker T. Washington Papers.

66. Penn and Bowen, *The United Negro*, 521–22.

67. Pickens, *Nannie Burroughs and the School of the 3 B's*, 13, 5.

68. See Collier-Thomas, *Jesus, Jobs, and Justice*, 127–32.

69. Daniel, *Women Builders*, 114.

70. Burroughs's statement is quoted from NHB, *First Annual Report of the Executive Committee*, 6.

71. Harrison, *The Dream and the Dreamer*, 26.

72. Penn and Bowen, *The United Negro*, 49.

73. Big Bethel AME Church still exists today. It was founded by enslaved African Americans in the 1840s and has the largest African American congregation in the historic Sweet Auburn neighborhood of Atlanta, Georgia. Big Bethel is also where the historically Black Morris Brown College started and where civil rights movement leaders such as Martin Luther King Jr. met to organize demonstrations. See "Big Bethel History," accessed September 14, 2022, https://www.bigbethelame.org/History.

74. Lawrence, notes from interview with NHB.

75. Quoted from NHB, "The Colored Woman and Her Relation to the Domestic Problem," 1902. See Graves, *Nannie Helen Burroughs*, 204.

76. NHB, "The Colored Woman and Her Relation to the Domestic Problem," 324.

77. NHB, 325, 327.

78. NHB, "Industrial Education—Will It Solve the Negro Problem?" *Colored American Magazine* 7, no. 4 (March 1904).

79. NHB.

80. NHB.

81. Pius, *An Outline of Baptist History*, 95–96.

82. Pickens, *Nannie Helen Burroughs and the School of the 3 B's*, 43.

83. Pickens, 43, 24.

84. NHB, postcard to Terrell, December 3, 1905, Correspondence, 1904–1905, Mary Church Terrell Papers, LOC.

85. The alliance was a group of Baptist leaders from countries across the world. Hornsby-Gutting, "'Woman's Work.'"

86. Alice Gantt, "Women's Day," n.d., NHB Vertical File, Moorland-Springarn Research Center, Howard University.

87. Gilkes, *"If It Wasn't for the Women,"* 147.

88. Stewart, "Designing a Campus," 143.

89. 1906 Meeting Minutes, Box 1, Folder 32, National Baptist Convention Records, Southern Baptist Convention Historical Library and Archives.

90. Samuel William Bacote, "Mrs. Ella Eugene Whitfield," in Bacote, *Who's Who*, 101–2.

91. Higginbotham, *Righteous Discontent*, 161; Bacote, "Mrs. Ella Eugene Whitfield," 101–2.

92. See chapters 3 and 4 for discussion of Woman's Convention and NACW support for the NTS after the school opened.

93. Bacote, "Mrs. Ella Eugene Whitfield," 102.

94. Harrison, *The Dream and the Dreamer*, 72.

95. Lawrence, notes from interview with NHB.

96. Pickens, *Nannie Helen Burroughs and the School of the 3 B's*, 8.

97. National Baptist Convention, *Journal of the Fortieth Annual Session*, 110.

98. Pickens, *Nannie Helen Burroughs and the School of the 3 B's*, 20.

99. Hammond, *In the Vanguard of a Race*, 53–54.

100. NHB to Mary Church Terrell, January 21, 1908, February 20, 1908, Correspondence, Jan.–June 1908, Mary Church Terrell Papers, LOC.

101. In 1926, for example, Terrell donated to the NTS when a building on campus burned down. See NHB to Mary Church Terrell, July 8, 1926, Correspondence, July–December 1926; Mary Church Terrell to NHB, April 14, 1925, Correspondence, Jan.–June 1925; NHB to Mary Church Terrell, April 10, 1925, Correspondence, Jan–June 1925, Mary Church Terrell Papers, LOC.

102. 1909 Meeting Minutes, Box 1, Folder 32, National Baptist Convention Records.

Part Two

"THE ONLY SCHOOL EVER FOUNDED BY AN ORGANIZATION OF NEGRO WOMEN"

"It is the only school ever founded by an organization of Negro women. . . . Graduates are at work in nearly every State in the Union, Africa, Haiti, and Puerto Rico. . . . It is the only school for Negro girls between Maine and Georgia, in the midst of a population of over three million colored people."

—Nannie Helen Burroughs, *Making Their Mark: Results of the Lives of Graduates*

CHAPTER 3

"The National Training School for Women and Girls Will Materialize"

A Timeline of Patriarchy, Land, and Ambition

On May 14, 1908, Nannie Helen Burroughs wrote to Booker T. Washington:

> We thought at first not to open the school before building the other building, but there are quite a number of women and girls anxious to enter, and we feel that we must begin the work as soon as possible. I am now preparing our Convention to open in the fall. . . . After you have thoroughly examined the merits of the case, could you possibly write us a letter of recommendation?[1]

Two weeks later, on May 28, 1908, Booker T. Washington wrote a letter to the National Baptist Convention president criticizing Burroughs's idea of establishing the NTS. He also placed a bid "for his daughter" on the land where Burroughs planned to build the school.[2]

Burroughs responded in capital letters:

> THE NATIONAL TRAINING SCHOOL WILL MATERIALIZE, and if after we are in operation, you feel that the work deserves a kindly mention, we shall certainly appreciate a statement to that effect.[3]

Maggie Lena Walker gave Burroughs the extra five hundred dollars she needed to outbid Washington for the land that became the NTS campus.[4]

To establish a school managed by Black women with the unique mission of reforming household work and creating new career possibilities for Black women and girls in the early twentieth century was a remarkably radical undertaking. Burroughs insisted that the institution remain private and out of the hands of white government officials so that Black women would remain in charge of the school and its curriculum. She had to constantly make the case for the significance of the NTS and her educational philosophies to draw financial support for the school. Simultaneously looking beyond the physical boundaries of her school, Burroughs also wanted to inspire a national Black movement to reform domestic service. In the process, she confronted racism, sexism, and elitism. Some of the most powerful and financially resourceful men in the country scoffed at her philosophy that Black women's household work was essential to Black economic and political progress. They also resented Burroughs's insistence that they support a single-sex school managed by Black women.

While Burroughs's goal was to grow the NTS with donations from only Black people, she was ridiculed in Black business leadership circles. In 1909, the same year she opened the NTS, she was mocked by National Negro Business League members for championing domestic workers and women's household work. National Negro Business League president Booker T. Washington invited Burroughs to deliver a speech about the "Negro Servant Girl Problem," or the lack of domestic service training for Black women and girls. Although Washington had refused to endorse the NTS, Burroughs accepted his invitation to speak at the league meeting without hesitation. She took advantage of this rare opportunity to assert the importance of domestic workers in front of a large audience of business owners who could provide financial assistance to the school. As prominent leaders of their respective communities, they could also support her in her efforts to create a national movement for labor reform in household employment.

Immediately after walking up to the podium, Burroughs declared to the crowd of predominantly Black men that she was a "friend of the working woman," or the "thousands of hard working women who are toiling and sweating over the wash-tub, over the ironing-boards, and in the cook kitchens struggling to maintain themselves." The audience applauded. Their show of approval, however, took a sharp turn after she told them that Black men needed to value women's household work as essential to the social and economic progress of the Black community.

As she put it, "We have complained about conditions on the outside, but on the inside there are some weaknesses and prejudices to overcome."[5]

To illustrate her point she told the audience that she was appalled when a former sharecropper boasted at a business meeting that he had purchased acres of land without crediting his wife for his upward economic mobility. As Burroughs explained, "his poor hard-working wife, who also had no education, and had never been to school, who had been working all her life to help him buy and pay for those hundred acres of land, she was at home, still working, and still being worked far beyond the sound of any applause or commendation." Burroughs did not stop there. She told the audience that they needed to respect not only the work their wives did at home but Black women who worked in white people's homes. She instructed the audience to "not be ashamed to doff your hat to her [domestic worker] when you meet her in the street" and "don't shun her or fail to speak to her just because she might not have on fine clothes."[6]

Some attendees applauded. Others erupted in laughter that was so loud that it was difficult for the note taker for the meeting to hear the rest of Burroughs's speech. Booker T. Washington remained silent. Burroughs persisted by arguing that the National Negro Business League needed to advocate for living wages in household employment. As she asserted, "Some of our teachers find it difficult to exist on from $7 to $10 per week, and yet the Negro servant girl is expected to maintain herself and go decently on from $2.50 to $3 a week, as a rule."[7]

The crowd erupted in laughter again.

Washington did not bring the meeting to order. He introduced the next speaker.

The speaker boasted that he had recently reentered the room after leaving in the middle of Burroughs's speech to tend to more important matters.[8]

While Burroughs could not rely on the National Negro Business League to support her school in its early years, she was determined to grow her institution, even if it meant approaching white philanthropists for funding. In 1912 she sent a letter to Booker T. Washington asking him to request funding for the NTS from Julius Rosenwald, German

Jewish immigrant philanthropist and founder of the Rosenwald Schools. Rosenwald accumulated his wealth from heading the profitable national retailer Sears, Roebuck, and Company. Moved by Booker T. Washington's rise from slavery and his commitment to education, Rosenwald worked with him on expanding educational opportunities for Black people. While in close collaboration with Washington, Rosenwald funded five thousand Black schools across the rural South. Burroughs knew no other Black leader had the ear and respect of Rosenwald like Washington did. He was her best chance of securing funding from this major philanthropist.[9]

Responding disdainfully to Burroughs's request, Washington wrote, "As I see it, the colored people in Washington have more money spent on them per capita than any set of colored people anywhere in the world. . . . I am wondering if it would really be fair to take money away from colored people in other parts of the country where the per capita expenditure is as low as 56 cents in many cases." Instead of asking Rosenwald for money, Washington continued, Burroughs needed to seek help from Black public school teachers in Washington. He declared, "Notwithstanding the high pay they receive, how many Washington school teachers do you ever see in any prominent national gathering for the betterment of our race? . . . I know you are not responsible for these conditions . . . but still these are conditions that one must face when trying to help someone else give away money."[10]

As president of her own trade school, Burroughs was no longer the young and deferential woman who rarely challenged Washington's dismissive responses to her. In a fiery three-page letter challenging Washington's gender and regional biases, she wrote, "It seems to me on this same line of argument, the Y.M.C.A. of Washington, should have been refused help by Mr. Rosenwald. On the other hand, I believe that you and Mr. Rosenwald will find some delight since he helped the men in a work that is definite in aim and national in scope, to help the women whom I represent whose work is very definite in aim and the scope of which is certainly national." Burroughs continued,

> I want you to keep prominently before you, the fact that the National Training School is not the property of Washington. They are simply

expected to contribute their part as the people of Alabama are expected to contribute their part to Tuskegee. If Alabama had to bear all of the burden, I am afraid that you would not have a Tuskegee, although the Negroes of Birmingham hold more money than the Negroes of any other City. . . . But, geography does not regulate our interest when we are really anxious to help people, nor do we withhold light from a man in the dark because someone else with light refuses to let him walk by it.[11]

Addressing Washington's comments about Black teachers in DC, Burroughs reminded him that she was a "product of the public schools of that city." Knowing the challenges confronting Black teachers in Washington, she asserted that "they are to be pitied rather than censured." According to her, the NTS filled an important gap for Black girls that was not being met by the present institutions. She asserted that Howard University, for example, was an institution operated by the government and the NTS catered to girls who could not get into Howard and whose mothers work long hours at domestic service. The mothers wanted "to put [their daughters] in a school that will be a home." Burroughs left Washington with this declaration: "I do not want you to give a single cent, if you do not believe that we richly deserve it. I would rather walk the streets, and beg the money, nickel by nickel, than to receive it at the hands of someone who feels that the cause is not deserving of it."[12]

In a brief letter, Washington told Burroughs that the decision would ultimately be left up to Rosenwald. Burroughs responded: "While you say that you will be guided largely, by the wishes of Mr. Rosenwald, I know on the other hand that Mr. Rosenwald will be largely guided by your wish in this matter." She invited him to visit the campus to develop a deeper understanding of her mission for the NTS.[13]

Several months passed, with no response or visit from Washington, and Burroughs sent a follow-up letter. Later she received a letter from Washington that read: "I fear that it is not going to be possible out of the present appropriation from Mr. Rosenwald to secure you the donation suggested. . . . I have been holding your letter for some days, hoping that the way would be open for me to comply with your request."[14] Burroughs persisted. She urged him to read about the dire learning conditions of Black girls and boys in cities from Washington to Boston. They were harassed by racist white teachers and students who resented the mere presence of Black students in their schools. She reminded him that most Black women in northern cities worked in domestic service and needed a boarding school for their daughters. It was too expensive for them to send their daughters down South to Spelman College. She enclosed a letter from a mother as proof.[15] Washington did not budge.

During the course of more than ten years of correspondence with Washington, Burroughs developed a strong partnership with his wife, educator Margaret Murray Washington. She too had been on the receiving end of Washington's disdain for smart and ambitious women. Burroughs and Margaret Washington also shared the belief in promoting landownership, education, and manual labor among Black women and girls to achieve Black economic independence.[16] Margaret visited Burroughs often and challenged Booker T. to change his views about the NTS. Still, he refused to support the school. In one of his last letters to Burroughs before he passed into history in 1915, he confessed, "Mrs. Washington has given me a very interesting and encouraging report concerning her visit to your school. I wish some time to visit it myself. I wish that your school was not in Washington."[17]

The NTS hit an especially rough patch during the Depression. Working-class Black people were disproportionately impacted by the economic crisis and their donations to the NTS declined sharply. Burroughs decided to approach white philanthropists directly for financial assistance. She wrote to philanthropist John D. Rockefeller for a contribution. Although he was the head of an oil monopoly and the country's first billionaire, he sent Burroughs one dollar with a note that read: "I shall be interested to know how, as a business woman, how you plan to make use of this dollar." Burroughs purchased and roasted peanuts with the dollar and mailed the peanuts to Rockefeller with a note saying that if he autographed them, she could make money from the dollar.[18] He neither complied nor sent her a contribution.

Despite continued objections to her and the NTS, Burroughs's effort to center the needs and aspirations of Black women and girls in education was something special and groundbreaking. The overwhelming response to the NTS made clear that a school for Black women and girls in Washington, DC, was greatly needed. And as Burroughs established the most extensive domestic science program in the country there, she also charted new career pathways for generations of Black women and girls in the United States, Africa, and the Caribbean.

Notes

1. NHB to Booker T. Washington, May 14, 1908, Box 36, Reels 32–33, Booker T. Washington Papers.

2. Booker T. Washington to NHB, May 28, 1908, Box 36, Reels 32–33, Booker T. Washington Papers. In an informal interview with Una Lawrence, Burroughs told Lawrence that Booker T. Washington claimed to want the land for his daughter. See Lawrence, notes from interview with NHB.

3. NHB to Booker T. Washington, May 30, 1908, Box 36, Reels 32–33, Booker T. Washington Papers.

4. Lawrence, notes from interview with NHB.

5. National Negro Business League, *Report of the Tenth Annual Convention*, 176, 177.

6. National Negro Business League, 176–78.

7. National Negro Business League, 178.

8. National Negro Business League, 178.

9. NHB to Booker T. Washington, August 19, 1912, Box 36, Reels 32–33, Booker T. Washington papers; James D. Anderson, *The Education of Blacks in the South*, 153.

10. Booker T. Washington to NHB, August 29, 1912, Box 36, Reels 32–33, Booker T. Washington Papers.

11. Booker T. Washington to NHB, September 2, 1912, Box 36, Reels 32–33, Booker T. Washington Papers.

12. Washington to NHB, September 2, 1912.

13. Booker T. Washington to NHB, September 12, 1912, Box 36, Reels 32–33, Booker T. Washington Papers.

14. Washington to NHB, November 15, 1912, Box 36, Reels 32–33, Booker T. Washington Papers.

15. Washington to NHB, October 30, 1913, Box 36, Reels 32–33, Booker T. Washington Papers.

16. Rouse, "Out of the Shadow of Tuskegee," 33–34, 39–40.

17. Washington to NHB, September 30, 1913, Box 1, Folder 23, Una Lawrence Collection.

18. "Our 'Miss Burroughs' Was a Very Special Person," *Washington Star*, May 3, 1978.

CHAPTER 4

"To Command Respect and Good Living"

Curriculum Building to Organize Women of the Race, 1909–1961

On September 16, 1909, at 7:45 p.m., a thirty-year-old Nannie Helen Burroughs stood before members of the Woman's Convention at the National Baptist Convention meeting in Columbus, Ohio, and gave a speech outlining an ambitious new labor agenda.[1] This agenda was to improve the working conditions of Black domestic workers and create new pathways of employment for Black women through her National Training School for Women and Girls in Washington, DC. Burroughs declared, "Two-thirds of the Negro women who earn their living work in service. The industrial schools now operated are not meeting the demands. . . . Women and girls will come [to the NTS] for the definite purpose of preparing themselves to take positions as cooks, laundresses, chambermaids, ladies' maids, nurses, housekeepers, dressmakers, stenographers, book-keepers and clerks, and will be able to command respect and good living."[2] Burroughs's speech that evening marked a momentous occasion after a hard-fought battle for authorization from the National Baptist Convention to establish a school for Black women and girls across the African diaspora, irrespective of their class status and religious affiliation.

The once-distraught and unemployed high school graduate was now the president of a school of her own design. Burroughs also accomplished her personal goal of attaining a career that would enable her to take care of her mother. In the early 1900s, Jennie remarried and took on the last name Bell. By 1910 she had separated from her husband, and Burroughs purchased a home for her in Philadelphia.[3] By the 1920s, Jennie was living on the NTS campus helping Burroughs operate the school, and she remained there for the rest of her life. Reflecting Jennie's supportive role at the NTS, students and staff affectionately called her "Mother Bell."[4] Burroughs's cousins and aunts from Orange, Virginia, also stepped in over the years to help her carry out her vision at the NTS.[5]

Burroughs saw education as the most important tool in her immediate possession to organize women and girls into changing economic and political institutions to benefit themselves and their communities. While several other educators in Burroughs's orbit shared the same philosophy, what made her approach to education unique was her deep political and financial investment in domestic science as a pathway for tackling Jane Crow. Her curriculum building was driven by her motto: "Until we realize our ideal, we are going to idealize our real."[6] Knowing that most Black women were barred from jobs outside domestic service, she committed most of her efforts toward designing a domestic science curriculum to transform the slave-like working conditions of household employment and organize domestic workers into becoming leaders for economic empowerment and civil rights. Along with NTS faculty, she created rigorous scientific courses to give students a competitive edge over the European immigrant women who were entering the ranks of household employment in northern cities. They also wanted students to maximize their chance of attaining any domestic science–related career of their choosing. Whether domestic science graduates decided to labor as domestic workers or as domestic science teachers, they would be able to confidently demand the wages that matched their knowledge and skills.

By taking their political work as Black teachers seriously, Burroughs and NTS faculty insisted on their citizenship right to nourish the minds of Black women and girls through a combined trade and academic curriculum. As Burroughs declared in an NTS faculty meeting, "This is a trade school, but we can't teach a trade without giving an academic background." She asserted that they needed to "offer the literary subjects in order to round out the necessary qualifications for useful citizenship."[7] Unlike white women, the majority of Black women had to work for wages, and they needed to learn a wide array of skills to increase their employment options. Burroughs was part of a community of women institution builders, known as the Fab Four of education, that included Lucy Craft Laney, Mary McLeod Bethune, and Charlotte Hawkins Brown. Collectively, they argued that Black women and girls deserved to live lives full of intellectual curiosity, hard work, and enjoyment, and they laid the foundation for making this type of life possible through blended classical and trade curricula at their respective schools.[8] Margaret Murray Washington is not considered part of the Fab Four, but she worked with Hawkins, Laney, and Bethune and had an especially close friendship with Burroughs. When Margaret's husband, Booker T. Washington, rebuffed Burroughs's requests for support, Margaret was always there to support the NTS and Burroughs's other initiatives.[9] Burroughs respected Margaret's pedagogical approaches and ideas as an educator herself who helped Booker T. build the women's curriculum at Tuskegee Institute.

Burroughs's expansive curriculum and educational mission of improving Black women's working and living conditions resonated with the needs and desires of Black people across ethnicity, socioeconomic class, and region. Over the school's fifty-two-year existence, Burroughs received hundreds of letters and phone calls from parents, aunts, uncles, and cousins in occupations ranging from domestic workers, clergymen, members of the Brotherhood of Sleeping Car Porters, sharecroppers, missionaries, housewives, and teachers to unemployed workers who were eager to enroll their loved ones in the NTS.[10] So many people wrote to Burroughs for application materials that neither Burroughs nor NTS staff members could reply to all of the inquiries in a timely manner.

Building a School to Meet the Needs and Wants of the Race

The general reasons why people were anxious to send their daughters to the NTS remained consistent throughout the Jane Crow era. The reasons differed and overlapped in relation to regional location, socioeconomic status, and age. Across the wide spectrum of needs, concerns, hopes, and aspirations, what was abundantly clear was that the NTS was crucial for Black communities. Mothers from the South wrote to Burroughs with urgency wanting to provide their daughters with opportunities that were not available in southern rural towns. Black people far outnumbered the number of primary and secondary schools available to them in the South. While southern Black teachers were determined to provide their students with the best possible education, without federal and state funding, most Black schools were overcrowded and severely underfunded.[11]

With limited educational opportunities, especially in the rural South, Black girls had few options but to work alongside their mothers as sharecroppers or domestic workers. Mothers considered the NTS a rare opportunity for their daughters to obtain a quality education outside of the Deep South in a school managed by a Black woman leader like Burroughs who cared about the future of Black girls. As one mother anxiously wrote, "I have been waiting to hear from you. I tried to contact you at the school by phone, but no one answered. . . . Please try to find room for my daughter. . . . I am actually begging for you to please find room for her. . . . I want her to go to your school."[12] Domestic workers in the South and North wanted their daughters to attend the NTS for education and safety. In a country where there were no laws to protect Black girls from sexual assault and physical abuse, mothers were concerned about staying away from their daughters for long hours. Some mothers looked to the NTS to provide care and nurturing that they were unable to provide. A mother from Chattanooga, Tennessee, expressed to Burroughs that she was worried about her teenage daughter's safety while she worked long hours in household employment. As she put it, "I would like to send her right away. . . . While she is a nice little girl, I would like to keep her that way."[13] A domestic worker from New York City worked such long hours that she barely had time to see her daughter. She explained, "I am a young widow and work at night, and sleep in the day. . . . [I] go to work before Evelyn's bedtime. So, you see just how difficult it is to give her the proper attention she should have. I would like very much for her to enter your school."[14]

Jessie McConnell wanted so badly for her daughter to stand out from other applicants that she convinced her domestic service employer to send Burroughs a letter attesting to her and her daughter's character and abilities. McConnell's employer, Gundie Griswold, made sure to let Burroughs know that she was a respectable woman as the wife of an editorial board member of a newspaper in Omaha, Nebraska. Griswold continued,

Recently, Jessie McConnell (a colored woman) addressed you in regard to the possibility of her daughter Bessie Mae West coming to your school. She has asked me to write you. It is with great interest and pleasure I am doing so. . . . I can vouch for the honesty, moral standing, industry, faithfulness, and intelligence of both Jessie and [her daughter] Bessie Mae. They are unusual in their natural ability and comprehension generally. Honorable is the word for them. . . . I trust that Bessie Mae will meet your requirements and be afforded the benefits of your most excellent school.[15]

Iris Ramus from New York City offered Burroughs her employers' home address so that Burroughs could contact her employers directly. As she put it, "The above address is where I work. If you need to know more about me, you may write to this family in whose service I have been for a year and a half."[16]

Parents in the South were so anxious to send their daughters to the NTS that they tried to enroll them before they were old enough to attend the school. The fact that the NTS began offering courses at the sixth-grade level did not stop a mother from applying on her young daughter's behalf. As Burroughs wrote to the mother, "Regret we cannot accept Mary Nealy. She is below grade. We do not have fourth grade."[17] Other parents wanted a spot in the school for themselves. A mother from Pine Bluff, Arkansas, wrote that she was interested in the domestic science program because she wanted "training for more and better service." In her words, "I'm a young mother, but still have hope."[18] Fathers, uncles, and pastors wrote to Burroughs urging her to consider admitting girls into her school who they believed had great potential. Dr. Carter G. Woodson saw so much promise in the NTS that he convinced his niece Jennie Woodson to move from Virginia to Washington, DC, to enroll in the school.[19]

Just as the young Burroughs and her students at the Women's Industrial Club in Kentucky sought additional training and certification after graduating from high school, young women who were unmarried and did not have children wrote to Burroughs with hopes of obtaining employment and enrolling in continuing education courses at the NTS. Olivia Johnson of Keysville, Georgia, was in search of work and education opportunities in a bustling city. Committed to acquiring as much training as possible, she had moved to Atlanta to attend a business school after having attended Paine College in Augusta and Boggs Academy in Keysville. Johnson felt that an even brighter future awaited her at the NTS, where she saw herself working as a stenographer while taking continuing education courses.[20] Pansy Martin from Timmonsville, South Carolina, offered to use her resources from her rural community to convince Burroughs that she would be beneficial to the school while visiting the campus during the day to take courses. She wrote, "I shall be pleased to know if day students are allowed to attend the school? I wish to also advise I am from a rural community and would I be among those allowed to help pay my way with such [agricultural] products as mentioned in your circular?"[21]

Alma Jackson from Jackson, Mississippi, and graduate of Booker T. Washington High School in Houston, Texas, wanted to enroll in an NTS domestic science course. Concerned that she was too old to enroll at the NTS, she wrote, "The course that I am interested in is Home Economics. I note in the circular of information that this is an outstanding course in your school. I wonder if provision could be made for me at this late date."[22] Jackson had written the right person. Burroughs was keenly aware of limited education opportunities in the South and opened the doors to her school to adult women of all ages. As the 1930 US census report shows, students' ages at the NTS ranged from thirteen to forty-seven years old.[23]

While schools for Black women and girls were more accessible in the North, there were few all-Black schools in northern cities, and mothers wanted their daughters to attend schools with Black women role models.[24] Josephine E. Smalls, mother of a fifteen-year-old girl in Englewood, New Jersey, wrote to Burroughs that she wanted her daughter to attend the NTS so that she could develop friendships with Black girls and become rooted in southern Black culture. Her reasoning reflects why some parents still send their children to historically Black colleges and universities in the South today. As Smalls explained, the NTS was "just a little more countryfied" than the school her daughter was attending in New Jersey. After hearing back from Burroughs, Smalls replied, "It assures me that I've found the right woman for my daughter. . . . I think your viewpoint is what we need in our race. . . . If the women are trained, half the work is done . . . for the advancement and proper training of the race."[25] While hopeful about their daughters' futures, mothers worried about their migrations to the NTS. Women who had migrated northward knew the dangers that awaited Black women and girls when they traveled. A mother in Chicago asked Burroughs for more assurances regarding the logistics of her daughter's possible migration to Washington, DC. She wrote, "I want to send my girl to your school this fall, and I wanted to know if there was anyone I could send her with that was going to the school this fall. I don't feel that I could send her alone."[26]

The NTS programs and location were still selling points for loved ones in the North who wanted girls to attend a Black school specifically for women and girls. A family friend of a professor from Morris Brown College and a Spelman College graduate wrote to Burroughs from Roxbury, Massachusetts, about their eleven-year-old niece Evelyn. Evelyn could no longer live in Atlanta with her grandmother, but the family friend wanted Evelyn to have the experience of going to a school only for Black girls.[27] Mothers of older girls wanted to enroll their daughters in a school that was not as far away as Spelman College. Mrs. M. A. Wright wrote to Burroughs that her daughter was smart and fond of studying music vocally and instrumentally. She had recently moved to New Hampshire and withdrew her daughter from Spelman so that she could be closer to her. Her daughter, however, was not keen on enrolling in the predominantly white boarding schools in the New England area. As Wright explained, "She feels a little delicate about the boarding school in New England because all the girls are white." She asked Burroughs to enroll her daughter as soon as possible since a month had already gone by since the last time she was in school.[28]

While Burroughs admitted girls like Wright's daughter from well-to-do families, she also knew that Black girls were overrepresented in state welfare departments and needed a school that would accept them. The NTS developed a national reputation as a potential home and place of learning for girls in state custody. The director of case work at the Cuyahoga County Child Welfare Board in Cleveland, Ohio, was determined to keep a girl named Theresa out of jail. According to her, Theresa had lived in seven foster care homes and had become "boy-conscious" and lost interest in school, yet she believed Burroughs and NTS faculty could help her. As she explained, "we have so few schools for our older

Colored girls and we are informed that you have a staff of capable, under-standing women, who may help Theresa, that we are asking you to help us with this girl. Hoping that your answer will be in the affirmative."[29]

Alice Smith, who Burroughs considered her adopted daughter, came to the NTS from the New York State Welfare Department. Smith had learned about the NTS from hearing Ella Whitfield deliver a speech about it at a Baptist church in New Rochelle, New York. Smith recalled, "After hearing her speak, I tore a leaf out of a hymn book and wrote a note. What was on it, I do not know, but the desire in my heart was to go to school. I was a product of the New York Welfare [Department]. I had no people at all and I understood that at the age of sixteen you had to go into service and work the rest of your life. I wanted to go to school."[30]

When Burroughs received Alice Smith's note from Ella Whitfield, she called the welfare department and convinced them to send Smith to the NTS. Smith became a lifelong student at the school, taking all its courses, and was elected president of the student council. She also became a per-manent resident of the NTS and worked closely with Burroughs as a staff member. Reflecting on the school's influence on her life and her personal relationship with Burroughs, Smith asserted, "What I do know is that it [the NTS] opened a new world for me. . . . If she [Burroughs] thought anything about you, you were the hardest person she was going to work on."[31] According to Smith, "Miss Burroughs helped you to overcome and to become. The sky was the limit. She would help you to do whatever you wanted to do. She was a teacher, mother, and friend to me. She was everything. All that I am, that's any good, I owe first to God and then Nannie Burroughs."[32]

The exact number, names, and ages of all students and faculty at the NTS each year of its existence is unknown due to two fires on the school's campus that destroyed school records. I have pieced together information about NTS students, faculty, and staff primarily from census data, student accounts, surviving school records, National Baptist Con-vention meeting notes, and stories that Burroughs and her allies wrote about the NTS. These records tell the story of how Burroughs built a campus and curriculum to inspire and prepare Black women and girls to harness pride in themselves and Black history to not only confront employment discrimination but to take their rightful place at the forefront of industrial capitalism. According to her, capitalism was built on the backs of Black people during slavery. As organized, knowledgeable, and above-average workers, Burroughs believed, Black women and girls could transform the US economy and attain their long overdue labor and civil rights.

Creating an Accessible School for Students and Teachers of the African Diaspora

Student enrollment quickly outgrew the physical capacity of the campus within the first decade of its establishment. In October 1909 the school started with nine students, who represented Cape Town, South Africa, and states across the US South; five assistant teachers; a dormitory matron; and Burroughs as president.[33] Delia Rudolph, the student from South Africa, was supported by the foreign missions fundraising that Burroughs had established through Woman's Day. The first cohort of faculty members included Julia Foster, May M. Wall, Hattie A. Shaw, Susie Harris, Nannie Goodall, E. Romaine Robinson, and Lula M. King. Burroughs was committed to hiring primarily Black women; she refused to hire white women who looked down on Black students and teachers and preferred off-campus housing. Burroughs hired three white women teachers—Jennie Peck, Florence Walter, and Martha Howell—who she insisted live on campus in the dormitories.[34] Burroughs's deep dedication to the school is evidenced by her decision to live on campus for her entire tenure as president. Staying on campus was cost effective and ensured that she remained connected to faculty, students, staff, and the community surrounding the school.

By the end of the first school year, there were thirty-two enrolled students and approximately $3,000 in new school funding.[35] This funding enabled Burroughs to hire two on-site dressmakers, Netti Benjamin and Netti Washington, to design student uniforms.[36] In 1911, eighty-three students enrolled at the NTS, and sixty-nine of those students lived on campus. Burroughs rented rooms in the local community to accommodate the remaining students.[37] By 1913 two more students from South Africa, Maggie Brownhill and Jennie Sumtumzi, and Clarice Gooding from Barbados were enrolled in the school.[38]

Figure 4.1. Nannie Helen Burroughs (*center*), Ella Whitfield (*bottom step, right*), and other NTS faculty members sitting on the steps of an NTS building, circa 1909. Nannie Helen Burroughs Papers, Prints and Photographs Division, Library of Congress.

Figure 4.2. The first cohort of NTS students standing in front of an NTS building circa 1909. Nannie Helen Burroughs Papers, Prints and Photographs Division, Library of Congress.

Figure 4.3. A group of NTS students posing for a school photograph circa 1910–1920s. Nannie Helen Burroughs Papers, Prints and Photographs Division, Library of Congress.

The class, age, ethnic, and regional diversity among students confirmed that Burroughs had made good on her promise of making the NTS accessible to Black women and girls from all walks of life. The strong representation of southern students during the first decade of the school was due to limited educational options in the South and the extensive ties Burroughs established with southern Black Baptist churches through the Woman's Convention. Years of Burroughs working and writing for the Foreign Mission Board were starting to bear more fruit. Interest from Caribbean and African students in the NTS was generated by stories about the NTS in the *Mission Herald* and the working relationships between Woman's Convention organizers and Baptist women in Africa and the Caribbean. Over the years, students came to the NTS from as far as Liberia, Nova Scotia, Brazil, Haiti, and Puerto Rico. The wide representation of countries in the student body was because of Whitfield's international travels and promotion of the NTS and the Woman's Convention's fundraising to cover the costs of international students' travel to the NTS.[39]

By 1920, ninety-two students, four teachers, two clerks, and a bookkeeper lived at the school. Student ages ranged from fourteen years old to thirty-five years old.[40] Seventeen-year old Jennie Poindexter, Burroughs's mother's niece, was part of this large student cohort. Attending the NTS must have been a welcome opportunity for her. She did not attend school until after she turned six years old. She worked on her family's farm for most of her childhood in Orange, Virginia.[41] Some students at the NTS in their twenties and thirties were widowed and were taking advantage of educational opportunities they had put on the back burner to take care of their families as mothers and wives.

The NTS supported the aspirations not only of students but also of teachers. Burroughs was as committed to providing jobs for women teachers as she was to making education accessible to Black women and girls. Teaching positions were not easy to come by, especially in the South, where many schools stopped at early primary and intermediate education levels and did not have the resources to pay teachers living wages—nor, at times, to even keep school doors open. NTS faculty member Jennie Peck lost her job as Dean of the Caroline Baptist Training School, a school for Black girls in Dallas, Texas, when it closed. In 1910 Burroughs hired her to become the first director of the Missionary Department. Although Burroughs provided jobs for white teachers like Peck, her primary aim was to employ Black women who were either underemployed or unemployed.[42] Teaching at the NTS was an especially attractive option for Black women during the Great Migration, when their teaching certification served also as a passport to travel, live, and work wherever they desired. It was also a rare opportunity to work in an exciting place like DC and at a school managed solely by Black women. Hattie Shaw, among the first cohort of NTS faculty, left Dallas to start and direct the Music Department. Maggie Wall Arter, another dedicated faculty member, left the South to establish a range of programs at NTS.[43] In 1920 all teachers at the NTS were Black women from the South.[44]

With no financial assistance from the National Baptist Convention, USA, Incorporated (formerly known as the National Baptist Convention), keeping the school open and teachers employed fell on Burroughs's shoulders.[45] William Pickens, field secretary of the National Association for the Advancement of Colored People, boasted that by 1921, 1,216 students had graduated from the NTS, and Burroughs had raised $322,051.54 for the school. In his field report, Pickens emphasized Burroughs's skill, hard work, and sacrifice to raise money during such a hostile period. As he noted, the money had been "raised by the oratorical power, the personal magnetism, the individual appeal, and the sweat and blood torture of the nasty Jim Crow travel of, this one Colored woman, aided and encouraged by a few devoted friends."[46] Ella Whitfield continued fundraising for the school after it opened. She traveled the world advocating for the NTS at times when Burroughs needed to stay at the school to manage it. Part of the money Burroughs and Whitfield raised went toward the salaries of NTS faculty. On average, annual salaries for Black teachers were much lower than those for white teachers. As an active member of the National Association of Colored Women, Burroughs was involved in their campaign to address wage disparities in the teaching profession. Burroughs aimed to pay NTS faculty salaries that were comparable to what white teachers earned and higher than what Black women teachers earned on average. In 1930–31, for example, NTS faculty were paid between $70 and $155 per month ($840–$1,860 per year).[47] Experienced full-time teachers at the NTS made the higher-end salaries. The national median salary of white teachers who taught full-time in 1930–31 was $1,360–$1,547 per year.[48] As late as 1939, Black teachers in the nearby state of Maryland were only earning an average of $765 per year.[49]

Burroughs was also in constant fundraising mode to construct new buildings with classrooms and dormitories to meet the needs of the growing student population. While expanding the campus, she integrated her belief that Black people needed racial pride for social and economic progress into every school building. She insisted that students learn about the accomplishments of Black leaders so that they could confidently assert and know for themselves that they were skilled and intelligent workers in a world that did not value them and their work. Few buildings on school campuses in the United States were named after Black people, much less Black women. On the NTS campus, except for the Mary G. Burdette Memorial Home, which was funded by a white women's missionary organization, the buildings were either monuments to Black leaders or represented Burroughs's beliefs in what it took to advance the Black community.

Constructing a Campus to Inspire Black Pride and Race Work

Burroughs dedicated Pioneer Hall, a three-story primary building of the NTS, to formerly enslaved leaders: Lott Carey, a statesman in Africa; John

Jasper, a philosopher and preacher; and William J. Simmons, a teacher and Baptist preacher.[50] She considered it important for NTS students to especially look toward Black women leaders as models. She named buildings after Ella Whitfield and Maggie Lena Walker, two women who had helped her establish the school. Whitfield Hall was one of the largest buildings on campus and doubled as a dormitory and recreational space. Maggie Lena Walker had sworn Burroughs to secrecy when she helped her outbid Booker T. Washington for the land on which she built the school. Burroughs was so proud that a Black woman with her own bank came to her rescue that she insisted on honoring her with a building. Walker Hall was a dormitory and infirmary. Inside all of the classroom buildings were pictures of Black leaders, including Toussaint Louverture, Sojourner Truth, Charlotte Hawkins Brown, and Paul Laurence Dunbar.[51] When passing students on this historically rich campus, Burroughs would often tell students to take pride in their own names and life histories and walk with their heads high like they were queens of Ethiopia.[52]

By 1930 Burroughs had built Community Service, a building across the street from campus that students managed to serve the Lincoln Heights community. Their community house included a library with more than

Figure 4.4. NTS students enjoying themselves, circa 1930s. Nannie Helen Burroughs Papers, Prints and Photographs Division, Library of Congress.

Figure 4.5. Pioneer Hall was Burroughs's residence and housed her office, the Music Department, dormitory rooms, reception rooms, a kitchen, and a dining room. Nannie Helen Burroughs Papers, Prints and Photographs Division, Library of Congress.

Figure 4.6. Ella Whitfield Hall. Nannie Helen Burroughs Papers, Prints and Photographs Division, Library of Congress.

Figure 4.7. Maggie Lena Walker Building. Nannie Helen Burroughs Papers, Prints and Photographs Division, Library of Congress.

four thousand books, a large room for community gatherings and entertainment, a pie and cake shop, and sewing materials.[53]

According to Burroughs, transforming society for the benefit of wage-earning Black women and girls also required an unwavering commitment to God. She built the campus on a hill for practicality and spiritual significance. The NTS was commonly referred to by students, benefactors, and community members as "the school on the hill" or "God's school on the hill," where Burroughs believed students would be safeguarded from "distractions" and "dangers" from the city but could also easily access and engage with the surrounding Black community.[54] A railroad track and trolley line at the bottom of the hill gave students, faculty, and staff transportation to engage in community learning and work throughout the District.[55] Students performed plays and sang at fundraising events for churches, the National Association of Colored Women, and Carter G. Woodson's Association for the Study of Negro

Figure 4.8. NTS community store and library, circa 1930s. Nannie Helen Burroughs Papers, Prints and Photographs Division, Library of Congress.

Life and History. Faculty used the trolley to take students to plays, musicals, museums, libraries, and theatrical performances to supplement what they taught students in their classes.[56]

Buildings that did not bear the names of Black leaders represented Burroughs's beliefs in the importance of spirituality, manual labor, and community engagement to Black economic and political empowerment. Students studied the Bible at the National Chapel on campus. The poultry plant promoted Burroughs's commitment to teaching students the importance of achieving self-sufficiency through community work. The plant provided revenue for the school and wages for student workers who worked in the plant to help pay their tuition. They raised chickens and prepared low-cost chicken dinners for the Lincoln Heights community during the holidays.[57] Burroughs was most proud of the completion of the Trades Hall in 1928, after a multiyear fundraising campaign to build it. It became the main administrative and classroom building on campus, and Mary McLeod Bethune delivered the keynote speech at the dedication ceremony of this important building to the everyday operation of the school. Trades Hall is now a national historic landmark and it is the only remaining building left of the NTS today.[58]

The Foundational Philosophies of the NTS Curriculum

With NTS faculty, Burroughs built a curriculum that reflected the meanings behind the buildings on campus. As education historian Alana D. Murray has argued, Burroughs constantly worried about fundraising, yet she had the benefit of not being under the surveillance of a school board system or white philanthropists. Thus, she had the independence to design the NTS's blended curriculum.[59] In 1909 the NTS consisted of sixth-grade to twelfth-grade classes, and the curriculum included programs in domestic science, missionary training, typing, shorthand, sewing, public speaking, English, drama, printing, bookkeeping, and music. By the 1930s NTS students could couple their trade courses with an array of academic courses, including Latin, Spanish, literature, business, sociology, psychology, music, and ancient and general history.

While Burroughs advocated for legislation to address structural inequalities, she also believed that Black people could help better their own lives through a strict adherence to Christian doctrines and presenting their best selves. The NTS was well-known for its motto of the 3 B's—Bible, bath, and broom. The Bible represented the school's focus on spirituality, and the bath and broom emphasized the importance of personal and spatial cleanliness. Burroughs believed everyone should strive for clean living on all fronts—including personal hygiene, healthy eating, and sanitation and organization of the home.[60]

For Burroughs, cleanliness was not a gendered responsibility. She held not only NTS students but also Black male business owners to standards of cleanliness. As she told members of the National Negro Business League Convention in 1915,

> It has been my observation and experience among many of our business men and women that they do not lay the proper stress upon the necessity

of keeping their places of business neat. . . . It is an open secret that some of the business establishments run by members of our race are so unattractive and so uninviting that they do not deserve and should not expect the patronage of anybody. . . . If you business men expect to win our trade or a goodly share of the trade of our community, you will have to keep your shops in order and you will have to keep yourselves in order. . . . I hold that no man has a right to be in any mercantile business who cannot keep himself clean, tidy, and presentable.[61]

Similar to other Black women educators of her time, she argued that women in any occupation needed to learn the "fine art of homemaking" because the "crux of the Negro problem is in the home."[62] In this sense, she argued that Black women and girls could address structural inequalities within their own abodes.

Burroughs's views about domesticity might appear jarring in the twenty-first century, but they were in line with the beliefs of many leading early twentieth-century Black educators, including W. E. B. Du Bois, Mary McLeod Bethune, Booker T. Washington, and Anna Julia Cooper. It is understandable how Burroughs and some of her contemporaries arrived at this type of conclusion when there were few to no federal and state resources for Black people in the early twentieth century and after the federal government failed to uphold Reconstruction-era promises. As she would later argue in a government study, the federal government needed to pass legislation to fix the national housing crisis that relegated many Black people to poor living conditions.[63] She also knew that the government would be slow to move on any program that benefited Black people, if they did anything at all. Black people could rely on only themselves and what was at their disposal in their own communities.

Educators like Burroughs saw domesticity as a realm that Black women could control and mold for the benefit of themselves and their families. They also carried the enormous task of disproving racist scientific claims that Black people were socially and physically unfit for citizenship rights. As she was preparing students to transform the labor market, she viewed tidiness as a way for Black people to assert their humanity and discipline while organizing for an equitable society. Untidiness, Burroughs preached, would lead to the downfall of any worker or business and would thereby compromise Black people's ability not only to compete against whites for jobs and business but to establish economic ownership of their communities and fight for their political rights.

Burroughs integrated her belief in the necessity of racial pride for Black empowerment into the curriculum by mandating that all students, no matter their trade emphasis, pass a written and oral examination on Black history before graduating from the NTS. Teaching Black history was a subversive act during the racial segregation era in the United States. As historian Jarvis Givens has noted, Black teachers were often subjected to violence and employment termination when they taught Black history and other related subjects that white townspeople and school officials deemed rebellious. This constant degrading and dangerous oversight of Black teachers is a reason Burroughs initially insisted on an all-Black women's board for the NTS and why she wanted to build the school with donations from only Black people.[64] While Burroughs did not face life-threatening violence like Black teachers in the South and in other parts of the country, what distinguished the NTS from other institutions was its Black history graduation requirement. According to Burroughs, knowledge about Black history would instill in students the confidence to take care of themselves and challenge racial and gender discrimination in any profession and the larger society.

For the first decades of the school, Burroughs and NTS faculty relied on Carter G. Woodson's *The Negro in Our History* and *The Story of the American Negro* as textbooks for Black history lessons. It should go without saying that these books represented Woodson's exhaustive primary research of Black history. His books provided NTS students with detailed histories of precolonial Africa, slavery in the United States and Africa, and the Reconstruction era in the United States. Burroughs also used as instructional materials rare archival sources from her own extensive research of Black history. As historian Charles H. Wesley remembered, Burroughs helped guide and counsel Woodson a great deal in his collection of Black women's history materials. Wesley was especially impressed with Burroughs's collection on Black women's organizations.[65] As a generous preservationist who wanted people to use her collection for scholar-activism, Burroughs loaned Wesley primary source materials that were essential to his premier book on the history of the National Association of Colored Women's Clubs.[66]

Dorothy Porter Wesley, librarian and architect of Howard University's renowned Moorland-Springarn Research Center, was married to Charles Wesley and was in awe of Burroughs's archive of rare photographs and literature related to African history. She spent three to four days in Burroughs's dining room looking through every document imaginable to find materials Burroughs had written and collected about John Chilembwe, a Baptist pastor who was a leader in the labor and anticolonial movements in Malawi. As Wesley remembered, Burroughs "had watched his career and made reports about him. . . . She helped him while he was building his career in the U.S. . . . The biography of Chilembwe was published and she is acknowledged in the book for providing much of the information about his early life."[67]

Although Burroughs had a rich collection of sources to use in the classroom, she worked collaboratively with NTS faculty to determine what they considered the most effective teaching methods and materials. Burroughs held monthly faculty meetings to discuss with faculty their ideas on how to improve the curriculum and overall instruction at the school. Any proposed changes to the curriculum were discussed at length, and final decisions were determined by a vote.[68] Committed to providing students with the latest methods of instruction, NTS faculty attended summer school for teachers at the Hampton Institute, where they exchanged pedagogical and curriculum ideas with Black teachers and principals from schools across the South, including Spelman College and Tuskegee Institute.[69] Teachers from Spelman College, Storer College, Tuskegee Institute, Talladega College, Morehouse College, Hampton Institute, Howard University, and several other historically Black colleges and universities visited the NTS campus to discuss curriculum ideas with Burroughs and NTS faculty.[70] While Burroughs's racial and gender politics were foundational to all of the trade and academic courses, she thought it was of special importance to the domestic science program. Of all the NTS trade programs, the Domestic Science Department was the most extensive, best funded, and most essential to Burroughs's vision of driving societal change for Black people.[71]

Driving Change through a Domestic Science Curriculum

Black women and girls had held domestic service positions since slavery, and Burroughs wanted to make sure they continued to do so and maximized their presence in all domestic science–related occupations. Explaining the Black nationalist aims of her pedagogical approach, Burroughs asserted, "unless we get busy and meet the demands for trained women, Negro women will lose their places in the homes and kitchens as surely as our thoughtless, antiquated [Black] men lost their places as barbers, whitewashers, waiters, and bootblacks."[72] According to Burroughs, if Black women were pushed out of domestic service positions, they would be unable to support themselves and their families, which would ultimately and detrimentally impact the entire Black community. Although Black women were most easily hired in household employment, domestic service employers in northern cities generally hired British, Scandinavian, and German women for the highest-paid position of governess, and Black women for the lowest-paid position of general household worker.[73] Burroughs and NTS faculty designed a robust domestic science curriculum to change this racial and wage hierarchy and better position Black women in household jobs. In fact, they aimed to create multiple forms of employment opportunities for NTS students by offering courses in homemaking, housekeeping, household administration, interior decorating, laundering, home nursing, and management for matrons and directors of school dining rooms and dormitories.[74]

Domestic Science Hall (renamed Alpha Hall by 1930) was the dedicated classroom building for domestic science students. Burroughs and faculty designed rigorous scientific lesson plans that they believed gave students a competitive edge in the labor market. Rather than teaching students how to serve employers, domestic science instructors prepared lessons that addressed the intersecting needs of students and employing families. In the domestic science courses, teachers did not emphasize submissiveness toward employers nor how to take care of employers' children. Teachers created domestic science tests and instruction materials that focused on knowledge about nutrition and food composition that students could use for themselves and in any domestic science occupation, whether they took positions as domestic workers or teachers. Offering these scientific lessons undermined prevailing twentieth-century racist and sexist scientific claims that Black women and girls were intellectually and morally incapable of learning science.

Bettie B. Henderson, who taught the introductory domestic science course, expected students to provide detailed answers to final exam questions about a range of scientific processes from describing the number of "elements enter[ed] into the body through the food that we eat" to "species of shrub [from which] tea is grown" to "the different types of sugar and the countries that produce each."[75] Henderson also taught students how to use this in-depth knowledge about food chemistry to achieve personal and community health. As historian Jennifer Wallach has argued, caring for one's health has been a form of Black resistance since the era of slavery. Achieving good health was a line of defense against structural racism and preparation for the work that needed to be done to demand full citizenship rights.[76] Similar to food justice activists and public health experts today, Burroughs argued that Black communities' disproportionate rates of chronic illnesses and infant mortality stemmed from a lack of access to quality medical services and nutritious and affordable foods.[77] Bettie Henderson was determined to equip domestic science students with scientific knowledge to help protect their physical well-being in the face of these systemic injustices that undermined their survival.

Henderson taught lessons about how to prepare balanced and affordable meals for themselves and potential employers. Most drawn to the benefits of these budgetary lessons for herself, Dolores Fields, a domestic science student, wrote in her final term paper that she would apply her newly acquired knowledge when she returned home. She asserted, "I learned how to plan my menu and balance my diet," "cut expenses," and "make my family healthy."[78] According to Burroughs, no one was above the art of cooking. All Black women and girls needed to learn how to make do with what they had to cook nutritious and inexpensive meals, even if they did not labor as domestic workers. She modeled this philosophy by cooking big dinners for students on Thanksgiving and Christmas. She was known for her eggless and butterless cake and meat dishes that she prepared from the wild animals on campus.[79] In addition to finance

Figure 4.9. Students in domestic science class, circa 1910–40. The charts on the wall show that the curriculum included a rigorous and scientific study of food composition. Nannie Helen Burroughs Papers, Prints and Photographs Division, Library of Congress.

management lessons, NTS faculty and Burroughs taught students how to protect themselves from bodily injuries in the kitchen. Students were quizzed on how to operate kitchen ranges to prevent combustion and were required to memorize the exact number of seconds it took a person's hands to burn when reaching into an oven or over a boiling pot.[80] Knowledge of how to operate household technology was beneficial to students both for the care of their own homes and when working in employers' kitchens.

NTS domestic science faculty taught students how to take care of employers' and their own future homes in the Mary G. Burdette Memorial Home. The home contained a large wraparound porch, a basement laundry room, four bedrooms, a dining room, a pantry and kitchen, a visiting

Figure 4.10. Combined lessons about spirituality, domestic science, and health studies, circa 1930s–1940s. The sign "We Desire" above the far right chalkboard indicates that good health was a goal taught in class. Nannie Helen Burroughs Papers, Prints and Photographs Division, Library of Congress.

area, and a fireplace. The building was named after the first president of the Women's Baptist Home Mission Society, who was also a supporter of the NTS. The society likely considered it a noble cause to donate funds for the construction of a model home they believed would assist students in learning how to become subservient "efficient" servants.[81] Contrary to the society's desires, Burroughs and NTS faculty taught students to think of the model home as not only a prospective employer's home but as a type of home they could aim to purchase for themselves. Students practiced furnishing the model home without going into debt and by avoiding stores that exploited Black communities with overpriced installment plans. In the dining room of the practice home, students gained an inside view of how to waitress, cater meals, and manage a business. With guidance from NTS faculty, students prepared and served meals to customers from the local community who dined on campus.[82]

Carter G. Woodson was a frequent customer of the NTS dining services, and he wrote an article to promote the student-run business. He wrote that he was served by a domestic science student from Arkansas who prepared a meal "cooked according to scientific methods . . . with a domestic touch seldom found in public places." He concluded that "Miss Burroughs had given her [the student] the fundamentals in catering."[83] Considering Woodson's respect for Black women's work, it is no coincidence that he used the word "catering" to communicate to readers that NTS students were skilled and specialized workers.[84] Catering, or the cooking, organizing, and presentation of meals for formal affairs, had been a respected form of labor in both white and Black communities since the mid-1800s. Since slavery, Black women and men had established their own catering businesses as their preferred alternative to domestic service and sharecropping.[85]

Waitressing, another skill students learned from working in the dining hall, was a job that many women preferred over domestic work. Waitressing jobs did not always pay more than household employment, but they had defined work hours and duties. Waitresses were not expected to care for other people's children, and they were not under the constant surveillance of domestic service employers. According to the occupational census from 1900 to 1930, primarily white immigrant and white American women were employed as waitresses.[86] NTS domestic science faculty created waitressing lessons to counteract this employment discrimination in the restaurant industry. Burroughs also used the dining hall as an intimate setting for students to learn from prominent race leaders. After graduation ceremonies, commencement speakers would often dine with students in the dining hall. In 1917, for example, Mary Talbert, then vice president of the National Association of Colored Women, delivered the commencement address. Afterward, Talbert and Mary Church Terrell, first president of the National Association of Colored Women, dined with students as their special dinner guests.[87]

Burroughs was a multifaceted labor strategist and educator. She knew that service work was not an ideal occupation for Black women. In fact, the breakdown of students across the various school programs during the first years of the NTS revealed that most students had ambitions outside of domestic service. In 1911, for example, students registered

Figure 4.11. NTS dining room, Mary G. Burdette Home. Nannie Helen Burroughs Papers, Prints and Photographs Division, Library of Congress.

for a variety of programs, and music was the most popular: the Music Department enrolled forty-three students; Dressmaking Department, thirty-four; Missionary Department, seventeen; Business Department, twelve; Millinery Department, ten; Public Speaking Department, nine; Hairdressing, Manicuring, and Massaging Department, nine; and Domestic Science Department, seven.[88] As someone who resisted her mother's recommendation to become a domestic worker, Burroughs saw the value in creating new lines of employment for Black women.

Diversifying the Curriculum to Challenge Segregation in the Labor Market

While pushing for domestic service reform, Burroughs and NTS faculty developed a flexible and dynamic trade curriculum for Black women and girls to assert their rightful place in any profession of their choosing—and particularly those professions dominated by men or white women. W. E. B. Du Bois saw great promise in Burroughs's ambitious curriculum and made a point of advertising the NTS in *The Crisis* for several years.[89] In addition to the domestic science program, Burroughs established a missionary program. As mentioned in chapter 2, Burroughs's views about missionary work were layered. While she upheld the imperialist notion that everyone should commit to the Christian faith, she also preached that Abyssinia, now known as Ethiopia and Eritrea, was the birthplace of Black people and Christianity. She saw missionary work as a gateway for women to assume leadership positions in the church and in education. Graduates of the missionary program often became teachers and school administrators.[90] These opportunities for NTS missionary graduates dovetailed with Burroughs's insistence that Black women and girls travel and aim to become financially self-sufficient. As a faithful supporter of the NTS and all initiatives related to Burroughs, Reverend Walter Brooks accepted her invitation to teach the first cohort of students in the missionary program. Brooks kept in touch with NTS students after they graduated from the program and collected donations from his church to send them essentials for their students in Africa.[91] He also rolled up his sleeves to do manual labor at the NTS. Reverend Brooks is remembered for lending a helping hand when Burroughs needed to move furniture in the school buildings.[92]

In addition to missionary training, Burroughs was especially motivated to create clerical courses based on her own experience of being denied a federal office clerk job even after passing the civil service exam required for hire. Clerical work was initially dominated by native-born white men, but this trend shifted when native-born white women began dominating the profession when more managerial positions were created for white men. Federal clerical positions were certainly harder for Black women to come by during President Woodrow Wilson's administration. Black people were practically excluded from "good paying" federal jobs in DC.[93] As Eric Yellin argues, Wilson did not pass a law or policy demanding federal segregation, yet he agreed with it and was unwilling to intervene when administrators in federal departments separated Blacks and whites within the same facilities from working side

Figure 4.12. Walter Brooks (*center*) among missionary program students and teachers, circa 1909. Nannie Helen Burroughs Papers, Prints and Photographs Division, Library of Congress.

by side or when they cut the wages, hours, and promotional opportunities of Black federal workers.[94] Taking their cues from a purposely silent president, federal agencies and employers refused to hire Black women for clerical positions. By 1920 only 3 percent of clerk positions in the nation's capital were held by Black women.[95] Burroughs vowed to change this trend by establishing stenography courses at the NTS.

Burroughs had such an inclusive vision of the clerical profession that she vowed to train disabled students in secretarial work. In his promotional article of the NTS clerical training courses, Carter G. Woodson recalled that he met a disabled graduate of the NTS from North Carolina who worked as a secretary at a Black-owned business in Washington, DC. He wrote,

> Not long after I had occasion to dictate a letter in the office of a colored man who heads one of the largest business enterprises controlled by Negroes, I had some doubt about his secretary, a physically deformed girl from North Carolina, who has such difficulty in locomotion that she has to support herself by taking hold of the objects as she passes through the

building—just the very sort of girl that the public schools would not have taken up time with, one who could never get into a university without such help. This girl, however, took that dictation with such ease, worked it out so thoroughly, and handled the affair in such a secretarial fashion that I immediately inquired as to where she received such thorough training. ["]At Miss Burroughs' school["] was the reply.[96]

More than likely Dr. Woodson was referring to Carrie Pettipher, who Burroughs proudly described as having just as interesting and challenging of a story as Hellen Keller. Burroughs had so much confidence in Pettipher that she hired her as a secretary for the NTS.[97] Pettipher's employment at a Black company and at the NTS reveals the importance of Black businesses and schools in providing job opportunities for Black women who might have been denied jobs elsewhere in their fields of expertise. The NTS also provided teaching jobs for women graduates of Howard University. By 1931 two Howard University alumni—one of whom had been teaching at the NTS for fourteen years—were full-time faculty at the NTS.[98]

The NTS curriculum included several other industrial trade courses in which Black women were grossly underrepresented, including sewing, printing, and commercial laundry work. Mary White Ovington, cofounder of the National Association for the Advancement of Colored People, revealed in her study *Half a Man* that employers justified not hiring Black women for industrial jobs by claiming that white American and white immigrant women refused to work alongside them.[99] Although factory jobs became available to Black women during World War I, employers stopped hiring Black women when men came back from the war. Table 4.1 shows the scope of the situation that Burroughs and her colleagues were taking on and highlights how the NTS curriculum was a direct challenge to the systemic and intersecting racial, class, and gender inequalities in the industrial labor market.

While Burroughs and NTS faculty prepared students to dismantle occupational race and gender prescriptions, they also offered internship opportunities with the aim of teaching students how to start their own businesses. Working as a private seamstress for clients was preferred over laboring under the harsh working conditions of textile factories

Table 4.1. Demographics of women in clerical and industrial fields, 1900–1930

	1900	1920	1930
Clerical occupations			
Black women	3,014	7,921	10,862
Immigrant white women	40,697	90, 949	114,387
Native-born white women	544,770	1,322,749	1,858,914
Printing, publishing, and engraving			
Black women	101	76	413
Immigrant white women	1,159	541	2,488
Native-born white women	14,728	1,033	27,456
Laundry owners, managers, and officials			
Black women	—	131	63
Immigrant white women	—	347	276
Native-born white women	—	578	596
Stenographers			
Black women	177	1,970	216
Immigrant white women	5,994	32,232	38,735
Native-born white women	79,981	303,956	732,171

US Bureau of the Census, "Color and Nativity of Gainful Workers," *Twelfth Census of the United States, 1900*, 11 and 14; US Bureau of the Census, "Color or Race, Nativity, and Parentage of Occupied Persons," *Fourteenth Census of the United States, 1920*, 346–47, 358–59, 357–58; US Bureau of the Census, "Color and Nativity of Gainful Workers," *Fifteenth Census of the United States, 1930*, 74, 77, 79, 85. The 1910 census included information about the sex of workers in the printing trades only by state. Data regarding the race and sex of commercial laundry workers and managers were not available in the 1900 and 1910 censuses.

and piecemeal factory work at home. As evidenced by the 1911 Triangle Shirtwaist Factory fire in New York City, garment companies were not regulated, and they regularly subjected seamstresses to life-threatening conditions and everyday cruelties such as penalties for taking restroom breaks. As Eileen Boris and Cynthia Daniels have argued, harsh requirements and low wages extended into piecemeal work that women performed inside of their own homes for factories.[100] NTS courses in nonfactory sewing provided a critical avenue for Black girls and women to move into more autonomous lines of work. Students were taught to sew by hand and machine to prepare for a variety of private customer preferences and to adorn themselves and decorate their own homes. Burroughs was ecstatic when students secured the types of jobs that she had imagined for them when building the curriculum. In her promotional

Table 4.2. Demographics of women working as seamstresses, 1900–1930

	1900	1920	1930
Black women	11,452	26,961	20,433
Immigrant white women	27,086	37,479	22,571
Native-born white women	107,474	110,245	112,839

Does not include factory workers. US Bureau of the Census, "Color and Nativity of Gainful Workers," *Twelfth Census of the United States, 1900*, 11 and 14; US Bureau of the Census, "Color or Race, Nativity, and Parentage of Occupied Persons," *Fourteenth Census of the United States, 1920*, 345; US Bureau of the Census, "Color and Nativity of Gainful Workers," *Fifteenth Census of the United States, 1930*, 77.

school pamphlet, she boasted that NTS alumna Frankie Turner graduated from the sewing program and secured a job making gowns for First Lady Eleanor Roosevelt.[101] Table 4.2 helps explain Burroughs's enthusiasm about students like Frankie who broke into private sewing, a field dominated by white women.

Most Black women and girls as young as ten years old worked outside sewing and clerical trades in the most exploitative lines of work as sharecroppers or domestic workers.[102] Like with her domestic science program, Burroughs worked at challenging the perception that manual labor was undignified work and agricultural work was unskilled labor through her farming and horticulture program.

While Booker T. Washington did not support the NTS, his wife and Tuskegee educator Margaret Murray Washington became a lifelong friend of Burroughs. Burroughs and Margaret Washington supported each other's institutions and exchanged pedagogical ideas throughout their partnership. As the daughter of a washerwoman and as someone who labored as a domestic worker to pay her way through school, Washington shared Burroughs's profound respect for manual laborers and domestic work.[103] Together, Burroughs and Washington promoted the philosophy that agricultural work was a skill that all students should learn for everyday survival given the absence of healthy food sources in many Black communities. They also encouraged their students to use their agricultural skills to grow and sell their own crops instead of for white landowners. Burroughs and Washington believed that their students could enjoy horticulture as a profitable and creative profession in an economy that often relegated Black women and girls to sharecropping. Similar to Margaret Washington's two-year horticulture program at the Tuskegee Institute, Burroughs established a horticulture program for NTS students to urge them to go into business for themselves selling ornamental flowers.[104] With help from students and faculty, Burroughs transformed the open land on the campus grounds into a farm and garden where students could practice their agricultural and horticulture skills. They raised animals and cultivated crops and plants for their own use and to sell to community members. Profits from the sales helped students pay off their tuition. Burroughs was especially proud when students could start their own businesses after completing the program. Burroughs boasted that Christina Jean Francois, a thirty-year-old Haitian student, took what she learned from the horticulture program back home and became a professional gardener in Haiti. Burroughs was also proud to announce that Susie Green, another NTS alumna, received support from the US Department of Agriculture to start her own gardening business in Washington, DC. [105]

The NTS curriculum was ever-evolving and responsive to shifts in the economy, culture, and politics. During World Wars I and II, the NTS offered courses in manufacturing work so that students could take over jobs once held by men who were then overseas fighting in the wars. Burroughs's insistence on training students for factory jobs was a direct challenge to employers' beliefs that Black women were intellectually incapable of operating what was considered advanced industrial technology such as factory machines. Employers used this prevailing mythical belief to justify not hiring Black women for factory jobs. As historian Carroll Pursell has demonstrated, Black people advanced technology during the Industrial Age through their inventions. Building on this tradition of experimentation, Burroughs developed industrial programs to move students from the bottom to the forefront of industrial capitalism.[106]

In the early years of the NTS, Burroughs was adamantly against beauty culture. She accused Black women who straightened their hair and wore makeup of trying to look like white women. Burroughs shifted her thinking when she saw lucrative entrepreneurial opportunities become available to Black women in the 1920s and 1930s. Probably influenced by her National Negro Business League colleague Madam C. J. Walker, Burroughs argued that beauty industry jobs were Black women's jobs and they needed to hold onto them at all costs. Always aware of labor market changes and trends, Burroughs knew that beauty culture professions had become popular among Black women across socioeconomic class. Committed to building a curriculum that was responsive to the occupational desires of Black women, by the 1930s she had added barbering and beauty culture courses to the curriculum.[107]

As part of her broader advocacy and networking, Burroughs promoted the transgressive work that students were doing in the classrooms through photography. Beginning in the 1910s and throughout the 1930s, Burroughs commissioned Scurlock Studio to take photographs of students at work in the classrooms and on the farm. Her decision to work with the company underscored her belief in supporting local Black-owned businesses. Scurlock Studio was a prominent Black photography company in Washington, DC, dedicated to recording the achievements of Black people in the nation's capital. Burroughs's placement of a

Figure 4.13. Clerical training class, circa 1910–1920, Scurlock Studio. Scurlock's studio was the only one of its kind dedicated to documenting the lives of African Americans in the nation's capital (Zax, "The Scurlock Studio"). Nannie Helen Burroughs Papers, Prints and Photographs Division, Library of Congress.

photograph of Abraham Lincoln in the stenography classroom (fig. 4.13) emphasized how she viewed this type of student learning in NTS classrooms as an assertion of their citizenship rights.

Teaching the Value of Black Entrepreneurship

Most Black institutions of the early twentieth century believed in the importance of establishing Black-owned businesses to generate wealth and meet the needs of surrounding communities. The Hampton Institute had a community nursing program. Tuskegee University had a mobile health clinic and agricultural extension courses. Spelman College had a community garden and nursing program. In addition to the dining hall and poultry plant, the NTS had a public laundry named Sunlight Laundry where students gained practical experience in operating industrial machinery and running a commercial laundry business to benefit themselves and their communities. Gaining this type of entrepreneurial experience was important, since many Black women with home-based laundries had lost clientele due to the rise of commercial laundries. Burroughs advocated for Black laundresses to hold on to their trade, yet she also wanted students to position themselves at the forefront of industrialization by going into the commercial laundry business for themselves.[108] For women who could not create their own businesses, laundry work was a portable skill that they could take with them during the Great Migration to wherever they wanted to live and wherever they wanted to work—inside of their own homes or in a commercial laundry.

Like with the domestic science curriculum, Burroughs and NTS faculty taught what they considered superior cleaning methods to help differentiate students from white women competing for the same jobs. Their lessons were also important to the everyday survival and protection of Black women and girls. Burroughs and NTS faculty stressed to students who took an interest in working at Sunlight Laundry that they needed to clean the linens until they were in pristine condition. The motto for Sunlight Laundry was: "Where All Clothes Are Washed Right. Where All Clothes Are Kept White." The motto reflected the pride that historian Blair Kelley refers to in her discussion about laundry work as a skilled and independent form of labor that Black women had taken pride in learning and passing down through generations in their family since slavery. Laundry work sustained Black families, but it could also be dangerous work for Black women, especially in the South. Black women taught their daughters and granddaughters how to clean linens thoroughly to protect themselves as much as possible from white clientele who accused laundresses of damaging or losing their linens. Unfounded claims could easily result in lynchings, imprisonment, or loss in wages.[109]

For the first decade of the NTS, Burroughs promoted entrepreneurship while engaging in institution building in Washington, DC, and in Louisville. When she launched the NTS, she continued working with women in Louisville to keep the Woman's Industrial Club going.[110] While traveling between two cities to manage the NTS and the Woman's Industrial Club, Burroughs challenged the gross underrepresentation of Black women in the printing trades by creating spaces at the NTS and the Woman's Industrial Club to equip students with knowledge and job training for editorial, production, and managerial positions at print shops. Black women were often excluded from these positions due to discriminatory hiring practices that deemed them biologically incapable of industrial work that required higher-level thinking and problem-solving. White men were considered the epitome of intelligence, strength, and moral fortitude.[111] This myth was a major contributing factor to segregation in the printing trade. For the first half of the twentieth century white men owned and held supervisory positions in the majority of print shops in the country, and they were chief editors of most national newspapers (table 4.1).

Leading by example, Burroughs showed students at the Woman's Industrial Club and at the NTS how Black women could establish their own national printing company. In 1909, with L. G. Jordan, she cofounded a calendar and postcard company known as the Douglass Improvement Company, which they operated from the Woman's Industrial Club building.[112] They were ahead of the curve in making one of the country's first line of calendars and postcards featuring non-stereotypical representations of Black people. As Burroughs asserted in a promotional letter, "There is a growing tendency on the part of men who have race pride, and race ideals, to demand such pictures as will portray the bright side of life of the race. You have doubtless noticed that most of the drummers who come to you displaying calendars, show the beautiful WHITE

Figure 4.14. Burroughs poses for the Douglass Improvement Company calendar. Nannie Helen Burroughs Papers, Prints and Photographs Division, Library of Congress.

women, the pretty WHITE children; but there is not a jobber who will come to you, showing any of OUR beautiful women and children."[113]

Burroughs made clear at the 1909 National Negro Business League meeting in Louisville that creating jobs and promoting positive images of Black people were her motivating factors for establishing the company. She explained that she and Jordan "were trying to establish a business enterprise that will give employment to our young men and women" and specialize in "printing and furnishing various kinds of calendars designed and illustrated as to show the better side of Negro life."[114] The Douglass Improvement Company was so successful that local printing and engraving companies helped finance it with unlimited credit.[115] In 1912, three years after the company's founding, Burroughs launched a periodical known as *The Worker* from her printing department at the NTS. Her cousin Jennie Poindexter and other students worked in the printing department to fill local copying orders and help print copies of what became a popular religious and labor magazine that remained in print for more than a century.[116] Although Burroughs emphasized hard

Figure 4.15. Unnamed woman in a photo that also likely appeared in a Douglass Improvement Company calendar. Nannie Helen Burroughs Papers, Prints and Photographs Division, Library of Congress.

work, she also wanted students to love and enjoy what they did for a living and life outside work.

Teaching How to Leisure, Love, and Learn

According to Burroughs, a quality education was not solely about working hard and serving communities. She believed that labor justice included Black women's and girls' right to engage in enjoyable activities outside the classroom. Taking the drudgery out of Black women's working conditions meant finding love in one's work and overall life. Workers needed time for reflection and rejuvenation to do their jobs well. As she explained,

> Love, Learning, Labor, and Leisure are the lamps of life and the chief business of an institution of learning is to tell us where to find the oil, how to fill our lamps and how to trim them and keep them burning. . . . Great poets, philosophers, artists, preachers, teachers, and artisans are born in

the hours of leisure. The great thoughts that revolutionize the world and set new forces to work are born when man sits alone with God and in the world of nature.[117]

Black women and girls claiming the right to leisure and reflection was a radical educational philosophy. During most of the twentieth century, only well-to-do white housewives were considered worthy of engaging in leisurely activities, while Black women toiled in their homes and attended to white women's wants and needs. Encouraging students to engage in sports, swimming, and the arts was a subversive act that defied workplace and social limitations imposed on Black women and girls. As Ava Purkiss has argued, Black women also promoted physical exercise as a way of asserting themselves as first-class US citizens. Since emancipation, Black women's physical bodies had been under intense scrutiny, physical abuse, and stereotyped to justify the denial of their amendment rights. As Purkiss put it, Black women pushed back against these tropes to "fashion themselves as 'fit' citizens and wrestle with the social, physical, and representational uses of the Black female body."[118]

Burroughs implemented this philosophy into the recreational activities at the school. The NTS campus had a swimming pool where students had free time each day to hang out with their friends. Students had the option of joining one of the NTS basketball teams—the Falcons or Beats All—that competed with other teams across Washington, DC. Dedicated to advocating for youth and physical exercise, toward the end of her career, Burroughs purchased eighty acres of land in Constantine, Michigan, to serve as a national campsite for Black youth.[119] Along with physical exercise, Burroughs and faculty promoted civic engagement and overall well-roundedness. By the 1940s students could join a wide array of social activities and organizations at the NTS. They could run for class president or for student council representative. They could join a literary society and aim for induction into the honors society known as Zeta Rho Chi. They could edit and write for the *Co-op News: The Official N.T. & P.S. Paper*. Students organized school assembly events where faculty and administrators led discussions about romantic relationships, art, religion, politics, and culture.[120]

To help make learning fun and rewarding, Burroughs and NTS faculty

Figure 4.16. NTS students enjoying the campus swimming pool outside the print shop. Nannie Helen Burroughs Papers, Prints and Photographs Division, Library of Congress.

Figure 4.17. NTS basketball team. Nannie Helen Burroughs Papers, Prints and Photographs Division, Library of Congress.

created a range of annual prizes for various types of student performances. They gave awards to students in all levels of junior high and high school, and the amount varied between $2.50 and $5.00. Prize categories included best in Latin, social service, music, Bible, duties, plain sewing, personal appearance, dormitory room organization, and most exemplary all-around student. Maggie Lena Walker, who had become a member of the board of trustees, funded prizes for best business students at the beginning and advanced levels. Three prizes were dedicated to domestic science for highest average and the best-kept uniform and notebook. The student who won the highest average in domestic science received a one-year subscription to *Boston American Cookery*. The student who took the most copious and organized notes in the Negro History course won a prize for that. Finally, the valedictorian was awarded the Cornelia Aldis Memorial Prize, which was funded by a British woman philanthropist who left a lump sum of money to the NTS before she died.[121]

Persisting through Institutional Challenges

While growing the school, Burroughs constantly dealt with backlash from National Baptist Convention, USA leaders who attempted to take over her school by auditing the NTS financial records. Each time, she proved them wrong. She also hit a rough patch during the Depression, which led to a sharp decline in student enrollment. One key decision Burroughs took at this time to revive the school while staying true to its mission was to change the school's name. In 1931 she initiated a vote among the board of trustees to change the name of the NTS to the National Trade and Professional School for Women and Girls to distinguish it from the National Training School for Girls, a juvenile carceral institution for Black girls in DC.[122] Her vision for Black women and girls was far from the punitive mission of the reform school, and it frustrated her to know that people sometimes confused the two institutions simply because of the similarity in their names. In 1939 she formally changed the school's name on the deed from the National Training School for Women and Girls to the National Trade and Professional School.[123]

In an effort to expand the mission of the National Trade and Professional School, Burroughs attempted to create a junior college department that would serve as a feeder school to Howard University. She even organized a meeting with philanthropist Anson Phelps Stokes and Howard University's President Mordecai Johnson to discuss the details. Adam Clayton Powell Sr., Tuskegee University's President Robert R. Moton, and Reverend Walter H. Brooks attended the meeting to support Burroughs's idea. But Stokes and Johnson disappointed Burroughs with suggestions that she demand more tuition from her students and that she turn the National Trade and Professional School into a training school solely for preparing women and girls for Christian social service and leadership. Burroughs refused this approach. As she stated in a letter to Stokes, her objectives were to train her students to "help meet the increasing demand for specially trained women workers in many fields."[124] Despite Stokes's and Johnson's rejection of her idea, Burroughs established a junior college division of the National Trade and Professional School, and Stokes reduced his donations to her school.[125] Still, junior college alumni made history. Among the many graduates of the college was Agnes Nebo von Ballmoos, the first Black ethnomusicologist in US history.[126]

As Burroughs battled patriarchy from within the National Baptist Convention, educational leaders across the country recognized her as the trailblazing leader she had long been in education. At the invitation of Booker T. Washington's presidential successor Robert R. Moton in 1934, Burroughs became the first woman to deliver a commencement address at Tuskegee University. Throughout the years of the National Trade and Professional School, Burroughs stayed true to her commitment of providing a blended curriculum for Black women and girls. She also never abandoned her Black history course. In 1961 Burroughs's teachings about the importance of historical knowledge, self-learning, and entrepreneurial skills in the absence of businesses and schoolbooks that centered Black students came full circle. She had begun creating a textbook for students based on articles she had collected about the history of Islam and Christianity. Shortly after Burroughs passed away, her favorite student Alice Smith used the knowledge she had acquired in the NTS Black history course along with her own research about Africa to complete the textbook. She included articles about anticolonial and communist movements in Africa and quizzes for students to identify the names and photographs of African leaders including Haile Selassie, Kwame Nkrumah, and Sékou Touré. Alice entitled the new NTS textbook *The Congo: From Leopold to Lumumba* and published it from the art shop on campus for use in classrooms.[127]

———◆◆▶———

Throughout her career as NTS president, Burroughs knew that education alone would not change Black women's working conditions. As she built her trailblazing institution, she organized against structural inequalities that kept women and girls like her students from lives full of opportunity. Burroughs was able to drive so much change not only through education but also at the levels of worker organizing, research and policy, art and culture, and publishing and writing. Together, her methods reveal her concrete and widespread impact at the personal, community, and governmental levels for Black women's and girls' economic justice.

Notes

1. National Baptist Convention, *Journal of the Twenty-Ninth Annual Session*, 240.
2. Excerpt from Burroughs's speech at the 1909 National Baptist Convention; Charles Stewart, "Women to Solve Servant Problem," *Baltimore Afro-American*, October 2, 1909.
3. Population, Philadelphia, Pennsylvania, April 15–16, 1910, in US Bureau of the Census, *Thirteenth Census of the United States, 1910*.
4. NHB, "National Training School Girls on the Firing Line in Foreign Fields," *The Worker* 1, no. 1 (January–March 1934): 37–38, Box 333, Folder 3, NHB Papers.
5. See chapter 7 for further discussion about Burroughs's family and the NTS.
6. National Baptist Convention, *Ninth Annual Session of the Women's Convention*, 1909, 286; Hine, King, and Reed, *We Specialize in the Wholly Impossible*, xii.
7. Teachers' meeting notes, Box 311, Folder 8, NHB Papers.
8. Lucy Craft Lainey founded the Haines Normal and Industrial Institute in 1886 in Augusta, Georgia. Mary McLeod Bethune founded the Daytona Educational and Industrial Training School for Negro Girls in 1904 and later Bethune-Cookman College in 1941. Charlotte Hawkins Brown founded the Palmer Memorial Institute in 1902. See McCluskey, *A Forgotten Sisterhood*, 2.
9. See chapters 5 and 6 for further discussion about the relationship between Burroughs and Margaret Murray Washington.

10. Parents mentioned their occupations in the letters and school applications. For examples, see Box 112, Folder 1, NHB Papers.

11. Anderson, *Education of Blacks in the South*, 148–50.

12. Quoted from Alice Dixon to NHB on October 14, 1943, Box 163, Folder 1, NHB Papers. Most quoted letters in this chapter are from the 1930s and 1940s because there are no preserved letters from the 1910s and most of the 1920s due to a campus fire in 1926.

13. Letter to NHB, August 1937, NHB Papers.

14. Unknown to NHB, December 6, 1930, Box 143, Folder 5, NHB Papers.

15. Gundie C. Griswold to NHB, August 14, 1930, Box 143, Folder 5, NHB Papers.

16. Irish Ramus to NHB, January 22, 1931, Box 143, Folder 6, NHB Papers.

17. NHB to Mrs. Margaret Douglas, 1942, NHB Papers.

18. Ruby Hawkins to NHB, Box 144, Folder 3, NHB Papers.

19. Pryde, "My Personal and Family Reminiscences," 103.

20. Olivia Johnson to NHB, October 13, 1933, Box 143, Folder 9, NHB Papers.

21. Pansy Martin to NHB, August 12, 1932, Box 143, Folder 7, NHB Papers.

22. Alma Jackson to NHB, September 27, 1931, Box 143, Folder 6, NHB Papers.

23. US Bureau of the Census, *Fifteenth Census of the United States, 1930*, National Training School, A11.

24. Easter, *Nannie Helen Burroughs*, 66.

25. Josephine Smalls to NHB, July 9, 1932, Box 143, Folder 3, NHB Papers.

26. Lydia Cason to NHB, August 20, 1930, Box 143, Folder 5, NHB Papers.

27. K. C. Clugh to NHB, February 17, 1931, Box 143, Folder 6, NHB Papers.

28. Mrs. M. A. Wright to NHB, October 22, 1910, Box 36, Reels 32–33, Booker T. Washington Papers.

29. Marilla Greene to NHB, September 26, 1933, Box 143, Folder 5, NHB Papers.

30. "Reminiscences of Dr. Nannie Helen Burroughs."

31. "Reminiscences of Dr. Nannie Helen Burroughs."

32. "Our 'Miss Burroughs' Was a Very Special Person."

33. Downey, *A Tale of Three Women*, 5.

34. Population, District of Columbia, in US Bureau of the Census, *Thirteenth Census of the United States, 1910*; Downey, *A Tale of Three Women*, 5.

35. Easter, *Nannie Helen Burroughs*, 62.

36. Population, District of Columbia, in US Bureau of the Census, *Thirteenth Census of the United States, 1910*; Daniel, "Nannie Helen Burroughs," 116.

37. Easter, *Nannie Helen Burroughs*, 62.

38. National Baptist Convention, *Journal of the Thirty-Sixth Session*, 141.

39. National Baptist Convention, 140.

40. Population, in US Bureau of the Census, *Fourteenth Census of the United States, 1920*, 10A–10B.

41. Population, Orange, Virginia, in US Bureau of the Census, *Thirteenth Census of the United States, 1910*, 9B.

42. 1920 Meeting Minutes, Box 1, Folder 32, National Baptist Convention Records.

43. Lawrence, notes from interview with NHB.

44. Population, in US Bureau of the Census, *Fourteenth Census of the United States, 1920*, 10A–10B.

45. In 1915 the National Baptist Convention split into two organizations—National Baptist Convention, USA, Incorporated and National Baptist Convention of America—due to internal disputes concerning ownership of the National Baptist Publishing Board. The NTS was within the purview of the National Baptist Convention, USA, Incorporated. Brooks, "Unification and Division among Colored Baptists," 20–22.

46. Pickens, *Nannie Helen Burroughs and the School of the 3 B's*, 11.

47. NTS salary records, Box 47, Folder 6, NHB Papers.

48. "Median Salaries of Teachers," 911.

49. "Equal Salaries for Teachers," 10.

50. Stewart, "Designing a Campus," 151–52.

51. Downey, *A Tale of Three Women*, 23.

52. Easter, *Nannie Helen Burroughs*, 67.

53. Sadie Iola Daniel, *Women Builders*, 121.

54. The exact dates that the buildings were built are mostly unknown because of scant documentation in the school's records. R. R. S. Stewart culled city architectural records to obtain estimates of when buildings on campus were constructed. See Stewart's "Designing a Campus," 140–82.

55. Stewart, 149.

56. See chapter 8 for further discussion about student performances and field trips.

57. 1909 Meeting Minutes, Box 1, Folder 32, National Baptist Convention Records.

58. National Register of Historic Places, "Trades Hall."

59. Murray, *The Development of the Alternative Black Curriculum*, 20.

60. Wolcott, "Bible, Bath, and Broom," 93–94.

61. Excerpt taken from Burroughs's speech at the sixteenth annual convention of the Negro Business League. See National Negro Business League, *Annual Report of the Sixteenth Session*, 165–66.

62. NHB, *Making Their Mark: Results in the Lives of Graduates*, Women and Social Movements International Database, 1929.

63. See chapter 6 for further discussion about Burroughs's federal housing study.

64. Givens, *Fugitive Pedagogy*, 7.

65. NHB, Textbook orders list, Box 311, NHB Papers.

66. "Reminiscences of Dr. Nannie Helen Burroughs."

67. "Reminiscences of Dr. Nannie Helen Burroughs."

68. Teachers took copious notes of their meetings. See meeting minutes, Box 311, NHB Papers.

69. William Anthoney Aery, "Preparing for Better Service: Teacher-Students at Hampton From Many States," *Cleveland Gazette*, September 1, 1917.

70. For example, see Visitors Registry, 1910–1925, 29, 41, 44, 54, 55, 62, 87, Box OV 15, Manuscript Division, Library of Congress.

71. Higginbotham, *Righteous Discontent*, 214.

72. Charles Stewart, "Women to Solve Servant Problem," *Baltimore Afro-American*, October 2, 1909.

73. Dill, *Across the Boundaries of Race and Class*, 14.

74. Higginbotham, *Righteous Discontent*, 214.

75. Bettie B. Henderson, final exam for introductory domestic science course, Box 34, Folder 1, NHB Papers.

76. Wallach, *Every Nation Has Its Dish*, 5.

77. Jackson, "'To Struggle and Battle and Overcome,'" 58.

78. Dolores Fields, Domestic Science Exam, Box 166, Folder 2, NHB Papers.

79. Fannie Cobb Carter to NHB, June 6, 1931, Box 73, Folder 8, NHB Papers; "Reminiscences of Dr. Nannie Helen Burroughs."

80. Henderson, final exam.

81. Lawrence, notes from interview with NHB.

82. Carter G. Woodson, "Nannie Helen Burroughs's School Fills a Real Need, Says Dr. Woodson," *Afro-American*, May 14, n.d., Box OV 1–OV 17, NHB Papers.

83. Carter G. Woodson, "Nannie Helen Burroughs's School Fills a Real Need, Says Dr. Woodson," *Afro-American*, May 14, n.d., Box OV 1–OV 17, NHB Papers.

84. Woodson would later publish an article about the importance of Black laundresses. See Woodson, "The Negro Washerwoman," 269–77.

85. See Pilgrim, "Masters of a Craft," 269–83.

86. See US Bureau of the Census, "Of Occupations, Classified by Sex, General Nativity, and Color," General Tables, *Twelfth Census of the United States, 1900*, 11; "Statistics of Occupations: Colored Persons 10 Years of Age and Over Engaged in Each of 140 Groups of Occupations, Distinguished as Negro, Chinese, Japanese, and Indian, Classified by Sex, *Twelfth Census of the United States, 1900*, 14; "Colored Persons 10 Years of Age and Over Engaged in Each of 140 Group Occupations Who Were Employed During Some Portion of the Census Year, Classified by Sex and Months Employed," *Twelfth Census of the United States, 1900*, 85; US Bureau of the Census, "Color and Nativity of Gainful Workers: Gainful Workers 10 Years and Over, by Occupation, Color, Nativity, and Sex For the United States," *Fifteenth Census of the United States, 1930*, 85; US

Bureau of the Census, "Classified by Sex, Color, or Race, Nativity, and Parentage for the United States, 1920—Continued," *Fourteenth Census of the United States, 1920,* 359.

87. NHB to Mary Church Terrell, May 12, 1917, Correspondence, Jan.–June 1917, Mary Church Terrell Papers, LOC.

88. 1911 Meeting Minutes, Box 1, Folder 32, National Baptist Convention Records.

89. Du Bois to NHB, June 27, 1933, Box 7, Folder 35, NHB Papers.

90. See chapter 8 for further discussion about the work experiences of missionary program graduates.

91. Clarice Gooding to NHB, "National Training School Girls," 40.

92. Jerry A. Moore quoted in "Reminiscences of Dr. Nannie Helen Burroughs."

93. Yellin, *Racism in the Nation's Service,* 1, 4.

94. See Yellin, 113–20.

95. US Bureau of the Census, *Fourteenth Census of the United States, 1920,* 897–900.

96. Carter G. Woodson, "Instructors Teach Students Instead of Books in Nannie Burroughs' Training School: Unique System in Potomac Institution Brings into Action the Power of Individual Minds," n.d., Box 324, NHB Papers.

97. NHB, "Making Their Mark: By Their Fruits Ye Shall Know Them," 1934, 7, Box 309, NHB Papers; Carrie Pettipher, correspondence about Audrey, May 8, 1936, Box 24, NHB Papers.

98. NHB to Mordecai Johnson, March 23, 1931, Mordecai Johnson Papers, cataloging in process, Moorland-Springarn Research Center, Howard University.

99. See Ovington, *Half a Man,* 161–63. For discussion of hiring preference for white women to work in shops, see Vapnek, *Breadwinners,* 78.

100. For a comparative history of the early twentieth-century working conditions of white women and Black women who did factory work and piecemeal textile work at home, see Boris and Daniels, *Homework.*

101. NHB, *Making Their Mark: Results in the Lives of Graduates.*

102. See table 10, "Negroes 10 Years of Age and Over Engaged In Each Specified Occupation, Classified By Sex and Age Periods, for the United States: 1920," 423 and 431; table 9, "Foreign-Born White Persons 10 Years of Age and Over Engaged in Each Specified Occupation, Classified By Sex and Age Periods, for the United States: 1920," 414; table 8, "Native White Persons Born of Foreign or Mixed Parentage 10 Years of Age and Over Engaged in Each Specified Occupation, Classified by Sex and Age Periods, for the United States: 1920," 405 and 413, all in US Bureau of the Census, General Tables, *Fourteenth Census of the United States, 1920,* Women's Bureau Records, Washington, DC.

103. Rouse, "Out of the Shadow of Tuskegee," 31.

104. Guy-Sheftall, *Daughters of Sorrow,* 148; Weiss, *Robert R. Taylor and Tuskegee,* 226–27.

105. NHB, *Making Their Mark: Results in the Lives of Graduates.*

106. Pursell, *Hammer in Their Hands*, xi–xvii.

107. Roberts, *Pageants, Parlors, and Pretty Women*, 68–71; Easter, *Nannie Helen Burroughs*, 64–65; Downey, *A Tale of Three Women*, 15; Walker, "'Independent Livings.'"

108. See chapter 76 for further discussion about the NTS laundry.

109. Kelley, *Black Folk*, 70–74.

110. "Reminiscences of Dr. Nannie Helen Burroughs."

111. Stein, *Measuring Manhood*, 16, 38.

112. NHB, Memo to National Negro Business League, April 7, 1908, Box 36, Reels 32–33, Booker T. Washington Papers.

113. NHB to Emmett Scott, April 7, 1908, Box 36, Reels 32–33, Booker T. Washington Papers.

114. *Report of the Tenth Annual Convention*, 176.

115. Lawrence, notes from interview with NHB.

116. For a list of student workers in the printing department, see the ledger in Box 73, NHB Papers. See chapter 8 for further discussion about *The Worker*.

117. NHB, "Let Your Lights Shine," Box 46, NHB Papers.

118. Purkiss, *Fit Citizens*, 2–3.

119. "Social Life on Campus for Pleasure of Student Body," *Co-op News*, Box 312, Folder 11, NHB Papers; "Final Rites: Dr. Nannie Helen Burroughs," 1961, Mordecai Johnson Papers.

120. "We Salute Our President," "Zeta Rho Chi Honor Society Organized Here," "Extra Instructional Activities," "Assembly Programs Prove Interesting," *Co-op News*, Box 312, Folder 11, NHB Papers.

120. NHB to Maggie Lena Walker, August 23, 1933, Maggie Lena Walker Collection, Maggie Lena Walker National Historic Site, Richmond, Virginia.

122. NHB to Anson Phelps Stokes, January 3, 1931, Box 53, Folder 904, Anson Phelps Stokes Family Papers, Yale University Library Manuscripts and Archives.

123. Anson Phelps Stokes to NHB, March 2, 1939, Box 53, Folder 904, Anson Phelps Stokes Family Papers.

124. NHB to Anson Phelps Stokes, January 3, 1931, Box 53, Folder 904, Anson Phelps Stokes Family Papers.

125. Anson Phelps Stokes to NHB, November 1, 1938, Box 53, Folder 904, Anson Phelps Stokes Family Papers.

126. See chapter 7 for discussion about Agnes Nebo von Ballmoos.

127. NHB and Alice Smith, *The Congo: From Leopold to Lumumba*, Box 324, Folder 4, NHB Papers.

Part Three

THE ENERGY OF TEN HANDS AND A RADICAL VISION

[White women] will oppose any movement that will, in the end, prevent them from keeping their cooks and house servants in the kitchen twelve or fifteen hours a day and storing them away in cellars, up over garages, or in attics. . . . The only possible way for the Domestic Workers to get what others will demand and finally get, is to organize their own unions.

—Nannie Helen Burroughs, *Twentieth Annual Session of the Woman's Convention*

CHAPTER 5

"Show the World What Negro Women Can Do in a Labor Movement"

Black Women's Organizing against Jane Crow Unionism, 1917–1928

In the late 1910s and throughout the 1920s, with Black women facing relentless inequality and discriminatory labor practices across the United States, Burroughs and her comrades took matters into their own hands by establishing worker organizing initiatives. This chapter outlines their extraordinary worker organizing and advocacy during what I call the Jane Crow unionism era, a period when labor union leaders excluded Black women wage earners from union agendas and leadership positions.

As Black women mobilized workers through their own organizations, white domestic terrorism against Black people was on the rise. Black people had hoped their involvement in the US fight for peace and democracy abroad during World War I would result in citizenship rights for them at home. To the contrary, white mobs attacked Black communities soon after the war ended. Hostile whites resented the Great Migration of Black people to northern cities for higher-paying jobs in the wartime industry as well as their growing demands for equal citizenship rights. The tensions were so high that George Edmund Haynes, specialist in Black affairs for the US Department of Labor and husband of Burroughs's co-organizer Elizabeth Ross Haynes, wrote a report that called for urgent government action and that documented thirty-eight race riots and several lynchings of Black women, men, and children initiated by whites across the country during what is referred to as the "Red Summer of 1919." The labor front mirrored the hostility Black people faced in their everyday lives. While leaders of the American Federation of Labor, the largest US labor organization, claimed to welcome Black members, they

refused to challenge racism and sexism in workplaces or in their own organizations. Leaders of national and international women's labor organizations made clear that attaining labor rights for white women industrial
workers in the United States and abroad was at the top of their agendas.

Through worker organizing, Burroughs and her co-organizers fought
against discrimination in labor organizations and racial and gendered
violence during what philosopher Alain Leroy Locke dubbed the "New
Negro" era. In his 1925 Harlem Renaissance anthology *The New Negro:
An Interpretation*, Locke announced a new African American: proud,
bold, and unapologetically entitled to all rights of US citizenship. As evidenced by Burroughs's career, Black women had been developing what
historian Treva B. Lindsay calls a "New Negro womanhood" since the
late nineteenth century, a national movement with its own political ur-
gencies and expressions of citizenship entitlements particular to Black
women.[1] While working within these overlapping New Negro movements during the 1920s, Burroughs developed multiple methods for asserting her demands for Black women's labor justice.

A "New Negro" fire had been burning inside Burroughs since before
she graduated from M Street, and that flame grew in the 1920s. Her organizing and philosophies were integral to the vibrant labor resistance,
writing, and theorizing that emerged from organizing for civil, wom-
en's, and workers' rights. Now in her forties, Burroughs's worker organizing through institution and curriculum building were expanding and
reaping even more results. Burroughs's co-establishment of the Woman
Wage Earners' Association, the first National Association of Colored
Women's advocacy organization for Black women workers in Washington, DC, her coauthorship of the first Black women's international labor petition, and her establishment of the National Association of Wage
Earners, the first national Black women's labor organization for domestic workers, were testaments to her national and local recognition as an
economic justice expert and leader.

In the process of trying her hand at worker organizing in new ways,
Burroughs expanded her strategies for attaining labor justice by deep-
ening her collaborative relationships with labor reformers, politicians,
philanthropists, and grassroots organizers. As with her organizing for
the industrial club in Louisville and her school in DC, Burroughs could

not have pulled off her courageous plans without her loyal network of friends. Most notably, Burroughs's once doubtful mother, Jennie Bell, who encouraged Burroughs to take the safe route and abandon her efforts to become an educator, was fully on board with Burroughs's idea to unionize domestic workers. After witnessing her tenacious daughter far surpass her expectations, Bell was convinced that taking risks could in fact result in the "wholly impossible."[2] It must have meant a lot to Burroughs that Mother Bell, as National Association of Wage Earner organizers respectfully called her, became a member of the association. Bell's support was buttressed by Burroughs's mentors, allies, and co-organizers; Mary McLeod Bethune, Maggie Lena Walker, Mary Church Terrell, Carter G. Woodson, and Walter Brooks were right by Burroughs's side as she embarked on a historic and groundbreaking journey of worker organizing during the contentious Jane Crow Unionism era.

Acting Locally and Globally to Inspire Black Women's Labor Organizing

Burroughs's labor organizing was a crucial intervention into the race and gender problems of US and international labor movements. During the 1920s there were no national or international labor organizations that represented the interests of Black women and girls in general or Black domestic workers in particular. Their exclusion from the agendas of labor organizations was glaring. Over two million Black women and girls as young as ten years old worked as sharecroppers and domestic workers. White male leaders of the American Federation of Labor prioritized addressing the working conditions of white immigrant and US-born industrial workers, and they did not see the importance of advocating for domestic workers of any race.[3] Just as congressional leaders would not pass labor legislation to regulate domestic service, white male labor leaders argued that household employment was a private matter, and that unions should not interfere in it.[4] Burroughs directly challenged this claim by arguing that domestic service was real work that needed regulation just like the industrial trades.

While the majority of Black workers hired for factory jobs were men, Black women had made inroads in garment, iron, and steel factories.

Still, the American Federation of Labor refused to address racial and gender discrimination in the industrial trades or to condemn local white unions that barred Black members.[5] The federation claimed to welcome all Black industrial workers because it needed them to grow and solidify the movement, but it refused to share decision-making power with Black members. Samuel Gompers, the federation's longest-serving president, insisted that bringing up the race problem in the organization and in workplaces would only compromise the solidarity of the labor movement and thereby serve the interests of exploitative employers who did not want to see a unified labor force.[6] Gompers was not even committed to addressing the working conditions of white women. Frustrated with their marginalization in the federation, a group of white women labor activists started the Women's Trade Union League and advocated for white US-born and immigrant women workers in factories, mills, and retail stores.[7] Burroughs pushed back against the pervasive neglect of Black women's labor needs and interests, calling out their marginalization in labor movements, and taking on leadership roles in organizing against racial and gender inequities in the workplace.

Burroughs urged Black women to consider worker organizing as a solution. She declared,

> You know what a power the American Federation of Labor is in safeguarding and protecting the rights of millions of men. You know how vigilant the National Trade Women's Union League of America is in demanding rights for white women who are engaged as industrial workers. Both of these organizations demand that their members be well paid and well-treated. Our women have no organizations standing with them and for them in their struggle for economic advancement and protection. . . . We are lacking in common sense and constructive initiative if we sit down and wait for white women to do what we can do for ourselves.[8]

Convincing Black people nationwide that a labor organization was beneficial to them was no small feat. As Asa Philip Randolph discovered when organizing Black sleeping car porters, Black people were well aware of the long history of racial discrimination in labor unions and therefore did not see unionization as a pathway for making their lives better. In addition to their deeply rooted distrust of labor unions, Black people feared that they would lose their already tenuous jobs if they joined a union. Household employment in particular was undoubtedly a field left to the whims of individual employers. While confronting these challenges, Burroughs had to make the case to Black women of the New Negro era, who were increasingly determined to seek employment outside of domestic service, that a domestic workers' organization would benefit all Black women and their communities. As she argued, Black women's fates were intertwined across occupations. No matter the work environment, they all experienced racism and sexism, and no organization but a Black women's association was willing to go to bat for them.

Understanding that all Black women wage earners needed representation, Burroughs advocated for Black women who worked inside and outside households. In 1917 she cofounded the Woman Wage Earners' Association with her former teacher and by then Delta Sigma Theta Sorority soror Mary Church Terrell, and other NACW leaders, to unionize Black women in all professions as a direct protest to their exclusion from unions and federal government jobs.[9] They organized free weekly education and lecture sessions for the general public, primarily advertised to women and girls, to learn and discuss the issues impacting Black women workers. Sadie T. Henson, a local parole officer who Burroughs would later work with on another labor unionizing initiative, was among the first speakers in the public lecture series. The officers of the association knew people in the federal employment bureau, and they leveraged those connections to aid local Black women in securing federal jobs.[10]

In addition to Black women establishing their own labor organizations, Burroughs believed that another important avenue for organizing Black women workers was to seek common ground and organize with white women labor activists. In 1919 Burroughs and her NACW coworkers coauthored a petition that was presented at the inaugural meeting of the International Congress of Working Women in Washington, DC. The meeting was one of the largest gatherings of women laborers and organizers in global history, representing countries in Europe, Asia, and Latin America. Burroughs and her nine co-organizers asserted the significance of Black women wage earners to this global gathering by coauthoring a petition that Margaret Dreier Robins, president of the Women's Trade Union League, presented at the meeting.

Their petition was a detailed and intersectional analysis of the labor exploitation of Black women and their significance to the world economy. They asserted, "We, a group of Negro women, representing those two million Negro woman wage earners, respectfully ask for your active cooperation in organizing the Negro women workers of the United States into unions that they may have a share in bringing about industrial democracy and social order in the world." They appealed to the league to incorporate Black women's labor issues into their agenda because Black women had "very limited means of making their wishes known and of having their interests advanced through their own [men] representatives."[11]

Congress leaders rebuffed the petition, deciding not to act upon the authors' request to create a cross-racial partnership.[12] Robins, who chaired the meeting, adjourned the meeting immediately after the petition was translated and read in French, leaving no time for discussion. The congress's decision not to discuss the petition was likely rooted in their disinterest in addressing racial inequities in labor and their overall refusal to address labor exploitation in household employment.[13] They proceeded with an international conference without a focus on equal labor rights for women of all races, silencing Black women's particular concerns. They also excluded issues pertaining to domestic workers in the draft resolutions on policies to protect primarily white women in industrial trades that Robins sent to the first International Labor Organization meeting that year. After the meeting, Burroughs and her NACW co-organizers were convinced that Black women needed to form a labor union of their own. While disappointed and angered by the congress's dismissal of Black women workers' concerns, Burroughs found white women reformers who she would later partner with in her determination to start a Black women's labor organization.

Burroughs and her NACW co-organizers were more determined than ever to start their own Black women's labor union after they read about Black women's working conditions in a US Department of Labor study on women in industrial service. As Burroughs explained, "After reading this report, a few colored women talked the matter over seriously and decided not to stop until we shall have organized all Negro working women into a Labor Union."[14] Just two years later, in 1921, Burroughs and her co-organizers established the National Association of Wage Earners to "show the world what Negro women can do in a labor movement."[15] On November 11–14, 1921, they launched the organization as a national labor conference hosted by the Young Women's Christian Association and the John Wesley African Methodist Episcopal Zion Church.[16] Burroughs planned for the ceremony to take place on Armistice Day, the same day President Warren G. Harding held a conference in Washington, DC, of major political and military leaders from Great Britain, China, Italy, and other global powers to promote world peace. Burroughs wanted to send a strong message to participants, congressmen, and the White House that Black women were not at peace. They were at war in the United States, and improving their working conditions was just as important as attaining world peace.[17]

Starting her own organization gave Burroughs more freedom to lead with her distinct philosophy of centering domestic workers in the Black Freedom Movement for labor rights. As president of the association, Burroughs led the first national labor organization of the early twentieth century dedicated to improving the working conditions of Black women in household employment. The association designed comprehensive plans that included collective bargaining for living wages. Similar to labor unions, the National Association of Wage Earners—an important and intermediary precursor to the formalized domestic worker-led unions that emerged in the 1930s—advocated for standardized working conditions for domestic workers and had strike clauses.

The association's largest launch took place in 1924, shortly after Burroughs raised the money to purchase the national headquarters for the organization. A considerable percentage of the funds came from association members' and officers' recruitment of members to the organization. After operating the association for three years without an official building, Burroughs proudly declared that the headquarters would be a place that all association members could call their own.[18] She was immensely proud to welcome workers and national leaders into the building to check out and aid in the collective work of the National Association of Wage Earners. Just as she had insisted on building the NTS in the nation's capital, she was intentional about placing the association headquarters and thereby Black women's labor concerns in the heart of national politics and on the same footing as the demands of white labor unions. Burroughs made this sentiment known when she declared, "Race leaders have been talking for years about a National Clearing House at Washington. The thing is a reality. It took Negro women to do it. . . . Both of the white labor organizations have headquarters in Washington, because this is the center for molding sentiment on national problems. Negro women certainly scored when they purchased headquarters in Washington!"[19] Burroughs's elaborate and meticulous planning of the two-day dedication ceremony for the headquarters revealed just how excited she was about the possibilities of her groundbreaking organization and its headquarters.

The Grand Opening of the National Association of Wage Earners Headquarters

On the morning of November 11, 1924, a large crowd of people made its way to the headquarters to witness the celebration of the historic National Association of Wage Earners. The ceremony was a big deal, and so was the association itself. Several hundred people from multiple cities attended the two-day dedication ceremony to witness the launch of the first national labor organization of the early twentieth century dedicated to advocating for Black women wage earners.[20] The range of people who participated in the ceremony and endorsed the association reflected Burroughs's organizing prowess and her belief in the power of education, legislation, labor unions, the church, reform movements, and the National Association of Colored Women to building a Black women's labor movement.

The dedication ceremony was a multiracial gathering of people who visited the headquarters "during the entire day and far into the night to see the dream that had come true."[21] In the words of young people today, there were "big hitters in the building"—well-known people from domestic workers, social reformers, and NACW leaders to politicians, philanthropists, and clergymen. Supporters who could not attend the ceremony made sure to express their enthusiasm about the National Association of Wage Earners. Mary Anderson, head of the Women's Bureau of the Department of Labor, congratulated association members through a telegram and pledged her support to the organization. Burroughs made sure to mention at the ceremony that opera singer Marion Anderson had wanted to be at the ceremony but could not attend because of her touring schedule. She sent a statement full of well wishes to everyone, especially association members, and conveyed her support of a Black women's labor movement.[22]

Allies publicized their support of the association in newspapers. Universal Negro Improvement Association leader Amy Jacques Garvey wrote an article about the headquarters encouraging readers of her association's newspaper the *Negro World* to support the National Association of Wage Earners. As Garvey declared, the association's headquarters "stands out in bold relief as a monument to one who spares no efforts in consummating in plans that she deems makes for good." According to the Black nationalist leader, Burroughs's success in establishing the headquarters "should encourage every member of the race to lend his or her support to the association and convince others, whose specialty is in another phase of life, that in 'union there is strength.'"[23]

In true Black Baptist church fashion, the two-day dedication ceremony was an ornate affair that featured several influential speakers and hymns sung over the course of several hours. Burroughs's integration of prayer and song throughout the event made clear that she believed spiritual fortitude was necessary for establishing a Black women's labor union. The dedication service began at the National Association of Wage Earners' headquarters at 11 a.m. and concluded around 4 p.m. The NTS quintette opened the ceremony with a church musical selection, and Reverend Charles E. Stewart of Mother Bethel AME Church in Philadelphia followed with the opening prayer to bless the building and association members. Afterward, Burroughs delivered a presentation about the association and her expansive vision for the headquarters. She told the audience that the building was "dedicated for the service of all people" and had a five-point mission: "To study the conditions of women in industries and seek to promote their welfare; To make the Colored woman an efficient, productive factor in the labor world; To open new avenues of employment; To make working women of whom a community will be proud; and To make a community sentiment that will be proud of its working women."[24] As always, Reverend Walter H. Brooks was present to

HEADQUARTERS NATIONAL ASSOCIATION OF WAGE EARNERS
1115 RHODE ISLAND AVE., N.W., WASHINGTON, D.C.

Figure 5.1. NAWE headquarters, circa 1925. The building still exists and has been converted into a residence. Nannie Helen Burroughs Papers, Prints and Photographs Division, Library of Congress.

support Burroughs. He showed his support for her and the association by delivering the dedicatory address to the headquarters. Anson Phelps Stokes, secretary of Yale University and philanthropic investor in the NTS, delivered a dedicatory prayer.[25]

Philanthropist and social reformer Charlotte Everett Hopkins delivered the welcome address before attendees toured the building. Similar to Burroughs, Hopkins was outspoken about exploitative working conditions in domestic service, and she believed that Black schools could transform Black women's working and living conditions.[26] At the ceremony, Hopkins vowed to work with the association to "giv[e] them [domestic workers] better houses in which to live."[27] The housing she promised to members was likely apartments in the Ellen Wilson Memorial Homes community that Hopkins had worked with First Lady Ellen Wilson to establish as an alternative to alleyway homes. After Hopkins delivered the welcome address, attendees went on a tour of the massive house that was the National Association of Wage Earners official headquarters.

Burroughs's educational philosophy that Black women deserved equal access to education, safe housing, social amusements, and training for multiple professions and entrepreneurial opportunities guided how she made use of space in the National Association of Wage Earners headquarters. The headquarters was a large four-story home located near public transportation where Black working-class women without cars could easily access it. She created spaces where association members could learn and practice domestic science, engage in social activities, and create an additional stream of income for themselves and revenue for the association.

While Burroughs advocated for Black capital enterprise, she also believed association members should own their means of production and sell their products at affordable prices for other working-class women. The National Association of Wage Earners motto was "We can buy from ourselves and earn money selling to others."[28] Burroughs made plans to transport power machines into the basement to build a profit-sharing factory where association members could make domestic worker uniforms for mail-order sales at affordable prices for Black women. Burroughs believed that wearing uniforms would communicate to employers and employees that domestic service was a skilled profession and that they should adhere to the workplace standards set by the association. A percentage of the sales from manufacturing the uniforms would go to members and the association.

As Burroughs explained at the time, white-owned factories made huge profits from Black women purchasing domestic worker uniforms, yet factory owners refused to hire Black women to work in those factories. At the association's factory, Black women would instead take the lead in manufacturing products for their own benefit. Explaining the larger significance of the factory, Burroughs asserted that establishing it "means employment; it means influence; it means respect from others; it means strength for all. . . . We can build up a great enterprise."[29]

The National Association of Wage Earners business offices, practice dining rooms, kitchen, and parlor for socializing with visitors were on the second floor of the headquarters. Similar to the practice home on the NTS campus, the dining rooms were open to the general public for association members to practice organizing private dinner parties, serving families in private homes, and serving customers in restaurants. The demonstration rooms throughout the house doubled as training spaces for women who wanted to become dormitory managers. Again as she had done with the NTS campus, Burroughs adapted the space to meet the needs of Black women at and beyond the workplace. On the fourth floor were four bedrooms—one practice bedroom and three to provide emergency lodging for association members and Black women travelers to DC who could not find rooms in racially segregated hotels.[30] Burroughs's ultimate goal was to create a "chain of dormitories" in DC for domestic workers who did not want to live inside their employers' homes. She planned to build dormitories to address housing discrimination, the absence of laws to protect Black women from sexual violence, and the low wages of domestic service, which made it difficult for many Black women to find safe and affordable housing.[31]

During the second day of the dedication ceremony Burroughs and association members discussed the nuts and bolts of bringing their unionization vision into fruition. On the early afternoon of November 12, 1924, association members and officers and representatives of other organizations convened at Shiloh Baptist Church and did not leave until past 8 p.m. Shiloh Baptist Church was Carter G. Woodson's church home, and he likely facilitated Burroughs's relationship with the church. In addition to her connection to Woodson, Shiloh was an ideal place to hold the association meeting, since it was among the most prominent churches at the center of Black culture, public education, and leadership in DC.[32] A quintette of NTS students opened the meeting with the antislavery song "Battle Hymn of the Republic" to prepare participants for discussions about the specific challenges that lay ahead of them in their organizing against labor injustices.[33] After the song and prayer, the national officers of the association took center stage. The officers were also leaders in the National Association of Colored Women, and they had been directing initiatives to improve Black women's working conditions in domestic service in their respective states. Among the officers were Burroughs's closest allies, including Mary McLeod Bethune, vice president, Daytona Beach, Florida; Maggie Lena Walker, treasurer, Richmond, Virginia; and Margaret Murray Washington, board of directors member, Tuskegee, Alabama.[34] Burroughs relied on the national influence and resources of all the officers to bring widespread visibility and resources to the association.

National Association of Wage Earners officers delivered educational speeches about the labor issues confronting Black women who lived inside and outside their employers' homes. They also discussed media and rhetorical strategies for creating a national discourse in support of labor protections for Black women. In a speech entitled "Selling an Idea," executive secretary Minnie L. Bradley presented the officers' vision and goals for the organization. Burroughs updated attendees about the "work done since organized"—by which she meant recruitment—and association officers joined together with domestic worker members to present "How We Propose to Put It Over," their ideas for making long-lasting change through the four-point agenda that Burroughs had introduced the day before.[35] After more prayer and song, Mary McLeod Bethune called a platform meeting to discuss the National Association of Wage Earners agenda in-depth that evening. The speeches that followed Bethune's meeting made clear that association members and officers intended for their organization to become a federally recognized labor union.

National Association of Wage Earners members, officers, and allies often referred to the organization as a union and Burroughs's request for Ethel Smith, a labor activist of the Women's Trade Union League, to deliver a speech—entitled "The Value of Organization to Workers"—further underscored their unionization goal.[36] Smith had worked with Burroughs on the Minimum Wage Board of the District of Columbia on efforts to end the gender wage gap, or the unequal wages between women and men. Burroughs was one of the few members on the committee who spoke out against the racial and gender wage gaps that disproportionately impacted Black women. Smith might have accepted the invitation to speak at the dedication ceremony out of respect for Burroughs's advocacy and influence on her own thinking about women's labor issues. While there is no evidence that the National Association of Wage Earners and Women's Trade Union League worked on specific campaigns together, Burroughs collected labor reports produced by the league, and she cited their data about union wages in National Association of Wage Earners promotional pamphlets to encourage people to join the association.[37] Underscoring the unionization intentions of the association, Harlem Renaissance writer and Burroughs's friend Alice Dunbar-Nelson asserted that Burroughs "conceived the idea of a Domestic Servants Organization, with rules, regulations, and projects similar to the unions among men laborers and skilled workmen." According to Nelson, "It was a magnificent idea, and with her customary smashing skill, Miss Burroughs put it across in quite a bit of territory of the United States."[38]

In anticipation of the National Association of Wage Earners growing into a union that advocated for domestic workers and Black women wage earners in other occupations, Eugene Kinckle Jones, executive secretary of the National Urban League, spoke about how Black women could forge work opportunities for themselves in the industrial trades. Everyone in attendance knew that an organization with such an ambitious agenda would require an expansive structure. As historian Mary-Elizabeth Murphy has mapped with great precision, Burroughs recruited local grassroots organizers to the National Association of Wage Earners who recruited a diverse occupational membership to the organization. Sadie T. Henson, a truant officer and president of the association's District Union chapter, led a discussion about how to establish local union chapters across the country after delivering her address, "How to Make the Work of the Local Unions Effective." Henson led by example as one of the association officers who recruited the most people to the organization by energizing her extensive Black working-class and middle-class networks in DC.[39] The widespread enthusiasm for the association and its membership of several thousand workers was a testament to association members' effective coalition-building, the officers' skills, and, more generally, the great need for a Black women's labor union in a Jane Crow unionism era.

Burroughs and the National Association of Wage Earners in a Nation of Protesting Workers and Labor Reformers

Burroughs's labor philosophies and her creation of the National Association of Wage Earners were integral to and at the forefront of Black people's and women's labor resistance across the United States. While leading the association, Burroughs again linked up with her co-organizers Reverend Walter Brooks and Mary Church Terrell to challenge racial segregation in housing that relegated low-wage Black workers to dangerous and health threatening living conditions. In 1924 they teamed up with prominent Howard University professor Kelly Miller to plan and co-lead a mass meeting at the university to strategize with students and the local Black community about how to pressure the federal government into outlawing racial segregation in housing.[40] Their partnership was rooted in their shared belief that demanding labor rights was inherent to Black people's movement for civil rights, which included equal access to safe and affordable housing. Burroughs and Miller were on the same page about education and disrupting the negative stigma associated with domestic service. In his essay "Surplus Negro Women," Miller challenged racial and gender inequities in the labor market and criticized Black people who looked down on domestic workers and other manual laborers.[41] He was a proponent of Burroughs's blended curriculum for addressing the labor problem for Black women and girls and donated regularly to the NTS throughout his career at Howard University.[42]

Burroughs was also ideological companions with leading white women labor reformers. Similar to Leonora O'Reilly, union organizer and co-founder of the National Association for the Advancement of Colored

People, and Rose Schneiderman, president of the National Women's Trade Union League and its New York state branch, Burroughs saw women's labor rights as intricately tied to political and social rights. O'Reilly, Schneiderman, and Burroughs argued that women wage earners were breadwinners who contributed to their households and deserved wages, voting rights, and labor union representation equal to that of men. As Annelise Orleck has documented, Schneiderman would take her activism a step further in the 1930s by advocating for equal wages between Black women and white women in the same occupations. Schneiderman also knew that Black women had few options but to take on domestic service jobs to keep themselves, their families, and their communities afloat. She, as did Burroughs, pushed for the unionization of domestic workers and their inclusion in labor laws.[43]

What distinguished Burroughs's ideologies from her white women labor reformer contemporaries is that she believed Black domestic workers were best positioned to lead a national labor movement for all workers. Unlike her white counterparts, Burroughs also had the larger undertaking of challenging both racial and gender discrimination in the labor market. Her methods for achieving a Black domestic-worker-centered movement, however, overlapped with the ideologies and methods of other Black labor leaders. She shared A. Philip Randolph's and Du Bois's perspective that unionization was essential to achieving economic and political justice for Black communities. More specifically, Burroughs and Du Bois were of like minds that Black people could not trust white people to fully support their demands for labor rights and representation. When international and national chapters of the American Federation of Labor promised to welcome Black men into their ranks, Du Bois rightfully warned Black men not to celebrate but to wait and see if the federation would fulfill its promise. He argued that white union leaders would never share decision-making power with Black men. Consequently, Black men needed to form their own independent unions.[44]

Similarly, while Burroughs advocated for National Association of Wage Earners members to collaborate with white housewives to improve household working conditions, she believed that an independent Black domestic workers' union was necessary and inevitable. As she argued, white women who hired domestic workers would never see Black women as their equals. She bluntly expressed this view at a Woman's Convention meeting shortly before establishing the National Association of Wage Earners. As she told the audience, white women "will oppose any movement that will, in the end, prevent them from keeping their cooks and house servants in the kitchen twelve or fifteen hours a day and storing them away in cellars, up over garages, or in attics. . . . The only possible way for the Domestic Workers to get what others will demand and finally get, is to organize their own unions."[45]

Burroughs's intellectual and organizing work did not go unnoticed by white women and Black men labor reformers. They respected her labor philosophies, supported her worker organizing initiatives, and worked with her in a variety of capacities. As I discuss in detail in the following chapter, Ethel Smith of the Women's Trade Union League invited Burroughs to join a government committee to end the gender wage gap among service workers in DC. The overlaps between Burroughs's and Du Bois's labor philosophies resonated with Du Bois, and he took special interest in the National Association of Wage Earners. He asked Burroughs to send him a photograph of the headquarters so that he could feature a story about the organization in *The Crisis*. His decision to support and publicize the association was part of his long-term commitment to document the organizing and working conditions of domestic workers, as evidenced by his inclusion of Isabel Eaton's "Special Report on Negro Domestic Service in the Seventh Ward" in the *Philadelphia Negro* and his documentation of a Black laundress organization in early twentieth-century Galveston, Texas, in his Atlanta University study.[46] Recognizing Burroughs as a labor leader and expert, in 1924 Du Bois and National Association for the Advancement of Colored People field secretary William Pickens invited her to speak at their conference, on the same stage as US Secretary of Labor James Davis, about labor issues confronting southern Black workers who migrated north for employment.[47]

Burroughs's philosophies and organization were integral to a period of robust organizing concerning Black service workers. In 1925, a year after the National Association of Wage Earners' headquarters officially opened, Randolph cofounded and led the Brotherhood of Sleeping Car Porters and Maids. The brotherhood was an independent and unprecedented organization of Black Pullman porters and maids who demanded higher wages, more rest time and bargaining power, and shorter work hours from the railroad Pullman Company.[48] Burroughs's National Association of Wage Earners agenda overlapped with those of the brotherhood and the Ladies' Auxiliary of women who joined Black porters at the organizing frontlines. The association, brotherhood, and Ladies' Auxiliary led the way in organizing Black service workers on a national scale for the first time in US history. As the National Association of Wage Earners organized service workers employed in private homes, the brotherhood and its Ladies' Auxiliary organized public service workers employed by the Pullman Company, a private business.. The three organizations also worked at dispelling the persistent and centuries-old master-servant ideology, rooted in slavery, that Black people were inherently inferior and in service to whites. Collectively, they argued that Black service workers deserved respect and standardized wages and working conditions commensurate with their status as highly skilled professionals, whether they worked in private homes or in railroad company cars.

While brotherhood leader A. Philip Randolph centered manhood rights and Black men workers in his fight for labor rights, he saw eye-to-eye with Burroughs on the important role of education in organizing against racial discrimination and poor working conditions. Randolph endorsed her work at the NTS in *The Messenger*, the official organ of the Brotherhood of the Sleeping Car Porters, dubbed the most dangerous publications of its time by the US Justice Department.[49] According to Randolph, the NTS and Burroughs were powerful forces in the movement for changing Black women's working conditions. The editorial team nominated and inducted Burroughs into the periodical's AfraAmerican Academy to formally recognize her contributions to education and labor movements. As their dedication to her read, "Many people have to accept low pay and poor working conditions merely because of incompetence and ignorance. Over 20 years ago, Miss Burroughs decided to alter this latter widespread condition among black women workers. So, she founded the National Training School for Women and Girls in Washington DC. . . . That is her life's work; her contribution to Negro progress."[50] Randolph remained in contact with Burroughs and later tapped her to advise him and labor rights activists Roy Wilkins and Ella Baker on their organizing of the historic 1957 Prayer Pilgrimage to Washington to urge the federal government to force southern states to adhere to the 1954 *Brown v. Board of Education* decision that outlawed racial segregation in schools.[51]

United Negro Improvement Association leader Amy Jacques Garvey supported Burroughs's worker organizing as well. Just as bold and outspoken as Burroughs, Garvey publicly endorsed not only the National Association of Wage Earners, but Burroughs's overall vision and work for economic justice. She saw Burroughs as a comrade in the labor struggle for Black liberation and declared her a "great race woman." Garvey and Burroughs shared the Black nationalist ideology that racial pride, entrepreneurship, and education were essential to changing Black women's working conditions. As Garvey asserted,

> Much praise should be given the president, Miss Nannie Helen Burroughs, for the untiring and purposeful efforts she has put forth to better conditions for women workers. . . . Miss Burroughs's life has been one continued militant fight under many adverse circumstances to place the members of the race on a plane of recognition. . . . Negro women must be awakened to a realization of their future in the labor world. They are—and need to be more so—efficient, productive factors in the world of industry.[52]

Burroughs integrated her philosophy that racial pride, education, entrepreneurship, and unionization were key to worker organizing into the infrastructure of the National Association of Wage Earners and its headquarters to effect change for Black women in the labor world.

With much sacrifice, Burroughs and staff operated the National Association of Wage Earners headquarters like a union and Black worker center for nearly a decade.[53] Like Black worker centers today, the headquarters was a place dedicated to improving Black people's working conditions through education, research, grassroots organizing, employment services, and training programs. The headquarters was a prime meeting spot where Black women produced literature about domestic workers; attended public lectures about economic issues confronting Black women; received job training; applied for jobs; and strategized campaigns for collective action against racial, class, and gender inequalities that impacted their working lives.[54] The association's motto was "A Labor Organization with a Constructive Program," and its members employed unionizing strategies to accomplish their nine-point agenda, which included securing "a wage that will enable women to live decently" and "influencing just legislation affecting women wage earners." They compiled the complaints, concerns, and wants of their members and negotiated with employers for fair working conditions, vacation days, and standardized wages through the contracts of the National Association of Wage Earners's employment agency. There was a strike clause in the constitution if employers did not adhere to the working conditions set by the organization.[55] Together, the mission, headquarters, constitution, and actions show that the organization's work was adjacent to labor union organizing. Alongside organizations such as the Brotherhood of Sleeping Car Porters and its Ladies' Auxiliary, the National Association of Wage Earners played a significant role in redefining service work and advancing new ideas for charting an unprecedented course for Black service workers in the United States.

The National Association of Wage Earners's Inclusive Strategies and Governing Structure

Since she was a young adult speaking at Woman's Convention and National Negro Business League meetings, Burroughs had urged Black women and men across socioeconomic class to value the manual labor they had done since slavery as skilled work and honor domestic workers as pillars of Black communities. As president of the National Association of Wage Earners, Burroughs put her words into action by developing an inclusive governing structure and recruitment strategy to form a united Black labor organization that advocated for household workers. Taking an expansive Black self-determinist approach, she welcomed all Black wage earners—women and men—to the association. As she declared in a recruitment pamphlet, "This is an organization for every worker—skilled or unskilled. This is an organization for every woman—high or low, servant or secretary, college president or field hand. Working together we can advance to a place of influence and respect in the Labor World."[56]

Like NTS staff and students, association organizers affectionately referred to Burroughs's mother as Mother Bell. She was one of several hundred domestic worker members of the association's District Union.[57]

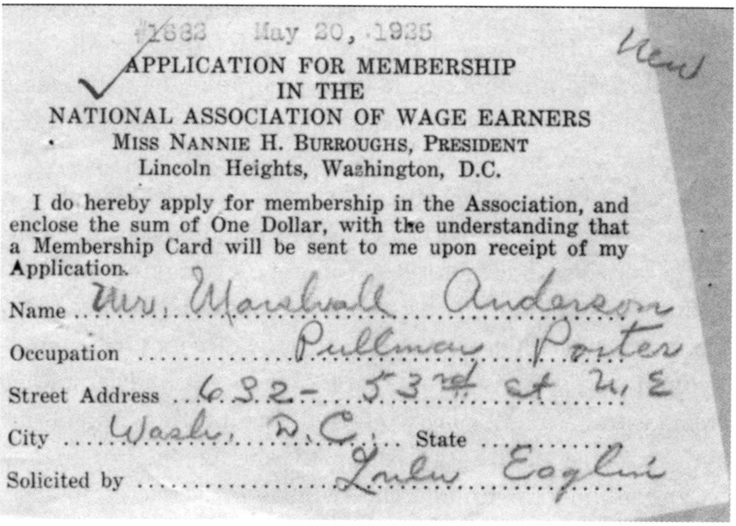
#1683 May 20, 1925

New

APPLICATION FOR MEMBERSHIP
IN THE
NATIONAL ASSOCIATION OF WAGE EARNERS
MISS NANNIE H. BURROUGHS, PRESIDENT
Lincoln Heights, Washington, D.C.

I do hereby apply for membership in the Association, and enclose the sum of One Dollar, with the understanding that a Membership Card will be sent to me upon receipt of my Application.

Name .... Mrs. Marshall Anderson ....
Occupation .... Pullman Porter ....
Street Address .... 632–53rd st. N.E. ....
City .... Wash. D.C. .... State ....
Solicited by .... Lulu Eaglin ....

Figure 5.2. National Association of Wage Earners membership card of a Pullman Porter. Nannie Helen Burroughs papers, Library of Congress.

While the majority of association members were domestic workers in Washington, DC, women and men in a variety of professions in small towns and large cities in other states, including New York, New Jersey, Connecticut, North Carolina, Georgia, Texas, Maryland, and Colorado, were members as well. Jeremiah Hawkins, the mayor of North Brentwood, Maryland, joined the association in 1924. Registration cards show that members worked as farmers, teachers, barbers, pullman porters, educators, chauffeurs, professors, pastors, tailors, firemen, secretaries, housewives, contractors, engineers, doctors, postal workers, dentists, insurance agents, printers and engravers, and hair and scalp specialists. High school students, NTS students and alumni, and students of Storer College, a historically Black college in West Virginia, also joined the organization.[58] Although the majority of recruiters of the association were women, some of the men who were members recruited their spouses and teachers in their communities to the organization.

The cross-class and mixed-gender membership of the association reflected the extent to which the gender and racial segmentation of the labor market affected Black people's lives. The labor market for Black women workers was so skewed toward domestic service, and because helping those workers was at the center of the association's mission, members who did not work in household employment probably had done so at some point or were inspired to join the association because of loved ones who did. The association's officers respected domestic workers, as they were not too far removed from household employment themselves. While the officers operated in middle-class and elite networks, their mothers had labored as domestic workers, laundresses, and sharecroppers. As a low-wage educator, Burroughs always lived a precarious life, and her earnings were not drastically different from household employment wages. Considering that Burroughs was a champion of the working class, she might have preferred a domestic-worker-led management structure for the association, but she needed the financial resources and influence of middle-class women leaders to establish a solid foundation for the organization and shoulder the maintenance costs of the headquarters.

Burroughs's closest friends and colleagues she had worked with on previous labor initiatives held some of the most important positions in the association. Reverend Walter Brooks was a member and helped Burroughs recruit members from his Nineteenth Street Baptist Church.[59] Burroughs depended on Mary McLeod Bethune and Maggie Lena Walker collectively to provide benefits and housing for members, recruit people to the association's chapters outside of Washington, DC, and amplify the organization's reputation through their national leadership positions and experience. As she declared, "The women composing the National Association of Wage Earners are not dreamers nor theorists. They occupy important positions in other big movements requiring initiative and constructive ability."[60] Burroughs relied on vice president Mary McLeod Bethune, who in 1924 became president of the National Association of Colored Women, to bring national attention to the National Association of Wage Earners. Bethune extended her stardom and incredible recruitment skills to the organization. Between 1924 and 1925, Bethune recruited 150 members to the association, and she presided over national meetings about the National Association of Wage Earners.[61]

In 1925 Maggie Lena Walker, treasurer, established timely and critical resources for the association. She created a death benefits fund for members through the International Order of St. Luke, an African American benevolent organization she led. Immediately after joining the organization, members received a sealed certificate confirming that their beneficiary would receive one hundred dollars to go toward members' burial costs upon their deaths.[62] Walker's investment was crucial for members since most domestic service employers did not provide life insurance benefits, and most domestic workers did not make enough money to bury their loved ones or to put aside funds for their loved ones to bury them.

Walker went a step further in supporting Burroughs by approving the Nannie Helen Burroughs Council, a Washington, DC–based club of the International Order of St. Luke that not only contributed to the National Association of Wage Earners death benefits fund but provided life insurance for NTS staff members who split their time between managing the administrative duties of the school and the association. This council also helped cover the salary of a doctor to treat patients in the northeastern section of DC, which would have included NTS students and some of the National Association of Wage Earners's District Union members.[63] Funding from the Nannie Helen Burroughs Council went a long way in recruiting people to the association, maintaining health services for community members, and keeping women employed at the NTS while Burroughs invested her earning into building the association.[64] In addition to Walker's timely and generous support, Elizabeth Carter, chair of the National Association of Wage Earners investment board and former member of the Woman Wage Earners' Association, supervised the Young Women's Christian Association building in Washington, DC, where she offered affordable lodging to National Association of Wage Earners members.[65]

Burroughs relied on local grassroots organizers and educators who did not have nationally recognizable names but were instrumental to growing the District Union chapter in Washington, DC. Sadie T. Henson and Lucy Holland were especially effective organizers, and they recruited the most members to the organization in DC. Henson had worked with Burroughs on the Woman Wage Earners' Association's projects, and, with her experience as a housekeeper and truant officer, she labored at the intersections of working-class and middle-class Black communities and thereby knew women and men who labored inside and outside the service industry. In February 1923 alone, Henson recruited fifty-three women and men who were employed as domestic workers, teachers, and doctors.[66] Maggie Wall Arter, teacher and director of the NTS Sunday School for children, recruited a wide range of workers from laundresses and housekeepers to students and teachers to the DC, West Virginia, and Maryland chapters.[67] Henson, Arter, and Holland were dynamic strategists who crafted the on-the-ground messaging, ran everyday recruitment operations, and worked with Burroughs on planning community meetings. Between NACW leaders and local strategists, National Association of Wage Earners organizers used their knowledge of the economy, politics, and extensive community networks to ensure that their vision of a cross-occupational alliance became a reality. At least 1,800 members from thirty-seven states and the nation's capital joined the National Association of Wage Earners between 1921 and 1926.[68] Two-thirds of the members were based locally in Washington, DC, and 46 percent were domestic workers.[69]

Prioritizing the specific needs of domestic workers did not stop Burroughs and association members from also advocating for Black women in other low-wage occupations. A recognizable percentage of the District Union membership consisted of federal charwomen, workers who cleaned government offices and buildings. When the federal Personnel Reclassification Board passed new policies that cut back on the wages of part-time charwomen, the District Union collaborated with protesting charwomen and association members to ignite community organizing against the draconian policies. Without a union hall, they held a massive mobilization meeting at a local elementary school. In the process of that campaign, more federal charwomen joined the association's District Union chapter.[70]

While the National Association of Wage Earners participated in campaigns against discriminatory labor policies, Burroughs believed that education, unionization, and Black entrepreneurship were the most immediate solution for addressing Black women's low wages. The association itself was a Black women's profit-sharing enterprise. It cost one dollar to join the organization, recruiters were paid twenty-five cents from membership dues for each person they recruited or for each association button or pamphlet they sold. The organization opened a mail-order supply house at the headquarters where association members mailed affordable uniforms, aprons, and caps to domestic workers.[71]

The association owned and established a Black-owned employment agency for domestic workers to help regulate the homes in which association members worked. As Elizabeth Ross, one of Burroughs's coauthors of the 1919 international petition, documented in her US Department of Labor study, Black women were often victims of exploitative employment agencies that deceptively promised them safe and living-wage domestic service jobs only to place them in homes where they were exploited and sexually assaulted. To counteract this dangerous and discriminatory practice, Burroughs advertised the National Association of Wage Earners as an employment agency that prospective employers needed to register with before hiring members.[72] News about the employment agency spread quickly across the city. Housekeepers' Alliance, an organization of white middle-class housewives in DC, studied the agency and attempted to create a similar service of their own to solve the "servant problem." Rather than considering the interests of domestic workers, however, the alliance created employment contracts that protected employers' demands.[73] The National Association of Wage Earners's agency clearly stood out as a service that had better intentions for domestic workers with its requirement of mutually agreed-upon work standards between domestic workers and employers.

The association's training programs reflected Burroughs's belief that education was essential to organizing to change working conditions. As with faculty at the NTS, instructors at the association's headquarters trained members for a range of career possibilities in the service industry, including waitressing and dormitory management. The headquarters included designated work rooms where members could test their newly acquired skills, just as NTS students could apply their lessons at the school's Domestic Science Practice House. After completing the training courses at the headquarters, members received a card that specified the skills they had attained for the jobs they sought. The goal of the training classes, like at the NTS, was professionalizing service occupations to increase Black women's wages and respect for them as skilled workers.[74] Burroughs's decision to later offer more waitressing and management courses than domestic service training courses signaled that association members were more interested in seeking job opportunities outside household employment.

Financial Sacrifices of a Radical Vision

While presiding over the National Association of Wage Earners, Burroughs was also directing the Young Women's Work Department of the NACW's Business Department. In that role, Burroughs collected labor census data and was abreast of the changing job landscape and Black women's career interests. Knowing that general household work was not a preferred job for many Black women, in the late 1920s, Burroughs shifted from advertising the National Association of Wage Earners as an employment agency for general household workers to an agency for higher-wage service workers who waitressed and cleaned furnished apartments and hotel rooms.[75] Pursuing these jobs was a game-changer, as Jane Crow laws and majority-white labor organizations had made sure that white women held a monopoly over these service positions across the country.

Burroughs knew that creating training opportunities for higher-end service positions required a large investment in teaching materials. Similar to the restaurant on her school's campus, Burroughs and National Association of Wage Earners organizers dedicated a dining room and kitchen space in their headquarters for a local restaurant. They invited local community members and prominent Black leaders such as Howard University's president Mordecai Johnson and his wife, Anna, to patronize the dining services.[76] Within one year, Burroughs donated a total of three thousand dollars of her own money and NTS funds to the association's account to help defray the costs of the expensive grocery store bills that she accumulated to purchase the finest meats, cheeses, chocolates, eggs, flour, and sugar for trainees to practice cooking and serving at high-end restaurants and in the homes of elite families. She also wanted lodgers, visitors, and customers at the National Association of Wage Earners restaurant to consume high-quality foods. While running up an expensive grocery tab, Burroughs accumulated a nearly insurmountable rental bill at a local furniture store. She could not afford to purchase the furniture outright, but she was determined to create opportunities for trainees to practice cleaning and maintaining high-quality furniture and for lodgers and restaurant patrons to dine on the best furniture available.[77]

With no federal, state, or labor union support to back up the association's efforts, the organization was in debt by the late 1920s. Local grocery and furniture stores hounded Burroughs to pay off her bills for several years, but she persisted with her plans of making the association and its headquarters a powerhouse for Black women wage earners. Burroughs and association organizers continued their service training courses, hosted national pageants, organized fundraisers for the association and other Black organizations, and provided rooms for travelers and low-wage workers until 1931. "Mother Bell" and Burroughs's NACW friends remained committed to the organization, maintaining their membership through the association's most challenging period. Maggie Wall Arter, director of the NTS Sunday School, kept the everyday accounting and business operations of the headquarters going into the 1930s.[78]

Advancing Labor Resistance into Multiple Directions

Just as the National Association of Wage Earners hit its stride, on May 26, 1926, the administration building on the NTS campus burned down. Burroughs was devastated. She confessed, "I have been too grief-stricken to think clearly. . . . God has been good to us, and our friends have been faithful; but this catastrophe, at this time, when I am quite tired, seems more than I can bear."[79] The fire began in the kitchen and spread to the top two floors of the building, destroying the roof and several dormitory rooms. Due to teachers' heroic rescue efforts, no students who were attending class in the building were injured.[80] Years of fundraising work that Burroughs and her co-organizers had done to construct the building had turned into ashes. Soon after the fire, Burroughs's organizing for the National Association of Wage Earners slowed down significantly as she diverted her attention to fundraising to repair and fireproof the building. Taking her attention away from her dream of establishing a Black women's labor union to face the substantial damage done to her first love, the NTS, took a personal toll on Burroughs.

Given the precarity of Black women's work and lives across social class, the National Association of Wage Earners could not fully withstand such a large hiccup within the first five years of its existence. The association's national officers were already stretched thin with their own projects. Like Burroughs, Mary McLeod Bethune, Maggie Lena Walker, and other officers held work-intensive positions in the NACW and in their respective states and institutions. They were loyal friends of Burroughs, but they could not fill in for her while she focused on rebuilding her school. It was difficult for local working-class organizers to keep their recruitment efforts going full-time given the demands and low wages of their own jobs. One recruiter pointed out this flaw in Burroughs's vision and the association's organizing structure when she told Burroughs that she could not possibly expect her to become a full-time or even part-time organizer when members received only twenty-five cents' commission for each person they recruited. Burroughs probably would have paid organizers more commission if she'd had the money to do it. As educator, Harlem Renaissance writer, and Burroughs's friend Alice Dunbar-Nelson rightly noted in her article about the association, the very idea of establishing a long-lasting union-like organization required money and time. She explained that union organizing meant that "organizers and speakers must be on the go all the time, reaching the women in small towns, as well as in larger ones, and hammering, hammering away at the idea. And that takes money. And Miss Burroughs had no money. And not much time to do the work herself, since the life of her own school, the National Training School, depends upon her own efforts."[81]

Dunbar-Nelson also highlighted the limitations of Burroughs's philosophy that domestic science education would improve Black women's working conditions. She seriously doubted that white housewives would ever set aside their stereotypical beliefs about Black women to see them as professionals, no matter how much training Black women received. As she put it, "Caucasian females of the species" would not "be willing to accord her [Black women] the position of business employee rather than personal maid" much less "be willing to pay the price for this superior class of domestics." According to Nelson, the only way for Black women to protect themselves was by starting a labor union, but that was incredibly difficult, as evidenced by the challenges of the National Association of Wage Earners.[82] There was still no denying, as Nelson concluded, that what Burroughs had attempted was remarkable.

While Burroughs and her co-organizers were unable to meet their goal of recruiting ten thousand members, their audacious attempts and accomplishments are noteworthy. Even with a decline in national and local membership, Burroughs and her labor co-organizers continued working toward their vision for economic justice and did not fold the organization until the early years of the Depression. Burroughs and association members had what scholar-activist Robin D. G. Kelley calls "freedom dreams," or the ability to "imagine something different, to realize that things need not always be this way."[83] Members' freedom dreaming led to unprecedented outcomes. At a time when racial and gender segregation in schools, labor unions, and businesses was protected by law, the association represented a profoundly courageous and influential effort for change.

The National Association of Wage Earners was at the forefront and nexus of movements to change the conditions and status of women and Black workers. They pioneered a new way of looking at work itself by bringing attention to an occupation that lawmakers and labor unions considered outside the workplace. The association sent a loud message to lawmakers and employers that domestic service was actual work and that domestic workers were just as deserving of standardized working conditions as industrial workers. Because of the members' extensive network-building and collaborative practices, Burroughs advanced many of her goals, including creating an employment agency for Black women service workers and bringing Black people together across social class to advocate for better household working conditions with domestic workers for the first time in US history.

When the activities of the National Association of Wage Earners declined, Burroughs continued using the headquarters as a base to promote racial pride and Black entrepreneurship. As he had done with the NTS, Carter G. Woodson helped amplify the visibility of the headquarters to support national investment in Burroughs's projects. By this time in Burroughs's life, however, Woodson was not just her mentor. They were equal partners in their shared project of making and promoting Black history and Black businesses. As historian Charles H. Wesley recalled in his personal remembrances of working with both giants, Burroughs counseled Woodson on his multiple Black history preservation projects, and she raised money to support Woodson's Association of Negro Life and History, the largest Black history organization in the United States. Reflecting her confidence in Woodson's Black history initiatives and his respect for Burroughs's expertise, Burroughs gave part of her personal collection of rare Black history books and artifacts to Woodson for the extensive Black history collection he kept at his office.[84]

Burroughs and Woodson used the National Association of Wage Earners headquarters as a space to advance their combined interests in Black pride and business ownership. In 1927 they cohosted a banquet there in celebration of the National Benefit Life Insurance Company, the largest Black-owned insurance company in the United States at the time.[85] A few weeks after the dinner, Burroughs cemented her organizational partnership with Woodson by placing a deposit on her lifetime membership in the Association for the Study of Negro Life and History. Woodson was most pleased when she completed payment of her membership in 1944. He told her, "On behalf of the Association for the Study of Negro Life and History I desire to thank you sincerely for completing the payment of the $100 required for life membership. . . . As a life member you have set an example which I believe others will follow."[86]

Labor organizing was still a part of Burroughs's economic empowerment vision, and she never fully let it go. On November 11–12, 1928, Burroughs and National Association of Wage Earners staff celebrated the association's seventh anniversary at the headquarters, and they recruited fourteen new members to the organization at the celebration.[87] By 1931 the association was still operating as a boarding home and a job training site for service workers.[88] Regina Chandler, a local businesswoman who worked with Burroughs through the NACW and Young Women's Christian Association, marveled at how Burroughs had expanded the headquarters to include a cosmetology school for women interested in establishing their own businesses and becoming hair and scalp specialists.[89]

Burroughs stayed true to her word of making the headquarters a profit-sharing property for other Black women. She eventually converted the headquarters into a rental home for her family members and for local DC residents.[90] In her will, she left the building in the care of her former student and employee Carrie Pettipher, who Burroughs had nicknamed the "Black Helen Keller" and who Carter G. Woodson praised for overcoming tremendous odds as a disabled student to become an extraordinary office administrator. By the 1960s, Pettipher had gone into business for herself by starting her own realty service, and she managed the former National Association of Wage Earners headquarters under Pettipher Realty.[91]

————◆————

While Burroughs believed in the power of labor organizations and schools, she also recognized the importance of policy in changing Black women's living and working conditions. She integrated her education and unionizing goals into her political advocacy work for Black women wage earners as a researcher and leader of political organizations. Her integrative approach to legislative work was reflected in her scholarship and research methods, which enabled her to push for labor-related policies in several political realms. Burroughs began challenging workplace discriminatory practices in the 1910s, and by the 1930s she had become a political leader who advocated for Black women wage earners and organized against any structural inequalities in the legislative realm that stood in Black women's way of living wages and freedom from the confines of Jane Crow laws and workplace practices. And in her later years, Burroughs expanded the reach of her political legacies through her mentorship of younger generations of labor and civil rights leaders.

Notes

1. Lindsay, *Colored No More*, 25.

2. Burroughs often used the phrase "wholly impossible" to describe what she intended for Black women to achieve through their work to transform society. Hine, King, and Reed, *We Specialize in the Wholly Impossible*, xii.

3. The American Federation of Labor is still active and is now known as the American Federation of Labor and Congress of Industrial Organizations (AFL-CIO).

4. See my discussion of Lenora Barry, *Putting Their Hands on Race*, 126–27; and Susan Levine's discussion of the patriarchal beliefs of male leaders of the Knights of Labor, *Labor's True Woman*, 132.

5. Trotter, *Workers on Arrival*, 84–85.

6. See Foner, *Organized Labor and the Black Worker*, 76–77.

7. The Women's Trade Union League was founded in 1903. See Vapnek, *Breadwinners*, 78–79.

8. NHB, "Negro Women Unprotected," n.d., Box 3, Folder 42, Mark Solomon

and Robert Kaufman Research Files on African Americans and Communism, Tamiment Library and Robert F. Wagner Archives, New York University.

9. The other cofounders were Julia F. Coleman and Jeanette Carter. Carter, a labor organizer who had earned her law degree from Howard University's law school, was president of the organization. Parker, *Unceasing Militant*, 202. By 1915 Terrell and Burroughs were honorary members of Delta Sigma Theta Sorority. See "The Delta Sigma Theta Sorority," 85.

10. "Wage-Earners," *Washington Bee*, April 7, 1917.

11. NHB, Elizabeth C. Carter, Mamie R. Ross, Leilia Pendleton, A. G. Green, Eva A. Wright, Mary Church Terrell, Carrie Roscoe, Caroline Clifford, Elizabeth Ross Haynes, "First Convention of International Conference of Working Women," November 4, 1919, Folder 3, International Federation of Working Women Records, Schlesinger Library, Harvard University.

12. Vapnek, "The 1919 International Congress of Working Women," 166.

13. For a history of white women labor organizer's reluctance to fight for labor rights for white women domestic workers, see Phillips-Cunningham, *Putting Their Hands on Race*, 115–31.

14. US Department of Labor, Women in Industry Service, *First Annual Report*.

15. Quoted from a National Association of Wage Earners promotional flier about the headquarters. See NHB, "Negro Women Unprotected."

16. "My Dear Co-worker," November 2, 1921, Box 308, Folder 2, NHB Papers.

17. NHB, "My Dear Friend," Box 308, Folder 3, NHB Papers.

18. NHB, "The Way to Make Money," Box 308, Folder 2, NHB Papers.

19. Quoted from a National Association of Wage Earners promotional flier about the headquarters. See NHB, "Negro Women Unprotected."

20. In 2022 the house was valued at over $1 million. See "1115 Rhode Island Avenue, Washington, DC," Zillow, accessed November 8, 2022, https://www .zillow.com/homedetails/1115-Rhode-Island-Ave-NW-Washington-DC-20005 /407284_zpid/.

21. "D.C. Women Open Home for Girls: Four Story Building Dedicated to the Art of Home Making," *Baltimore Afro-American*, November 22, 1924.

22. "National Wage Earners Hold Annual Meeting: Miss Nannie Burroughs Heads Organization Interested in Women Workers," *New York Amsterdam News*, November 22, 1924; "D.C. Women Open Home for Girls."

23. Amy Jacques Garvey, "A Great Woman of the Race Who Works," *Negro World*, December 6, 1924.

24. Quoted from the official program of the dedication services. See National Association of Wage Earners file, Tamiment Library and Robert F. Wagner Labor Archives, New York University.

25. Phelps used his family's Phelps-Stokes Fund to sponsor Black, Native American, and African education initiatives. See "Administrative History,"

Phelps-Stokes Fund Records, 1893–1970, New York Public Library; Stokes, *Negro Status and Race Relations.*

26. For Hopkins's seminal study about Black education and working conditions, see Hobson and Hopkins, *A Report Concerning the Colored Women of the South*, 7, 9.

27. Quoted from the official program of the dedication services, Box 3, Folder 42, Mark Solomon and Robert Kaufman Research Files.

28. "National Wage Earners Hold Annual Meeting," *Chicago Defender*, November 22, 1924; "Women's Armistice Day Meet to Adjust Grievances," *Norfolk Journal and Guide*, November 5, 1921.

29. National Association of Wage Earners, "The National Association of Wage Earners: A Labor Organization with a Constructive Program," Box 3, Folder 42, Mark Solomon and Robert Kaufman Research Files.

30. "D.C. Women Open Home for Girls."

31. "Wage Earners Association," *Dallas Express*, December 6, 1924, 5, University of North Texas Libraries, Portal to Texas History, accessed January 29, 2021, https://texashistory.unt.edu/ark:/67531/metapth278520/.

32. "Our History," Shiloh Baptist Church, https://shilohbaptist.org/about-us/our-history/.

33. "The First Annual Meeting of the National Association of Wage Earners" Program, November 11–12, 1924, Box 3, Folder 42, Mark Solomon and Robert Kaufman Research Files. The song was written by an abolitionist in support of the Union troops. See "Battle Hymn of the Republic Song: The Story behind the Song," *The Kennedy Center: Resources for Educators*, https://www.kennedy-center.org/education/resources-for-educators/classroom-resources/media-and-interactives/media/music/story-behind-the-song/the-story-behind-the-song/the-battle-hymn-of-the-republic/.

34. Other National Association of Wage Earners officers included Minnie L. Bradley, executive secretary, New Haven, Connecticut; Elizabeth C. Carter, chairwoman of the investment board, New Bedford, Massachusetts; Lizzie Foust, registrar, Lexington, Kentucky; Georgine Kelly Smith, advisory council chair, New York; and Maude A. Morrisey, recording secretary, Pennsylvania. See "Domestic Practice House Is Planned," *Sunday Star*, May 18, 1924.

35. "The First Annual Meeting of the National Association of Wage Earners" Program.

36. "Union That Would Enroll Colored Domestics," *Washington Post*, November 18, 1924; "Wage Earners Association," 5.

37. See National Association of Wage Earners pamphlets, Box 3, Folder 42, Mark Solomon and Robert Kaufman Research Files; and clippings of National Women's Trade Union League reports in Burroughs's files, Box 308, Folder 3, NHB Papers.

38. Alice Dunbar-Nelson, "The Problem of Personal Service," *The Messenger* 9, no. 6 (June 1927): 184.

39. "The First Annual Meeting of the National Association of Wage Earners" Program. For an in-depth discussion of Henson's and other National Association of Wage Earners organizers' strategies, see Murphy, *Jim Crow Capital*, 25–29.

40. "Residential Segregation," *Hill Top*, April 12, 1924, 5.

41. See Miller, "Surplus Negro Women," 168–78.

42. Lawrence, notes from interview with NHB.

43. Orleck, *Common Sense*, 117, 153. For discussion about O'Reilly's involvement in the National Association for the Advancement of Colored People, see Moore, "Women and the Emergence of the NAACP," 480–82.

44. Bates, *Pullman Porters and the Rise of Protest Politics*, 11.

45. National Baptist Convention, *Twentieth Annual Session of the Woman's Convention*, 37.

46. Du Bois, *Efforts for Social Betterment*, 62; Isabel Eaton, "A Special Report on Domestic Service in the Seventh Ward," in Du Bois, *The Philadelphia Negro*, 426–509.

47. "U.S. Secretary of Labor to Address N.A.A.C.P. Philadelphia Conference," *Broad Ax*, May 17, 1924, 2.

48. Chateauvert, *Marching Together*, 19–20.

49. Kersten, *A. Philip Randolph*, 17.

50. "The AfraAmerican Academy," *The Messenger* 9, no. 9 (September 1927): 275.

51. A. Philip Randolph, Telegram to NHB, March 27, 1957, Box 24, Folder 10, NHB Papers.

52. Garvey, "A Great Woman of the Race."

53. For a discussion about contemporary Black worker centers, see Pitts, "National Black Worker Center Project."

54. Worker centers are committed to addressing the particular needs of a marginalized group. For example, see National Black Worker Center, https://nationalblackworkercenters.org/about/; National LGBTQ Workers Center, https://www.lgbtqworkerscenter.org/.

55. "Constitution: The National Association of Wage Earners, Inc." and "The First Annual Meeting of the National Association of Wage Earners Program," Mark Solomon and Robert Kaufman Research Files.

56. Quoted from a National Association of Wage Earners promotional flier about the headquarters. See NHB, "Negro Women Unprotected."

57. National Association of Wage Earners accounting notes prepared by M. M. W. Arter, November 12, 1928, Box 62, Folder 8, NHB Papers.

58. National Association of Wage Earners membership cards, Box 71, NHB Papers.

59. Membership card of Reverend Walter Brooks, Box 308, Folder 2, NHB Papers.

60. Quoted from a National Association of Wage Earners promotional flier about the headquarters. See NHB, "Negro Women Unprotected."

61. National Association of Wage Earners accounting notes, Box 62, Folder 8, NHB Papers; National Association of Wage Earners, *Fifteenth Biennial Session, Oakland, California, August 1–5, 1926*, 84.

62. National Association of Wage Earners, "My Dear Friend," Box 308, Folder 3, NHB Papers.

63. Mary J. Smith to Magge Lena Walker, October 11, 1928, Maggie Lena Walker Collection.

64. NHB to Maggie Lena Walker, June 19, 1933, September 5, 1928; Maggie Lena Walker to A. B. Johnson, February 9, 1928, Maggie Lena Walker Collection.

65. Phillips-Cunningham and Popp, "Labor Organizer Nannie Helen Burroughs," 26.

66. List of National Association of Wage Earners members submitted by Sadie T. Henson, 1923, Box 308, Folder 1, NHB Papers.

67. Recruiters' names are listed on the membership cards, Box 308, Folder 2, NHB Papers.

68. This is a count of the existing National Association of Wage Earners membership cards, but not all the cards were preserved.

69. Murphy, *Jim Crow Capital*, 25–27.

70. Murphy, 28–29.

71. National Association of Wage Earners promotional pamphlet; NHB, "The Way to Make Money," Box 308, Folder 2, NHB Papers.

72. For National Association of Wage Earners employment agency ads, see "Employment Agencies," *Evening Star*, March 27, 1925, March 29, 1925, April 1, 1925, September 24, 1928.

73. Housekeepers Alliance contract, 1924, Anna Kelton Wiley Papers, Box 265, Manuscripts Division, Library of Congress.

74. "A Domestic Service Practice House."

75. See examples of late 1920s National Association of Wage Earners ads in "Employment Agencies," *Evening Star*, September 24 and September 25, 1928.

76. NHB to Mordecai Johnson, September 28, 1926, Mordecai Johnson Papers.

77. National Association of Wage Earners Accounts Ledger, Box 62, Folder 7, NHB Papers.

78. National Association of Wage Earners accounting statements, Box 62, Folders 7–8, NHB Papers.

79. NHB, "Fire! Fire! Fire!," May 28, 1926, Box 204, Folder 1, Sarah Williamson Coleman Papers, Moorland-Springarn Research Center, Howard University.

80. "National Training School Damaged by Flames," *Broad Ax*, June 5, 1926.

81. Nelson, "The Problem of Personal Service," 184.

82. Nelson, 184.

83. Kelley, *Freedom Dreams*, 9.

84. "Reminiscences of Dr. Nannie Helen Burroughs."

85. "Banker Is Honored by Insurance Company," *Philadelphia Tribune*, October 6, 1927; "Rutherford Host," *Baltimore Afro-American*, October 15, 1927.

86. Carter G. Woodson to NHB, August 10, 1944, Box 32, Folder 19, NHB Papers.

87. M. M. W. Arter's notes, 1928, Box 62, Folder 8, NHB Papers.

88. National Association of Wage Earners accounting statement, Box 62, Folder 8, NHB Papers.

89. "Hair and scalp specialist" was a description used for beauticians in the 1920s and 1930s. For Regina Chandler's comments, see audio recording of NHB Papers dedication ceremony, September 23, 1976.

90. James Poindexter to NHB, November 23, 1942, Box 1, Folder 1, NHB Papers.

91. See receipts and notes of the Pettipher Realty Service, Box 114, folder 2, NHB Papers.

CHAPTER 6

"We Are in Politics to Stay"

Securing Labor Protections and Legislation, 1913–1955

Burroughs's legislative work was integral to unprecedented organizing for Black workers during the 1920s and 1930s. While she pushed for labor protections for Black women and girls through the National Training School for Women and Girls and the National Association of Wage Earners, she knew that Black women could never simply use a few methods to change their lives and the larger society. Black women's and girls' needs were urgent, and their labor and civil rights needed to be firmly etched in law. Burroughs approached the fight for economic justice on multiple fronts during and after the National Association of Wage Earners—through her political work and leadership on government committees and in women's organizations—and by doing so she helped shift the paradigm of how we recognize labor resistance itself. Her political organizing work makes clear that labor resistance did not only come in the form of worker organizing. Political advocacy and research were just as significant to the labor movement as strikes, unionization, and public protests.

Although she was skeptical of politicians, political organizing was exciting work for Burroughs. As someone who desired to take elocution courses after graduating from M Street, Burroughs had aspired to become a public figure since her late teenage years. In her mid-thirties, she dipped her toes into labor politics by advocating for Black women federal employees impacted by racial segregationist workplace practices during Woodrow Wilson's presidency. This fight was important to her politically and personally, since she had been denied a federal clerk position after earning high marks on a civil exam as a young adult. By her forties, she had gained influence from her advocacy for local workers and her presidency of a trade school, and she took on leadership roles in national and international political organizations that challenged the government and congressional leaders to take the needs of Black women wage earners seriously.

In 1922 Burroughs cofounded the International Council of the Women of the Darker Races of the World with her comrades Margaret Murray Washington, Maggie Lena Walker, Mary McLeod Bethune, and other NACW allies including Mary Church Terrell. With Washington as president, the council became the first independent Black women's international organization in US history. For almost two decades the council studied global racial, class, and gender disparities to address economic, education, and housing issues that impacted the working lives of Black women.

Council women always thought about Black women in comparison to other women who had been impacted by European imperialism. The council extended the "darker races" of their organizational name and agenda to include Asian women, as they saw parallels between Black women's postcolonial conditions and those of Asian women. As Ashley Preston noted in her history of Mary McLeod Bethune, Pan-Africanists believed that parts of Asia were part of the African diaspora. Africans, they argued, were present in countries such as India before the transatlantic slave trade and were enslaved by Arabs in parts of India during the slave trade. According to Pan-Africanists, Indians experienced similar oppression to African Americans as British colonialism, and the color caste system in India was similar to racial segregation systems in the United States.[1] Burroughs and council members brought together women across the African and Asian diasporas who proposed school policies and curricula and who collected data about women's working and living conditions to press governments to address systemic inequalities that disproportionately impacted African-descended and Asian women.

While sitting on the executive board of the council, Burroughs worked with her National Association of Colored Women colleagues to organize conferences about Black women's and girls' working conditions from prisons to classrooms. Burroughs also led a national women's movement against lynchings as the National Association of Colored Women's superintendent of the Department for Suppression of Lynching and Mob Violence.[2] Her activism against lynchings was integral to her economic justice agenda. There was no way Black workers could live freely and enjoy the fruits of their labor if they could be lynched at a moment's notice and without federal intervention. Black women and men worked under the constant threat of white employers' making false claims of robbery, sexual assault, or insubordination, that often led to lynch mobs. Burroughs directly challenged President Woodrow Wilson's deliberate silence on lynchings and racial segregation laws despite his own war slogan "Make the world safe for democracy." As she declared at a Woman's Convention meeting, unless Wilson actually applied his doctrine domestically, "our nation would be hissed out of court when the world gets ready to make up the case against Germany and try her for her sins."[3] Shortly after she criticized Wilson at the meeting, J. Edgar Hoover placed Burroughs on the Federal Bureau of Investigation's surveillance list.

Unfazed by Hoover's threats, Burroughs took on more political leadership roles in the Black women's movement for economic justice.[4] A firm believer that labor rights could not be obtained without voting rights, in 1924 she cofounded and presided over the National League of Republican Colored Women at a time when most Black people voted for Republicans. As president of the league, she challenged Republicans to outlaw labor exploitative practices and racial segregation policies that stood in the way of Black women's equal access to the ballot box. She also created a research instrument to collect national data to transform Black women's working conditions through voter mobilization.

Managing several major political projects and the NTS was no small task, especially considering that Burroughs juggled multiple personal and family health challenges along the way. As Susan L. Smith has argued, chronic illness and morbidity rates were high among Black women in the early twentieth century due to limited access to quality medical resources in Black communities.[5] Like Black women today, Burroughs and others also experienced high levels of stress that often led to health complications. They carried the stress of workplace, housing, and food disparities and were held to gendered familial expectations that women take care of their immediate and extended families.[6]

In the process of serving in several leadership capacities, Burroughs contracted a stress-induced illness that worried her closest friends. While recovering from her illness, she provided medical care and financial assistance to her aging and sick mother, who had moved from Philadelphia to live with her on the NTS campus. Burroughs was also responsible for her mother's sister Rachel Winston, who lived in Virginia and was battling an illness too. Burroughs could no longer look toward her confidant Margaret Murray Washington to shoulder some of the organizational work they had shared for more than a decade: just as the International Council of Women of the Darker Races hit a stride, Margaret became ill and passed into history. Afterward, Burroughs worked even harder to continue her best friend's legacy through the council.

Just when one would think Burroughs could not imagine adding anything else to her plate, she urged President Herbert Hoover to form an interracial Negro housing committee to conduct research and make policy recommendations to address the dire circumstances of Black communities. Accurately predicting that the financial crisis would disproportionately impact Black people, in 1929 she wrote an emotional letter to Hoover imploring him to address the fact that Black people's right to living wages and decent housing was "growing distressingly limited." She asserted, "I appeal to you, our beloved President, to study the situation or call a small conference." Burroughs also urged him to consider the state of Black children, especially in the "rural South where there is no law against child labor."[7]

It would take two years and worsened Depression-era conditions for Hoover to finally realize the importance of Burroughs's idea. In 1931 he commissioned the federal Committee on Negro Housing and appointed Burroughs as its chair. Their report was a direct extension of Burroughs's curriculum-building work at the NTS to counteract racial and gender discrimination in the US economy. Burroughs led the research team in producing the first federal study about the interlocking relationships between housing, health disparities, and what contemporary economist Michelle Holder calls the double gap, or the disparate wages of Black women in comparison to their white men and women counterparts.[8] Burroughs's mixed methods and intersectional approach to the *Report on Negro Housing* laid an early foundation for Title VII of the

Civil Rights Act of 1964 that outlawed employment discrimination and the Fair Housing Act of 1968 that prohibited discrimination related to housing. The study, quite frankly, also provides a valuable historical and methodological guide for students in labor studies, women's and gender studies, and policy programs, and for lawmakers developing policies today to address deeply rooted and persistent disparities that continue to impact Black people's lives. Another lasting legacy of Burroughs's political work was her mentoring of younger activists who shook up the country with their leadership in civil rights and labor rights movements.

Worker Advocacy in Washington, DC

Burroughs worked with Black women and white women labor reformers to effect change in Washington, DC. As early as 1913, Burroughs expressed her outrage about diminishing occupational opportunities for Black government employees during the Woodrow Wilson presidential administration to people with legislative influence and connections. She wrote a letter to Belle Case La Follette, a white suffragist and the first woman to graduate from a law school in Wisconsin, saying she was appalled by the racism that Black women employees experienced in the Bureau of Engraving and Printing. La Follette was moved by Burroughs's letter. She, too, was an outspoken opponent of discrimination in the workplace and she was married to Robert "Fighting Bob" La Follette Sr., former governor of Wisconsin and another fierce labor reformer. La Follette credited Burroughs for pushing her to launch the first legal investigation into racial segregation among women employees of the Bureau of Engraving and Printing. As she explained, Burroughs sent a letter to her "pleading for justice to the colored people and protesting against the segregation being instituted in the Bureau of Engraving and Printing."[9] She followed up on Burroughs's request by interviewing Black women at the bureau and writing a series of letters to the secretary of the treasury inquiring about segregation in federal employment.

In her letters, she included data that she collected from her interviews with the director and Black women employees of the Bureau of Engraving and Printing. La Follette reported to the secretary of the treasury that while no official segregation order had been put in place, the director of the bureau had been allowed to mandate that Black women printer assistants eat at lunch tables apart from their white women coworkers. The director also forbade Black and white women to work together on the same printing and engraving machines. He justified his actions with the false claim that Black women were fine with discriminatory workplace practices. La Follette interviewed Black women in the bureau to get their side of the story. They told her that they were not okay with the discrimination they had experienced. Shortly afterward, one of the interviewees was fired, and La Follette insisted that the secretary of the treasury follow up on her dismissal.[10] If it were not for Burroughs's initial push, La Follette's unparalleled activism against racial discrimination in women's federal employment during the Woodrow Wilson administration would not have happened.

Burroughs also found common ground and worked with Ethel Smith, legislative secretary of the National Women's Trade Union League. Similar to Burroughs, Smith believed that research, education, labor unionization, and advocacy for labor would solve problems for women wage earners. Smith was one of the driving forces behind the passage of the 1918 Washington, DC, minimum wage law, which established a wage of sixteen dollars per week for women and minors (girls and boys under eighteen years old). To prevent labor strikes, the law created a Minimum Wage Board of the District of Columbia to enforce the law and to ensure that the interests of businesses, workers, and the public were met in a variety of industries including the service, printing, and mercantile trades.[11] The board created committees to take on this large task of researching and representing such vast and often conflicting interests. Smith invited Burroughs to join the committee that represented public, employee, and employer interests regarding women and minor service workers in hotels, laundries, restaurants, hospitals, apartments, and clubs.[12]

Although the board explicitly stated that it would not investigate the working conditions of domestic workers, Burroughs was still interested in participating on the committee because of her desire to create living-wage opportunities for Black women and girls in a range of service occupations. Her committee gathered data about the cost of living for women to determine wages that would enable them to afford the costs for safe housing, adequate childcare, reliable transportation, healthy foods, and quality medical services. Under Burroughs's leadership, the committee disaggregated the quantitative data by race to account for how legalized racial segregation impacted the cost of living for Black women versus white women. As the committee reported, Black women had to pay higher prices than white women for safe housing and healthy foods.[13] According to Smith, the board and committees were successful in that they discovered that only one-third of women in service, mercantile, and printing were making minimum wage.[14] After exposing noncompliant employers, the board was able to raise the wages for two-thirds of women workers.[15] It is unclear from the board's report, however, how many of those workers were Black women and minors.

In the following years, Burroughs took her labor activism to conferences, where she advocated for Black women wage earners on a larger scale in her leadership roles in the National Association of Colored Women. As director of the Business Department of the NACW, she co-organized a conference in Chicago in collaboration with the Chicago Federation of Labor to advocate for legislation to address the tuberculosis outbreak among Black women and girl inmates and to stop the sale of garments that inmates were forced to make as prison workers.[16] In 1926 Burroughs represented the National Association of Teachers in Colored Schools at the NACW conference in Oakland, California, where she co-led the charge for resolutions concerning working and learning conditions in Black schools. Due to Burroughs's and other association members' advocacy at the conference, the NACW passed a resolution urging the federal government to allocate equal funding for Black and white schools in the South. They also passed a resolution demanding that the government raise the salaries of Black teachers such that they were equitable with the salaries of white teachers.[17] As they did with all other sitting presidents, the NACW followed up with President Coolidge to make their demands known. They reminded all presidents and lawmakers that they would only organize Black voters for politicians who addressed the issues outlined in their resolutions.

Burroughs leveraged her leadership roles in the NACW to advocate for Black women in labor reform circles in DC. She drew on her extensive research and knowledge about working conditions and inequalities in the workforce to confront white women who avoided discussions about how they contributed to the race and labor problem for Black women. Strategically selecting her audiences, Burroughs saw the Women's Industrial Conference in Washington, DC, organized by the Women's Bureau of the US Department of Labor, as a prime opportunity to speak to white women interested in addressing the labor exploitation of women. As one of the NACW's foremost labor experts, Burroughs went to the conference as the NACW representative for Black women workers in Pennsylvania and Mississippi.[18] Her participation in the conference attested to not only her political intentions but the NACW's insistence on advocating for Black women wage earners in front of policymakers and federal agencies. At the conference, Burroughs challenged conference attendees to think about their complicity in perpetuating racial and gender wage gaps through their avoidance of discussions about Black domestic workers. She told attendees, "First, the very fact that you have daily contact with 57 percent of the colored women of this country gives you an opportunity to apply and to try out some of the ideals that have been so beautifully expressed in this gathering." According to Burroughs, attendees said they wanted to address women's working conditions, but really they were only "looking after the interests of white women of this country." Instead of talking to each other, they needed to "sit around the council table and together plan [with Black women] to look after the moral as well as the physical condition of the colored women."[19]

Burroughs insisted it was in their best interest to organize with Black women. After all, she argued, Black women's household work benefited white women beyond measure. As she asserted, Black women were the "backbone of economic life as far as white women are concerned" because employing domestic workers gave white women the "opportunity to engage in all kinds of work and leisure in so many ways that I cannot now enumerate." At times, when addressing white women, Burroughs softened her language in an effort to avoid offending them so that they would keep listening to her. She continued, "We know that you are absolutely sincere. But here's the acid test. And there are women in this audience who are fair enough and brave enough to stand that test."[20] Burroughs made it clear that she was not arguing for higher wages, except in the form of a standardized minimum wage for all domestic workers. What Black women wanted from white women was respect and professional treatment in household employment. She urged them to stop subjecting domestic workers to sleeping in basements and in cramped spaces over their garages.

Burroughs concluded her address by leaving the ball in the attendees' court to make things better. She declared, "The colored women are not on trial in this country. It is a test of the sincerity and opportunity of the white women of this country rather than of the colored women. . . . Together we are going to see how well we can work it out, how efficiently we [Black women] can serve on the one hand, and how fine and how just you [white women] can be on the other."[21] While Burroughs always left the door open to finding common ground with white women, she was skeptical of white women's willingness to change their mindsets concerning race. At the end of the day, she believed that no organization, committee, or legal institution would be more invested in eradicating racial, class, and gender disparities than Black women themselves. She thereby had a two-pronged approach to addressing Black women's working conditions. While she worked with white labor reformers and politicians to create and enforce labor legislation, she cofounded political organizations with other Black women.

Working toward Pan-African and Asian Economic Justice

Burroughs always believed that the fates of women across the African diaspora were intertwined. As chair of the executive board of the International Council of Women of the Darker Races of the World, Burroughs worked at building the first independent Black women's international organization with her NACW comrades. Collectively, they established a movement to comprehensively improve women's working conditions in the African and Asian diasporas. While the council has been referred to as a short-lived organization, the eighteen-year duration of the council and its groundbreaking agenda were impressive, especially considering the officers' extensive work and other commitments.[22] As a collective, council members addressed all disparities that impacted Black women's working conditions by conducting in-depth research to demand that governments in the United States and beyond develop policies to improve women's lives.

In 1920 Burroughs and several NACW leaders decided to start the council, which was in full swing by 1922. Their agenda was to conduct in-depth studies of the histories, employment, schools, and housing conditions of Black women and girls in Africa, South America, and the Caribbean for policy purposes. As global analysts and activists, council leaders were keenly aware of how European colonialism and imperialism impacted women of non-European descent. To expand the influence of their organizing against global racism and sexism, they established a council chapter in Ceylon (now Sri Lanka), developed working relationships with Asian women, and studied gender and ethnic discrimination in India, Sri Lanka, China, Japan, and the Philippines.[23]

While developing collaborative political and research relationships with women across the African diaspora and in Asia, council members established a database of archival and ethnographic research that they used as supporting evidence for their demands that US and international governments create legislation to address the glaringly disparate working and living conditions of African-descended women and Asian women. Sharing Burroughs's ideology that education and racial pride were nonnegotiable components of labor resistance and racial justice, council members demanded that governments require schools to implement the council's archival research about the cultures, histories, and women leaders of Africa, Asia, South America, and the Caribbean into core curricula. Council members understood that education had been used as a weapon against colonized people to suppress their resistance to oppressive political and labor systems. After Black and Asian students learned about the activist and resilient histories of their people, council members hypothesized, they would have the confidence to challenge white supremacy and exploitation globally.[24]

The council was the brainchild of Margaret Murray Washington. She had conceived the idea before her spouse, Booker T. Washington, died in 1915, but she could not start the organization until several years later, due to taking on more responsibilities at Tuskegee after Washington's death.[25] The council would last until the early 1940s. Through the council, Burroughs worked with her NACW co-organizers on building a Black women's labor movement on a global scale. Collectively, Margaret Murray Washington (president), Mary Church Terrell (second vice president),

Figure 6.1. Margaret Murray
Washington, circa 1915.
Nannie Helen Burroughs
Papers, Prints and Photo-
graphs Division, Library of
Congress.

and Elizabeth Carter (recording secretary of the council) had worked
with Burroughs on establishing national labor organizations, but they
also had their eyes on changing the world.[26] The two closest comrades
on the council, Burroughs and Washington, hosted the council's conventions on their respective school campuses—the NTS and Tuskegee.[27]
Burroughs and Washington also transformed church rooms into strat-
egizing spaces for women's labor resistance and political organizing, securing meeting places for the council in Baptist churches.[28]

The organization was a perfect fit for Burroughs's Pan-Africanist
politics and came at what seemed like a perfect time for her cross-
organizational and institutional work for comprehensive labor justice.
The council's mission dovetailed with her work for legislative change, the
National Association of Wage Earners' and Woman's Convention's focus
on changing local Black women's everyday working and living condi-

Figure 6.2. Councilmembers Burroughs, Mary McLeod Bethune, and Charlotte Hawkins Brown at Tuskegee University. Courtesy of the Charlotte Hawkins Brown Museum and State Historic Site.

tions, and the NTS's goal of establishing curricula to create a labor world of equal opportunity for Black women and girls. The council also fulfilled an important need in transnational organizing. No other international organization was committed to studying and challenging intersecting racial, class, and gender inequalities. Preexisting organizations such as the predominately white International Council of Women marginalized women of color and their interests.[29] The leaders of Du Bois's Pan-African meetings were primarily men, and there were no defined agendas for addressing racial and gender disparities in the African diaspora. Never one to back down from challenging men's exclusion of women, Burroughs urged Du Bois to appoint Margaret Murray Washington as vice president or executive council member of his Pan-African Congress and invite International Council of Women of the Darker Races members to his meetings to ensure that women had a say in what he was planning. Du Bois obliged.[30]

On August 6, 1923, the council met on Burroughs's school campus, and Washington assembled a group of founding officers for their shared mission of researching the living and working conditions of women of African descent so that they could "work out plans by which we might all be benefited educationally, socially, and politically."[31] They also stressed

the importance of educating the world about global Black history to promote racial pride among Black women and students and provide them
with a more enhanced education. With a quality education, council
members argued, young people of African descent had a much better
chance of attaining better jobs and housing conditions.

Although most officers were US-born, they did not assume that they
were the all-knowing experts of all cultures and histories. They insisted
on working collaboratively with women in other countries and stipulated
in the constitution that vice presidents from every country in the African
diaspora would represent their respective communities. Adelaide Casely
Hayford, a teacher from Freetown, Sierra Leone, held the vice president at-
large position for Africa.[32] Vice presidents were elected to represent South
Africa, Haiti, and other specific countries in Africa and the Caribbean that
had working relationships with the council. While it is unknown whether
all vice president positions were filled, council officers traveled to and developed collaborative working relationships with Black women in Brazil,
Cuba, Puerto Rico, Haiti, Liberia, Senegal, South Africa, India, and Sri
Lanka.[33] In 1924 officers invited representatives from Cuba, Africa, India,
and the Virgin Islands to speak at a council meeting in a Baptist church
in Chicago about the pressing issues confronting women in their respective countries.[34] Members also used books, articles, and studies written
by women from the respective countries as foundational texts for council
committees' research about women's education and women's living and
working conditions in each country.[35]

Burroughs's leadership role on the council reflected an important
extension of her broader philosophy about uniting workers to combat
economic disparities. As at the NTS and National Association of Wage
Earners, the officers of the council drew on research and analysis to understand the struggles and advocate for women workers both in Africa
and in countries with significant diasporic populations. As Margaret
Murray Washington reported in 1924, representative council members
conducted several months of ethnographic research concerning women's
living and working conditions in parts of Africa and the Caribbean. The
council also made plans to produce research reports about their upcoming investigations into Ethiopia, Sierra Leone, and Liberia.

Directly taking on racial disparities in US labor, the council developed an in-depth course of study of the exclusion of Black workers from the American Federation of Labor and the long history of "economic basis of prejudice" from slavery until the 1920s. Specifically, the study authors argued that whites and African Americans had been pitted against each other to further the capitalist interests of slavery and the "ethical justifications of the slave system by slave owners through denial of equality to slaves."[36] They traced these legacies of slavery and capitalism into the 1920s, examining racial discrimination in labor unions and companies that used working-poor African Americans as strikebreakers. Council members examined how scientific racism, education disparities, and legal racial segregation kept whites in fear of Blacks and thereby kept "white and black workers antagonistic in [the] fight between capital and labor." Council officers also declared their commitment to challenging the forces that kept Black sharecroppers and industrial workers at the "bottom rung of the economic ladder and subject to all the oppression of the working class plus super-oppression because of race."[37] As far as they were concerned, the race problem could not be solved under the present capitalist conditions, which retained exploitative labor systems rooted in the history of slavery.

With the understanding that transforming women's working conditions across the world was a long-term project, Burroughs insisted that the council recruit Asian students and alumni from historically Black colleges and universities to keep the council going for several generations. The grandmother of famous entertainer Lena Horne, member of the first graduating class of Spelman College, was an active member of the council for most of its existence.[38] The council recruited to its membership students from India at the University of Chicago who educated the council with their research presentations about gender and ethnic disparities in India. The council also proposed to school boards curricula that centered the achievements and activism of Black women and Asian women in the face of colonialism for US and African schools.[39]

Organizational Work as a Labor of Love between Friends

While presiding over the council, Washington leaned most on Burroughs for counsel. She ran past Burroughs the names of people she wanted to invite to the council before presenting them to the entire executive committee. Before speaking with executive committee members, Washington also consulted with Burroughs about fine details and logistics, such as where and when the council should meet. Toward the end of her life, Washington especially depended on Burroughs to fight her battles as she tried to muster enough energy to run the council while managing her declining health. Both women were founding members of the NACW's committee to preserve the home of Frederick Douglass in Washington, DC. Some NACW members disagreed with Burroughs and Washington's vision for the preservation project and wanted to take over the memorial committee at a 1924 NACW meeting in Chicago, a city Washington had also chosen for the international council meeting to make it accessible to the University of Chicago students from India who had recently joined the council.

Fearing that Burroughs would not make it to the upcoming meetings, Washington pleaded with her to drop everything at once and travel to Chicago. She wrote, "My very dear friend, how can I do without seeing you before the Douglass Memorial Meeting? We have got one or two women who are ambitious and who are going to spoil everything unless we can have you right here with us to do it correctly. I dread going into that meeting without your presence. . . . I repeat that I cannot go on here by myself. . . . Nannie, you must get here. You must." Washington was worried that NACW president Hallie Quinn Brown would block her from the committee meetings. As she wrote to Burroughs, "Our President [Quinn] knows exactly how to ride over a lot of women whose backbone is almost worn out and this is why she takes good pains to leave some people out of her Conference."[40] Margaret Washington was one of those people.

While Booker T. Washington had passed away years before Margaret wrote that letter, his influence loomed large over her life and impacted her leadership and communication style. In whatever room she walked into, she was known as the wife of the great Booker T. Washington. She asserted the privileges that came along with her marital identity by consistently referring to herself as Mrs. Booker T. Washington in formal forums and correspondence to advance her own ideas and initiatives, but she was also limited in how she could express her disagreements and conflicting points of view in meetings. At all times, she represented one of the most esteemed Black male leaders in the world, yet sometimes her concerns were dismissed in contentious closed-door meetings in the physical absence of her husband. Margaret Washington depended on Burroughs's privilege of being free from the pressure of adhering to feminine decorum. As an unmarried woman from a working-class background with no children and not physically attractive by society's standards, Burroughs was not always expected to adhere to what was considered ladylike behavior. At times, Burroughs's confrontational communication style backed people down, and they consented to what she wanted. Usually up for good trouble, Burroughs rushed to Chicago to stand side-by-side with Washington to defend their leadership on the Frederick Douglass Memorial Committee and to help run the International Council of Women of the Darker Races meeting.

A year later, Burroughs needed Washington's help. Cofounding the International Council of Women of the Darker Races and presiding over the National Association of Wage Earners in overlapping years had taken a toll on Burroughs. She was struggling to keep the association together, and she reached out frantically to Washington for help. As she wrote, "Another matter, I asked you to go on our Board of the Wage Earners. If you do not tell me not to, I shall put your name on our next supply of literature. *I need you.*" As Washington's confidant, Burroughs must have known about her friend's health concerns and insecurities about the physical signs of her declining health. Burroughs ended her letter on this encouraging note: "Be good to yourself. You looked fine."[41] But a few months after Burroughs sent her letter, in 1925, Washington passed away. Undoubtedly, Washington's death deeply affected Burroughs. They were close and they went a long way back. Washington had supported the NTS at a crucial time during its beginning years—and at a time when her husband criticized Burroughs for establishing the school in Washington, DC. Moving forward, Washington and Burroughs had remained loyal to each other throughout their more than twenty-year friendship.

Although Burroughs really did not have the time to continue working on the council, she remained committed to Washington's vision and their shared Pan-Africanist project. She remained active on the executive council until 1940 and worked closely with proceeding presidents Addie Hunton (1925–1928) and Addie Dickerson (1928–1940) throughout the 1920s and 1930s.[42] According to Sheena Harris, historian and author of

Washington's biography, conducting and publishing a study about the impact of the US occupation of Haiti on the conditions of women and children was one of Washington's top priorities for the council. Deeply committed to this investigation, Washington wrote to Haiti's president Louis Borno about the International Council of the Women of the Darker Races of the World's project and appointed a representative from Port-au-Prince to the council.[43] After Washington passed into history, Burroughs saw the study to completion. She coauthored with Addie Hunton and the council's vice president for Haiti a study detailing how US economic policies severely compromised the independent status of Haiti. They demanded that the US emancipate Haiti from its imperialist powers and support the local government in developing legislation to address the working and living conditions of Haitian women and children.[44]

While Burroughs was passionate about Pan-African women's organizing, her most immediate commitment was achieving economic and political freedom for Black women in the United States. She never depended on politicians for justice, but she saw the value in voter organizing to influence legislation that would address Black women's needs and interests.[45] As Burroughs organized for better working and living conditions on local and global levels, she worked tirelessly to effect change at US ballot boxes, as she and her NACW co-organizers knew this was an essential tool for achieving labor, women's, and civil rights at home.

Creating a Labor Research Database through Voter Mobilization

In 1924 a large and determined group of NACW members representing forty-five states established the National League of Republican Colored Women—with Burroughs serving as the National President—to advance their movement for racial and gender equality and to send a strong message to the Republican Party that it needed to prioritize Black women's demands.[46] The official slogan for the league was "We are in politics to stay and we shall remain a stay in politics."[47] As with Black women community organizers today, the NACW had been an influential force in determining the outcome of elections for candidates of their choice. As members of the "Party of Abraham Lincoln," Black women had been organizing since Reconstruction to elect Republican politicians in opposition to the blatantly racist Democratic candidates. It was not until Franklin D. Roosevelt's administration in the 1930s that Black people began voting for Democratic Party candidates. Roosevelt's progressive politics and Black women's advocacy for his administration in comparison to Republicans' increasing alignment with southern white segregationists and refusal to push for civil rights convinced Black people to vote for the other party. Ahead of the curve, Burroughs and other league members made their frustrations with the Republican Party known several years before Black voters shifted more broadly to the Democratic Party.

The league was a political force to be reckoned with on legislative issues that impacted Black workers. As president of the league, Burroughs integrated demands for labor rights into the league's national campaign for voting rights. It was thereby symbolically fitting and fiscally efficient for Burroughs to house the league in the same building as the National Association of Wage Earners headquarters.[48] Mary Church Terrell (treasurer), Elizabeth Ross Haynes (chaplain), and Maggie Lena Walker (cochair of finance committee)—the same allies who had worked with Burroughs on labor organizing initiatives—worked closely with her once again to establish and manage the league.[49] Always thinking of the Baptist church and its enormous membership as a key organizing base for her initiatives, Burroughs made a concerted effort to connect members of the league and the Woman's Convention to form a coalitional push for labor and voting rights. As she explained at a 1924 Woman's Convention meeting, "For industrial and economic reasons, the ballot will be a sure defense for women in industries who should demand equal pay for equal service."[50] During her speech, Burroughs encouraged her convention sisters to join the league and organize their own suffrage clubs. She told them they needed to become more explicitly involved in politics. According to her, they needed to resist their inclination to think of women's work in churches as separate from political organizing.

While Burroughs pushed the league's agenda through churches across the country, she kept the working conditions of household workers at the forefront of her mind. She created questionnaires for league members to fill out that helped her research and measure domestic worker participation in local and national politics and any obstacles to voting. Her questions indicated how integral domestic workers were to "fighting discrimination and class legislation" and "helping our [Black] women become a factor in the body politic."[51] In her questionnaire, Burroughs expressed concern about the voter suppression of domestic workers. She included questions asking league members to document specific incidents of domestic service employers threatening to fire domestic workers if they exercised their right to vote. Keeping all economically vulnerable Black women in mind, Burroughs also asked members to report stories of whites forcing Black women to sell their votes.

By creating this research instrument, Burroughs produced a national database of information about the impact of voter suppression on Black women wage earners. Responses to her questionnaires confirmed why Burroughs took such an expansive approach to organizing against economic inequalities. Respondents from northern and southern cities listed many issues that were integral to securing labor representation for Black women wage earners, including protection from the Ku Klux Klan and construction of better-quality hospitals, schools, and housing.[52]

A proponent of publicly engaged research, Burroughs made sure that data did not lie dormant at the league's and National Association of Wage Earners headquarters. She put her research into action by orchestrating a letter-writing campaign to put pressure on the president and congres-

Figure 6.3. Burroughs circa 1924, when she was president of the National League of Republican Colored Women. Nannie Helen Burroughs Papers, Prints and Photographs Division, Library of Congress.

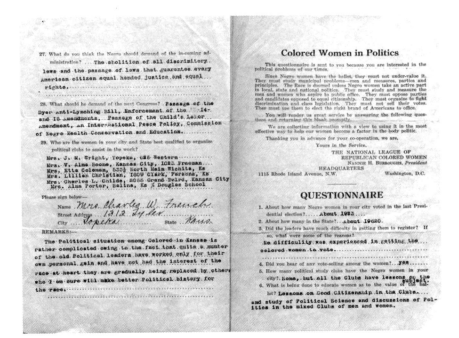

Figure 6.4. A questionnaire Burroughs created to measure Black women's voter participation. Nannie Helen Burroughs Papers, Prints and Photographs Division, Library of Congress.

sional members to appoint Black women to leadership positions in the Departments of Agriculture, Education, and Labor, where they could create policies that addressed the needs of Black women wage earners.[53] Under Burroughs's leadership, the league became an organization that federal appointees sought support from. In 1927 she led a two-day league meeting at the Young Women's Christian Association (YWCA) in Washington, DC, at which the secretary of labor, vice chair of the Republican National Committee, postmaster general, and secretary of the interior spoke to address the league's political and labor concerns and strengthen the league's support of the Republican Party. After the meeting at the YWCA, Burroughs insisted that President Calvin Coolidge meet with the executive board of the league to discuss civil rights issues that impacted Black women's living and working conditions. As Burroughs, Mary Church Terrell, Maggie Lena Walker, and other league

officers told Coolidge, he needed to exclude racist southern state representatives from Congress and issue a federal law against racial segregation. Confident in their political organizing track record, league officers
used their voter influence as their bargaining chip. As they told President Coolidge and other Republican politicians, they would not support
nor organize on behalf of any political candidates who did not commit
to enforcing the Thirteenth, Fourteenth, and Fifteenth Amendments.[54]

When President Coolidge announced he would not run for another
term, the league backed Republican presidential candidate Herbert
Hoover in his race against New York Governor Al Smith. Burroughs
and league members figured that Hoover would come closer to uphold-
ing the amendments than his opponent considering Hoover's campaign
promises for social reform. Strongly believing that Burroughs would ef-
fectively represent Black women's political interests in the presidential
race, the league launched a whisper campaign to get Burroughs elected
as chair of Herbert Hoover's 1928 presidential campaign. Although she
was not selected for the position, Burroughs did not hold back from in-
serting herself and Black wage earners into presidential politics after
Hoover was elected.

With incredible foresight, two months before the stock market crash
of 1929, Burroughs wrote to President Hoover that he needed to commission a study about the dire labor and housing conditions of Black children
and adults. In her letter to Hoover, she stated bluntly that Black people
needed but lacked political representation. As she put it, "A study of labor,
moral, and health conditions among the masses would be a challenging
revelation to you and to other Americans who believe that all citizens
should be given a fair opportunity to earn their daily bread and to live decent lives."[55] Strategically appealing to Hoover's social reform interests,
she told him that once he saw the appalling data, he would undoubtedly
create a course of action to remedy the many compounding problems that
had been impacting Black communities since emancipation.

Burroughs's powerful letter was convincing. The following year, in
1930, Hoover appointed her as a delegate to represent Black children
at his White House conference on Child Welfare and Protection.[56] The
next year, in 1931, Hoover commissioned the White House Conference
on Home Building and Home Ownership and appointed Burroughs as

chair of the Committee on Negro Housing. Burroughs's vision and persistence coupled with worsened economic conditions after the stock market crash led to the first federal study of compounding inequalities that impacted Black people's living and working conditions. While she never fully trusted politicians, she must have felt a sense of optimism after President Hoover finally acted on her unprecedented idea of commissioning such a historic study.

Taking on Government Policy Directly

On April 24, 1931, Burroughs and her twenty-member research team of Black labor scholars, researchers, educators, social workers, newspaper editors, and university presidents made their way to the White House to meet with President Hoover and members of his administration. The committee members represented organizations and schools that had been documenting Black people's working and living conditions in rural towns and urban centers for several decades, including historically Black colleges and universities, the National Association of Colored Women, the National Association for the Advancement of Colored People, the National Urban League, and the Association for the Study of Negro Life and History. Under Burroughs's direction, this esteemed committee produced one of the most extensive studies about structural racism and sexism that was foundational to economic disparities.

At their initial meeting, Hoover tasked committee members to identify what "can be accomplished by the Negroes themselves in the improvement of conditions of housing and homelife" and "what can be done by public authorities or other agencies to aid them in bringing housing conditions to higher standards."[57] Burroughs used this rare opportunity, however, to focus less on what Black people could do for themselves and more on what the White House and federal government could do for Black people. She also went beyond President Hoover's narrow charge. In her role as chair, Burroughs directed the committee to take an intersectional theoretical approach to the study of housing by uncovering systemic racial, class, and gender inequalities that impacted Black people's housing conditions, from unequal wages to underresourced schools to lack of medical services and to realtors who refused to sell inhabitable homes to Black people. The committee members' broad approach enabled them to produce a study that made it abundantly clear that Black people's housing conditions were intricately tied to their working conditions.

Burroughs was in good company to pull off such an expansive study. Most notably, as a writer and researcher, she was well acquainted with Charles S. Johnson, sociologist, labor researcher, and first Black president of Fisk University, who founded the historic *Opportunity: A Journal of Negro Life*, a sociological forum that covered issues regarding Black employment, education, housing, and the arts. While Johnson was editor in chief of the journal, Burroughs contributed articles to the publication, and Johnson covered Burroughs's writings, speeches, and National Association of Wage Earners.[58] As editor of the housing study, Johnson worked with Burroughs to compile and analyze the committee's data. Burroughs also knew committee member Lorenzo J. Greene through her friendship with Carter G. Woodson. Greene was the research investigator for the Association for the Study of Negro Life and History, and he had coauthored *The Negro Wage Earner* with Woodson. Their book was a groundbreaking social scientific study that traced the working conditions of Black people from emancipation to the 1920s. In some ways, the Committee on Negro Housing's research was a follow-up to Greene's and Woodson's study, as well as Burroughs's co-organizer Elizabeth Ross Haynes's ethnographic research about domestic workers that was heavily cited in Greene's and Woodson's book.[59] Burroughs also respected and had worked with housing study committee member Lena Trent Gordon, who had spoken at the ceremony for the National Association of Wage Earners headquarters, dedicated part of her career to conducting studies about the exploitation of Black adult and child workers as chief investigator of Philadelphia's Department of Welfare.[60] Given the intersections of Burroughs's and the committee members' work, there is no wonder how and why they wrote a seminal study.

The committee's findings and methodological approach broke new ground for federal studies. Across their diverse expertise and experience, Burroughs and committee members shared the view that access to safe, affordable, and comfortable housing was a citizenship right due to Black people. As they collectively asserted, "This population [Black people], it may be considered, is not now so essentially different from the American culture in size of family or requirement of security, comfort, cleanliness, and beauty. . . . It may be assumed that the normal basis for the establishment of an American home, with respect to location, equipment, care, and ownership, is not only acceptable but a requisite of that type of citizenship which is the objective of these inquiries."[61]

The committee presented a detailed, comprehensive, and well-supported case for federal government intervention in the improvement of housing options for Black people. The study's fundamental argument that the housing crisis could not be separated from an in-depth analysis of structural forms of racial and gender discrimination was supported by its synthesis of primary sources including photographs, interviews, ethnographic notes, surveys, redlining maps, and quantitative data concerning wages, demographics, and rent and mortgage inflation rates. Based on their research and community organizing experiences, committee members were well aware of the racial, class, and gender biases in the methods that employment offices and government officials used to collect data and write about Black communities. In addition to government data, committee members used data collected by Black organizations and Black colleges and universities.

Ahead of its time, the committee explained and highlighted forms of discrimination that scholar-activists and civil rights leaders organize against today in their movements for economic justice. They attributed the housing crisis for Black people to the following factors: redlining, the depreciation of property values of homes owned or rented by Black people, disproportionate rent rates for Black tenants, harassment of Black people who moved into white neighborhoods, and banks' refusal to issue loans to Black patrons. They also noted that city governments failed to construct housing for Black people who migrated northward for industrial jobs. As a result, Black migrant workers were relegated to sections of cities with no public transportation services and where "the paving, lighting, street clearing, and sanitary regulations are neglected."[62] Their special mention of the particular issues confronting southern Black migrants dovetailed with Burroughs's mission for establishing the NTS in DC in the first place. She believed that the gateway city to the North was the perfect place to intervene in the specific problems facing Black women and girls who left the South in search of better educational and job opportunities. Through their detailed assessment of the Great Migration, Burroughs and committee members made clear that the government needed to do its part in making sure Black people had a fair shot at attaining better lives, especially since it was their labor that helped strengthen northern economies.

At the heart of Burroughs's institution and curriculum building and activism in women's organization was the fight for equal wages. This foundational aspect of her career also defined the overall framing of the housing study. According to the committee, unequal wages along the lines of race and gender were at the core of many of the compounding factors that made it difficult for Black people to find safe, comfortable, and affordable housing. The committee provided data from its interviews with employers and employment agencies as evidence to support this important claim. Just as Burroughs's NTS curriculum challenged racial and gender stereotypes about Black women and girls, the committee debunked slavery-era myths about race that were used to justify the exploitation of Black workers. According to the committee, these stereotypes determined why Black people were the last hired and first fired, or in the case of the lowest-wage occupations, the first hired and the first fired. In committee members' interviews with employers at employment agencies, they found that employers often cited disparaging characteristics associated with Black people as the reasons why they no longer wanted to hire Black workers. According to those employers, Black workers were so unskilled, unreliable, and inexperienced that they were denied membership in labor unions. Other employers commented that they wanted to hire Black people but ultimately decided not to because white employees refused to work with them. Employers sided with white workers, who they considered reliable and skilled.[63]

The solution, however, was not to simply hire more Black workers or to compliment them with words of affirmation. As the committee wrote, "however enthusiastic individual white employers are of Negro labor, unless that enthusiasm is reflected in all situations with wages equal to those paid white workers, the Negro is at a disadvantage. In short, enthusiasm minus economic equality for the same piece and quality of work is exploitation."[64] Committee members conducted a quantitative analysis of wages to demonstrate how little Black workers were valued. Burroughs's experience of studying and organizing against the labor exploitation of Black women in her early organizing days was reflected in the committee's intersectional and mixed methods approach to analyzing wage inequalities. Their intersectional methodological framework enabled committee members to make a deep assessment of the housing crisis and its distinct impact on Black women and men.

The committee conducted an intersectional analysis of quantitative data it collected from the Department of Labor and Chicago's Urban League office to design charts comparing Black and white women's wages. To illustrate the pervasiveness of wage inequalities, the committee described Black women's wages in comparison to those of white women in a range of women's occupations, from domestic service and waitressing to factory work and stenography. The data led committee members to the conclusion that "Negro female workers receive less income than white female workers for the same type and quality of work." While the disparities in wages were glaring enough, the committee duly noted that the numbers did not tell the full story. Readers needed to take into account the many compounding factors that lowered Black women's wages even further than what was recorded by employment agencies and the US Department of Labor. As they asserted, "It is not enough merely to note the income labels in occupational types. Many of the women are heads of homes, either because of death, divorce, desertion, separation, or for other reasons. In many cases there is added responsibility because of children to be supported. Is there any wonder that these women experience difficulty in making 'both ends meet'?"[65]

The committee reached a similar conclusion about Black men workers, but they made careful note of their distinct gendered experiences. Unlike Black women, their wages were not drastically lower than those of white men, and they did not carry the weight of family responsibilities like Black women did. Black men, however, faced layoffs at higher rates because they were mostly employed in industrial trades that hired them only when not enough white men were available for hire or when white men employees did not object to working alongside Black men. By the 1930s, white immigrant women were no longer in competition with Black women for household jobs. They had greater access than Black women to other occupations, and when they could work those jobs, they took them or avoided domestic service altogether. In men's occupational realm, as time-saving machines replaced industrial workers, employers empathized with displaced white workers and preferred to hire them for the remaining jobs that needed to be filled by actual people. Employers also felt pressure from white residents to hire only white workers. White people boycotted companies who were accused of hiring Black workers when unemployed white men lived in the vicinity. When white men and Black men worked at the same companies, Black men had to deal with company policies that often allowed racial discrimination on the job. The committee documented these connecting issues for Black male workers across various occupations, including factory work, janitorial services, truck driving, restaurant and hotel work, and chauffeuring.[66]

The committee's comparative analysis of privilege and exploitation among workers enabled it to highlight parallels between the impact of economic inequalities on African Americans and immigrants of color. They reported that due to employment discrimination, Mexican immigrants and African Americans faced similar living and working conditions in Chicago, Illinois, and in Columbus, Ohio, that led to overcrowded housing in their communities. In Chicago African Americans and Mexicans lived in similar "outworn" tenement buildings. Far fewer Black and Mexican people were homeowners in comparison to whites, yet there were even fewer Mexican homeowners than African American ones.[67]

The committee's recommendations for remedying the labor problem for Black women and men reflected Burroughs's near-decade fight for labor union representation for Black women. As the committee noted, labor union leaders' refusal to fight against both racial and gender discrimination in the labor market compromised Black women's and men's ability to change their circumstances. Equal opportunities at labor union membership and leadership, the committee argued, would make a huge difference in Black workers' wages and working conditions. The committee concluded, "It is unquestionably true that the attitude and practices of unions vary toward the Negro worker. Some use direct, others subtle means to deny him membership. In some cases where membership is granted, similar measures determine the amount of work Negro workers secure." The committee ended its report with several policy recommendations to President Hoover and Congress, urging them to address the housing problem holistically and with special attention to the double gap and the overlapping yet distinct experiences of Black men and women workers in cities and in rural towns.[68] They asserted that this carefully detailed approach would lead to better quality of life for not only Black workers but all people of color wage earners.

Burroughs knew that her committee had produced a study that had enormous potential for transforming legislation in the US and abroad. She wanted to arm her people with the data to effect change, especially since she did not fully trust the government to act upon the findings. She enlisted the help of Carter G. Woodson and readers of his *Journal of Negro History* to help her circulate the research findings. As she wrote,

> Our report on Negro Housing comes from press on the 25th instant. . . . It should be studied by all who are interested in the social and manual aspects of the Negro problem. . . . I want the report to have wide circulation. . . . Will you devote one of your releases to a review of the book? It will help us in our efforts to do something about the findings. You will note from the recommendations that we do not mean to stop at nosing conditions. I shall consider any help you give, not only a help to the cause but a personal favor to your friend.[69]

Of course, Woodson, a dear friend and fellow labor studies scholar, obliged.

While extending the reach of the study through her friendship with Woodson, Burroughs maintained communication with President Hoover to build a bridge between the White House and the Black community in Washington, DC. She insisted that President Hoover learn about Black people's art, history, and political ideologies by attending Black cultural events. She wanted Hoover to learn more about Black people so that he would not look at them as simply research subjects. She took the initiative of reserving tickets for Hoover and his wife to attend a showing of the Pulitzer Prize–winning play *Green Pastures* at the Washington Auditorium, with African American actor Richard Harrison playing the lead character. As she told Hoover, "You and Mrs. Hoover have not attended any public benefit for our group since you have been in the White House. I know you are interested in the cause and I beg that you attend this benefit if possible."[70] She never let him forget that learning about Black culture and history was integral to addressing the economic disparities that Black people faced.

Juggling Care Work and Leadership Roles

Burroughs experienced a series of personal losses at the height of her political advocacy and legislative career in the 1920s and 1930s. On May 3, 1923, her father Reverend John Burroughs passed away at seventy-five years old from stomach cancer in Orange, Virginia, while in the care of his sister Mollie Frye.[71] By the time he died, John had become a respected clergyman, and he was buried in a special section for esteemed church officials in the graveyard of his church home Shady Grove Baptist Church.[72] Although Burroughs was not close to her father, he left an indelible impression on her life, and she was close to his sisters Virginia "Jennie" Holmes and Mollie Frye. When Holmes became ill in the 1920s, she appointed Burroughs as the executor of her estate. In 1928 Holmes passed away, and it took Burroughs nearly two years to settle her aunt's complicated business matters while managing the everyday logistics of multiple organizations and her school.[73]

Shortly after publishing the housing report study in 1932, Burroughs contracted what she believed was a cold that lasted for several months due to her stress-compromised immune system. Her colleague Fannie Cobb Carter, who would later become dean of students at the NTS, warned Burroughs to refrain from overextending herself. As she wrote, "we hope that you will not tax your strength for anything or anybody for your race and God have needed you. . . . You are our Moses and have been saved for this hour."[74] Carter's advice was easier said than done. Burroughs was the caregiver of Mother Bell, who had by then moved from Philadelphia to live with her on the NTS campus. Mother Bell had contracted the flu during the winter and could not shake it off.[75]

Burroughs was considered the successful and dependable member of the family. Her maternal cousins and aunts visited her often throughout the year and on holidays.[76] She cherished her relationships with them, and she supported them financially when she could. In the process of taking care of her mother, Burroughs supported her mother's younger sister,

Rachel Winston. In 1931 Burroughs wrote to Rachel, who was working as a domestic in Virginia at the time, that she was glad that her employers were being nice to her during her recovery from an illness. With sincere gratitude, Rachel responded to Burroughs, "I cannot thank you enough for the money that you sent me. I guess you think it is awful hard that you have to take care of your mother and me too . . . I truly hope and pray the Lord will bless you. Wish it was some Nannie's alike you because you is one that can be depend on. It's [a] great thing to have someone that you can depend on when you get in trouble."[77] Rachel had been worried about her older sister, Burroughs's mother, but Burroughs assured Rachel that she was "trying to take the very best care of her so that she will regain her strength" and that she believed her mother "would pull out all right." At the end of the letter, Burroughs communicated the importance of family to both her and her mother. As she told Rachel, "mother send[s] love" and "remember me to all of the family and friends."[78]

Notwithstanding her personal challenges and intense care work, Burroughs had established herself as a leading educator, researcher, labor organizer, and political leader for Black women wage earners by the 1930s. From being denied a teaching position in 1896 to leading national and international political initiatives throughout the 1920s and 1930s and chairing a historic federal commission on housing and labor in the 1930s was an arduous journey that highlights the depth of determination, knowledge, and skills that Burroughs developed over the years, and that ultimately helped her become a stay in politics. As she became older, she expanded her political legacies by using the influence she had gained to further advance her labor philosophies and help cultivate the next generation of Black political leaders.

Wielding Political Influence and Supporting the Next Generation of Labor Leaders

Burroughs continued pressuring the White House and the federal government to address employment discrimination and Black people's working conditions throughout the 1930s and 1940s. In 1933 a graduate of Howard University asked Burroughs to request that President Hoover investigate why he was declined a position in the fire department in Washington, DC, and was ineligible to apply for it again after passing a civil service exam. His situation was personally familiar to Burroughs as someone who had also been denied a job after making high marks on the exam. Burroughs was thereby moved to write two letters to the president within the same day, urging him to investigate the matter. And that he did. His personal assistant reported back to Burroughs that the young man could apply for the position again. Judging by the tone of the letter, the White House would see to it that the young man would not face the same roadblocks the second time around.[79]

After Franklin D. Roosevelt defeated Hoover in the 1932 presidential election, Burroughs worked at keeping an open line of communication with the White House. Just as she had done with Hoover, she pressed Roosevelt to do something about America's race and labor problem. In a personal letter to Roosevelt, she acknowledged what he had done for Black people economically, but she demanded that he condemn the racial discrimination that undergirded economic disenfranchisement. Burroughs asserted, "Are you going to let the American Negro down? . . . Material help for the Negro is not enough. . . . Democracies are not built on material things. . . . Equal rights for the American Negro are, therefore, far more essential than government paternalism. Being ill-fed, ill-clothed, and ill-housed are only the external manifestations, and physical tragedies [resulting] from a long train of base injustices." Burroughs concluded that Roosevelt would commit a serious act of betrayal toward the Black people who had voted for him if he continued to "remain silent on the question of race discrimination" and "unfair government practices in dealing with colored citizens."[80]

She held Roosevelt's feet to the fire when he ran for reelection. Burroughs told Black people to vote for any presidential candidate who promised to address racial and employment discrimination. While she signaled that Roosevelt was the best choice, she encouraged Black people not to become loyal to any political party, but to vote for the candidate that promised to address their economic concerns. According to Burroughs, "political bushwackers" were "trying to befuddle Negro voters" by telling them that they were wasting their votes on communist, socialist, Republican, or Democratic candidates. She encouraged Black voters to block out those arguments and use the ballot to vote into power the candidate who promised to address employment. Sending a strong signal to presidential candidates, Burroughs explained, "The ballot which the Negro holds in his hand, cost him two hundred fifty years of slavery and seventy years of service and indescribable sacrifice. It is his only deed of trust. He is going to use it to punish his enemies, reward his friends, and get him where he wants to go. . . . We should demand the balance of the jobs that have been withheld from us for over seventy years."[81]

Burroughs continued pushing congressmen to pass legislation for domestic workers. She blasted the federal government for excluding domestic workers from the Social Security Act of 1935, which would have guaranteed them social security benefits. Attempting to stir up outrage in Black communities, she published a scathing op-ed about the act in Black newspapers such as the *Atlanta Daily World* and *Norfolk Journal and Guide*. She asserted, "Society has always seemed to delight in penalizing those who wear caps, aprons, and work with their hands. . . . Now along comes the Federal Government . . . [which] by a sweeping legislative act of exclusion makes domestic workers the mudsill of the new social order."[82] Continuing her push for a domestic-worker-centered movement, Burroughs wrote another op-ed for the *Pittsburgh Courier* detailing the mistreatment of household workers. As she claimed, "The negro woman 'totes' more water; hoes more corn; picks more cotton; washes more clothes; cooks more meals; nurses more babies; mammies more Nordics; supports more churches; does more race uplifting; serves as mudsills for more climbers; takes more punishment; does more foregiving; gets less protection and appreciation, than do the women in any other civilized group in the world. She has been the economic and social slave of mankind."[83]

While Burroughs had no problem critiquing politicians, her public speaking skills and love for the country were not lost on them. On February 29, 1938, she became the first Black woman to deliver a national radio address. She was tapped to deliver a Columbia Broadcasting System speech in support of soldiers during World War II. Rather than making a race-neutral speech, Burroughs made clear that the war presented another opportunity for the United States to live up to democratic ideals as soldiers fought for democracy abroad. World War II, according to her, needed to inspire people at home to "repudiate race prejudice, discrimination, injustice, and hate."[84]

Burroughs further expanded her political influence through her support of younger leaders. Burroughs was overjoyed in 1938 when labor organizer Edgar Brown, at only forty years old, established the United Government Employees Union. She saw the organization as a big win for service workers. The United Government Employees Union was the first labor organization for Black federal government employees, including charwomen, or women who cleaned the offices of congressmen and other government workers.[85] Although Burroughs praised Brown for establishing the union, Elizabeth McDuffie, a Baptist church member and a maid in the Franklin D. Roosevelt White House, had cofounded the organization with Brown. McDuffie leveraged her intimate working relationships with Eleanor and Franklin D. Roosevelt to convince the latter to support the union and she insisted on including charwomen and domestic workers in the organization.

McDuffie shared Burroughs's philosophy that domestic science education would improve household working conditions and create more career opportunities for Black women to become domestic science teachers. McDuffie coordinated negotiations between Roosevelt, Brown, and congressmen to put federal dollars behind the construction of a United Government Employees Union–affiliated training center for domestic workers and domestic science teachers who wanted to become administrators and supervisors. News of the training center was music to Burroughs's ears. She praised the training center and noted that the government and Black people must not stop organizing "until domestic arts and household management are put on a level with other vocations and professions." As she claimed, "Education will do it."[86]

Burroughs also argued for the continuing importance of Black organizations to push the government to value Black workers. She was one of the first prominent leaders to back the Negro Industrial League. The league was established by younger labor activists Robert Weaver and John P. Davis to advocate for the inclusion of Black workers in the National Industrial Recovery Act, which guaranteed workers the right to collective bargaining. As historian Francille Rusan Wilson has documented, Burroughs helped Weaver gather key evidence for a presentation that he delivered in front of the leaders of the United Mine Workers about the unequal pay scales between Black and white coal miners. After his presentation, the United Mine Workers lent their support to the National Industrial League. John P. Davis invited Burroughs to join his Joint Committee on National Recovery. The committee represented the interests of Black workers during the New Deal era and investigated New Deal agencies and their treatment of Black workers. Soon after Burroughs joined the committee, it gained the support and participation of the National Baptist Convention, USA and several Black leaders.[87]

As part of Burroughs's agenda to elevate the political power of the Black church, she worked with younger generations of Baptists in their fight for equality. She stood shoulder to shoulder with Ella Baker, Jackie Robinson, and Congressman Adam Clayton Powell Jr. during panel discussions about the importance of organizing for workers' rights through the Baptist church.[88] Out of all the dynamic leaders in Baptist circles, Burroughs took a special interest in mentoring Dr. Martin Luther King Jr. King held Burroughs in high regard, calling her "one of the leading voices in the Negro race."[89] Burroughs and King were kindred spirits who shared a vision of bringing together labor and civil rights organizing to transform the United States into a true democracy. King would later articulate the importance of both movements when he declared that "the two most dynamic and cohesive liberal forces in the country are the labor movement and the Negro freedom movement."[90] Burroughs advised King on how to achieve this holistic vision by keeping in constant communication with him and offering him advice during his journey toward becoming one the world's most influential leaders.

She helped King organize Baptist women for his political initiatives by extending to him an open invitation to attend Woman's Convention meetings and speak to members about his civil rights and labor initiatives. King respected Burroughs's organizing skills and invited her to join the planning committee of the Southern Christian Leadership Conference's Institute on Nonviolence and Social Change. In the words of civil rights activist Ralph David Abernathy, as a committee member, Burroughs sold a record-breaking number of copies of King's book *Striving for Freedom*, and the proceeds went to the institute.[91] King expressed his appreciation to Burroughs for her mentoring and fundraising efforts. He wrote, "Let me thank you once more for the interest you have taken in our struggle. I can assure you that your moral support and financial contributions have given me renewed courage and vigor to carry on."[92] Civil rights organizing came at a cost for Black teachers who worked in the South. Burroughs worked with King to identify prospective teachers for the National Training School for Women and Girls who had been fired from their jobs in the South because of their affiliation with the National Association for the Advancement of Colored People.[93]

Throughout the 1940s and 1950s, Burroughs remained a committed Pan-Africanist and advocate for better housing in Black communities. At the invitation of younger activist Paul Robeson Sr., Burroughs joined Robeson, W. E. B. Du Bois, and other Pan-Africanists on the Council on African Affairs, an independent and nonprofit organization committed to advancing political and economic liberation for Africans and Indian migrants on the continent.[94] As Burroughs had been in the earlier phase of her legislative career, Robeson and the council were on the Federal Bureau of Investigation's surveillance list. But Burroughs still did not back down from engaging in what had been deemed radical activities by the Department of Justice. She was a member of the Council on African Affairs for seven years. Robeson saw Burroughs as a personal friend and a powerful ally for "shaking up" colonialism in Africa because of her politics and her leadership in the Woman's Convention. As he told her, "we know of your long and deep interest in Africa and the powerful influence of Black churches and their several million members could have in supporting the goals of the council."[95]

W. E. B. Du Bois, who was older than Burroughs but had a radically young spirit, reached out to her to work with him on demanding the US government change its exploitative policies toward Africa. Burroughs was among the first people to sign Du Bois's 1952 petition addressed to President Dwight D. Eisenhower and the US Delegation to the United Nations about "policies towards colonized peoples, especially in Africa, a matter upon which colored Americans had a moral obligation to make their views known."[96]

Always working on better conditions at home, when Burroughs became president of the Woman's Convention in 1947, she continued molding the auxiliary group into a politically active organization. Leading up to the hallmark 1954 *Brown v. Board of Education* decision, which outlawed racial segregation in schools, Burroughs raised money through the

Figure 6.5. Burroughs and Thurgood Marshall (*far left*), circa 1950s. Nannie Helen Burroughs Papers, Prints and Photographs Division, Library of Congress.

Woman's Convention for the National Association for the Advancement of Colored People's Legal Defense Fund to support the attorneys arguing the case. She invited the young lawyers to speak at convention meetings and she kept in close contact with Thurgood Marshall, one of the lawyers who would later become the first Black US Supreme Court justice, offering him spiritual and political advice throughout the trial. Burroughs's long fight against racial disparities in education gave Marshall encouragement to face the hostile opposition to his desegregation efforts. He told Burroughs, "I know that you know that all of us are forever indebted to you for the long hard fight you have made for our people. You will forever be an inspiration to all of us." He promised Burroughs that he would "finish the job that you and others kept going on through the present cases we are now handling."[97] Marshall made good on his promise. On May 17, 1954, the Supreme Court decided to outlaw racial segregation in public schools. This landmark decision, which she had worked toward throughout her career, must have made Burroughs proud.

⎯⎯⎯⎯⎯◆◆◆⎯⎯⎯⎯⎯

Burroughs employed a range of creative strategies to navigate hurdles along her rise to political prominence. While pushing for legislative change, Burroughs encountered profound challenges at her school during the Depression. NTS student enrollment declined sharply due to students' and their families' inability to pay for tuition. On top of losing funding from decreased student enrollment, philanthropists cut back on their donations to the NTS to preserve resources for their own organizations. The devastating loss in revenue made it impossible for Burroughs to provide students with opportunities to work their way through school. She had to make the unavoidable decision of shortening the academic school year to cut operating costs.[98] Throughout most of the 1930s, she focused on teaching smaller classes of students, fundraising to maintain the campus buildings, and rebranding the school with the hope of reopening the NTS at full capacity. In the process of relaunching the NTS, Burroughs took on more family responsibilities. Like most Black families during the Depression, Burroughs's family members lost their sources of income and struggled with chronic illnesses. As Burroughs was the respected breadwinner of the family, her aunts, uncles, and cousins reached out to her for help. Despite her nearly nonexistent salaries of a teacher, political organizer, and caregiver, Burroughs found ways to help them, while also continuing to care for her mother.

Burroughs found personal motivation and intellectual freedom in the arts and entrepreneurship to continue advancing her educational mission for Black economic empowerment during this incredibly difficult period. Underscoring her determination to keep going, Burroughs asserted that although she had willingly "sacrificed, slaved, and suffered in silence," she had "accepted the new challenge to find a way out and save the institution into which hundreds of friends have invested money, faith, and hope."[99] Burroughs had both an unyielding commitment for social change and activism and a deep intellectual and organizing versatility that not only saved her institution but advanced the overall labor movement for Black women and girls.

Notes

1. Preston, *Mary McLeod Bethune, the Pan-Africanist*, 93.
2. NHB to Mary Church Terrell, June 19, 1920, Correspondence, May–Sept. 1920, Mary Church Terrell Papers, LOC.
3. Brooks, "Religion, Politics, and Gender," 17.
4. Dosset, *Bridging Race Divides*, 30.
5. Smith, *Sick and Tired*, 20–21.
6. Frye, "On the Frontlines at Work and at Home."
7. NHB to President Herbert Hoover, August 19, 1929, NHB papers, Box 37, Folder 21, NHB Papers.
8. Holder, "The 'Double Gap' and the Bottom Line."
9. La Follette, "The Color Line," 6–7.
10. La Follette, 6–7.
11. Butler, *Two Paths to Equality*, 85–86.
12. *Second Annual Report of the Minimum Wage Board*, 3, 5, 13, 14.
13. For example, see *Second Annual Report of the Minimum Wage Board*, 42–44.
14. US Department of Labor, *Monthly Labor Review, June 1921*, 71.
15. Butler, *Two Paths to Equality*, 88.
16. National Association of Colored Women, *Minutes of the Fourteenth Biennial Session*, 36–37.
17. National Association of Colored Women, *Minutes of the Fifteenth Biennial Session Held at Oakland, California, August 1–5, 1926*, 50.
18. *Proceedings of the Women's Industrial Conference*, xii.
19. *Proceedings of the Women's Industrial Conference*, 100–101.
20. *Proceedings of the Women's Industrial Conference*, 100–101.
21. *Proceedings of the Women's Industrial Conference*, 100–101.
22. Downey, "Precursor to Women of Color Feminism," 272.
23. Margaret Murray Washington, "International Council of the Darker Races of Women of the World: Statement from the Organization," 1923, Containers 20–21, Reel 14, Mary Church Terrell Papers, Moorland-Springarn Research Center, Howard University.
24. "Constitution," circa 1920s, Subject File–1962, International Council of Women of the Darker Races of the World, Mary Church Terrell Papers, LOC.
25. Rief, "Thinking Locally, Acting Globally," 214.
26. Other officers included Addie Hunton (second vice president), Charlotte Hawkins Brown (corresponding secretary), Mary S. Josenberger (treasurer), Lugenia Burns Hope (Social Committee chair), Addie Dickerson (Foreign Relations Committee chair), Emily Williams (Education Committee chair), and Casely Hayford (vice president for Africa). Rief, "Thinking Locally, Acting Globally," 215; Washington, "International Council of the Darker Races."

27. "International Council Elects at Convention: Gathering of Darker Women's Conference in Washington Comes to an End," *Chicago Defender*, August 18, 1923.

28. Minutes, International Council of Women of the Darker Races of the World, 1924, Box 7, Reel 5, Mary Church Terrell Papers, LOC.

29. Parker, *Unceasing Militant*, 158.

30. NHB to W. E. B. Du Bois, March 1, 1929; NHB to Addie Hunton, October 20, 1923; Addie Dickerson to W. E. B. Du Bois, November 2, 1929, W. E. B. Du Bois Papers (MS 312), Special Collections and University Archives, University of Massachusetts Amherst Libraries.

31. Washington, "International Council of the Darker Races."

32. Adelaide Casely Hayford to Margaret Murray Washington, November 28, 1922, Box 102–12, Folder 240, Mary Church Terrell Papers, Moorland-Springarn Research Center, Howard University.

33. Washington, "International Council of Women of the Darker Races."

34. "Conventions," *Half-Century Magazine*, September–October 1924, 8.

35. Washington, "International Council of Women of the Darker Races."

36. Mary Church Terrell, "An Outline for a Study Program on Race Relations," 1, Subject File 1884–1962, International Council of the Darker Races of the World, Mary Church Terrell Papers, LOC.

37. Terrell, 2.

38. "Spelman Gives Three Honorary Degrees," *Atlanta Daily World*, May 26, 1987.

39. Margaret Murray Washington, "Account of Origins of the International Council of Women of Darker Races," November 10, 1924, Box 102–12, Folder 238, Mary Church Terrell Papers, Moorland-Spingarn Research Center.

40. Margaret Murray Washington to NHB, July 15, 1924, Box 31, Folder 5, NHB Papers.

41. NHB to Margaret Murray Washington, circa 1925, Mary Church Terrell Collection, Moorland-Spingarn Research Center.

42. Rief, "Thinking Locally, Acting Globally," 216–17.

43. Harris, *Margaret Murray Washington*, 139–41.

44. Balch, *Occupied Haiti*.

45. "Constitution: The National Association of Wage Earners, Inc."; "The First Annual Meeting of the National Association of Wage Earners" Program.

46. "Women Form Republican Voters' Club: League to Stimulate Interest at Polls," *Chicago Defender*, August 16, 1924.

47. NHB, "National League of Republican Colored Women," *National Notes: Official Organ of the National Association of Colored Women*, July 1928: 10.

48. NHB, "National League of Republican Colored Women," 10.

49. "Women Form Republican Voters' Club."

50. National Baptist Convention, *Twentieth Annual Session of the Woman's Convention*, 1920, 338–40, 383.

51. National League of Republican Colored Women Questionnaire, 1924, Box 308, Folder 8, NHB Papers.

52. National League of Republican Colored Women Questionnaire.

53. Murphy, *Jim Crow Capital*, 34.

54. "G.O.P. Women from Twenty-Three States in Session: G.O.P. Women Meet 3 Days at Capital," *Afro-American*, May 21, 1927.

55. NHB to Hoover, August 19, 1929, Box 37, Folder 21, NHB Papers.

56. National Training School for Women and Girls secretary to Hoover, November 8, 1930, Box 37, Folder 21, NHB Papers.

57. Hoover, Message to the Committee on Negro Housing.

58. For example, see Johnson, *Opportunity: Journal of Negro Life* 1 (1923): 32, 192, 252; Johnson, *Opportunity: Journal of Negro Life* 2 (1924): 128, 155, 380, 383.

59. Greene and Woodson, *The Negro Wage Earner*, vi, 228–43.

60. Rollo Wilson, "Philly Mayor and Director Praise Aides in Department of Welfare; Race Woman Chief," *Pittsburgh Courier*, August 3, 1929.

61. Johnson, *Negro Housing*, xv.

62. Johnson, 2–3, 9.

63. Johnson, 157.

64. Johnson, 158.

65. Johnson, 160–64, 159.

66. Johnson, 166, 164–65, 165–70.

67. Johnson, 10, 84, 124.

68. Johnson, 165, 114–18.

69. NHB to Carter G. Woodson, Box 47, Folder 5, NHB Papers.

70. NHB to Herbert Hoover, April 7, 1931, Box 37, Folder 21, NHB Papers.

71. Certificate of Death #16175, May 2, 1923, Bureau of Vital Records, Virginia Department of Health.

72. Notes, author's conversation with an employee of the state of Virginia's Orange County Historical Society, July 9, 2023.

73. Virginia B. Holmes, Certificate of Death #26041, November 21, 1928, Bureau of Vital Records, Virginia Department of Health; NHB to Mollie Frye, December 19, 1930, Box 1, Folder 1, NHB Papers; "Obituary: Virginia B. Holmes," *Evening Star*, November 20, 1928.

74. Fannie Cobb Carter to NHB, November 29, 1932, February 8, 1933, Box 5, Folder 8, NHB Papers.

75. "Deaths: Jennie Burroughs Bell," *Evening Star*, July 1, 1935; Fannie Cobb Carter to NHB, November 29, 1932, Box 5, Folder 8, NHB Papers.

76. James Poindexter to NHB, October 14, 1937, NHB Papers.

77. Rachel Winston to NHB, Box 1, folder 1, June 25, 1935, NHB Papers.

78. NHB to Rachel Winston, February 28, 1931, Box 1, Folder 1, NHB Papers.

79. NHB to Hoover, January 21, 1931, Box 37, Folder 21; William C. Hull to NHB, Box 13, Folder 10, NHB Papers.

80. NHB to President Franklin D. Roosevelt, Box 42, Folder 8, NHB Papers.

81. NHB, "From a Woman's Point of View: Vote for Justice and Jobs," 1936, Box 46, Folder 7, NHB Papers.

82. NHB, "Domestic Workers Excluded," *Atlanta Daily World*, January 21, 1937, 2, reprinted as "The Social Security Act Looks Down on Us Who Toil with Our Hands," *Pittsburgh Courier*, January 23, 1937.

83. Graves, *Nannie Helen Burroughs*, 38–39.

84. NHB, "Brotherhood and Democracy: Radio Address," February 29, 1938, Mordecai Johnson Papers. The 1943 revised version of the speech is at the Library of Congress; NHB, January 1, 1943, Box 46, Folder 20, NHB Papers.

85. NHB, "A New Day Dawns: Domestic Workers Will Get a Break," *Baltimore Afro-American*, June 11, 1938.

86. NHB.

87. Wilson, *The Segregated Scholars*, 235–38.

88. "Baptists in 63rd Meeting," *New York Amsterdam News*, October 18, 1958.

89. Martin Luther King Jr. to Bernice Cofer, Martin Luther King Jr. Papers, 1954–1958, Howard Gotlieb Archival Research Center, Boston University.

90. King, *All Labor Has Dignity*, xiii.

91. Ralph D. Abernathy to NHB, November 13, 1956, February 10, 1959, Box 1, Folder 5, NHB Papers.

92. James Wyatt, "Forging Path toward Better, More Just America," *The Capital*, April 23, 2023, 13.

93. Martin Luther King Jr. to NHB, March 8, 1958, Martin Luther King Jr. Papers, 1954–1958, Howard Gotlieb Archival Research Center, Boston University; Martin Luther King Jr. to NHB, September 18, 1956, Box 63, NHB Papers. Also see Carson et al., *The Papers of Martin Luther King, Jr.*, 370–71.

94. Paul Robeson to NHB, February 7, 1947, Box 25, Folder 2, NHB Papers.

95. Paul Robeson to NHB, April 8, 1954, Box 25, Folder 2, NHB Papers.

96. W. E. B. Du Bois to NHB, March 12, 1952, Box 47, NHB Papers.

97. Thurgood Marshall to NHB, November 18, 1953, August 27, 1954, October 7, 1954, Box 20, Folder 5, NHB Papers.

98. NHB, "Plan Is to Close Plant in Winter: Miss Burroughs to Tour Country with Players to Raise Funds," 1933, Box 46, NHB Papers.

99. NHB.

CHAPTER 7

"Interested in Making a Life"

Beginning Anew through Entrepreneurship and the Arts, 1929–1940

There was such a crowd last night that I did not try to get to you. I thank you for the opportunity of seeing your Pageant. I was astonished and gratified to note the way in which it [*When Truth Gets a Hearing*] gripped and interested the audience. . . . We have lots to learn from you.

—W. E. B. Du Bois to Nannie Helen Burroughs, May 17, 1929

I am very glad to have your impressions of the effect of the pageant upon the audience. I have really longed to see the masses of our people, and the others included, sufficiently interested in their own problems to sit still while they were presented in a serious and compelling way.

—Nannie Helen Burroughs to W. E. B. Du Bois, May 21, 1929

With barely two pennies to rub together, Burroughs confessed that she was "not only interested in making a living, but in making a life" during the Depression.[1] Similarly, she wanted Black people to not only survive this devastating period but to come out of it economically empowered. She integrated this charge into multiple aspects of her organizing as a playwright and the cofounder of the Northeast Self-Help Cooperative (renamed Cooperative Industries of Washington, DC, in 1936), the first cooperative in the District established by a Black woman. For Burroughs, driven by an impassioned vision of a new world, creative writing and entrepreneurship offered additional tools in her push for economic justice that was at the heart of her life's work.

228

In the late 1920s and 1930s, Burroughs tapped into the Black Little Theater Movement of the Harlem Renaissance era as a vehicle to press forward with her labor agenda of changing society for working Black women
and girls. The movement provided her with the opportunity to engage in
creative writing, which she genuinely enjoyed and had been doing since
her early days of writing short stories for fundraising in the Woman's Convention. The bold expressions of Black culture and pride in the arts during
this period also resonated with Burroughs. As a teacher-playwright, Burroughs created community platforms for Black women and NTS students
to advance Pan-Africanism and public education about racism, sexism,
and labor exploitation beyond the walls of a classroom. Her goal was to
inspire Black people to organize against disparities that affected Black
women and girls. Her body of plays included *When Truth Gets a Hearing*,
Slabtown Convention, and *Where Is My Wandering Boy Tonight?* Among
her multiple works, Burroughs made her loudest appeal for Black workers and economic justice in her play *When Truth Gets a Hearing*. As one
reviewer of the play wrote in 1929, "The story is built up carefully and
skillfully, point by point, relating to the ups and downs of a race who for
250 years have labored without reward for the advancement of civilization."[2] The play highlights the historical struggle among Black Americans
for justice and equality in the United States, alongside a broader Pan-
Africanist call for change. Burroughs wrote the first version of the play
in 1916, and with NTS students serving as the actors, she took a revised
version of it that more prominently foregrounded Pan-Africanism on the
road in the late 1920s and early 1930s. Maggie Lena Walker provided the
financial backing that enabled Burroughs and students to travel and perform the play in various states. By enlisting NTS students to act in the
play, Burroughs turned her creative writing skills into a pedagogical tool
to educate students and the public about the importance of labor rights
to Black freedom and inspire them to organize to that end.

Burroughs's plays were extensions of her organizing for labor rights
through the NTS, church, politics, and women's organizations. She was
a visionary leader, and in all her work, she looked for ways to inspire people in the Black community, especially women, to reimagine their lives,
their labor, and how they might support themselves and their commu-

nity. In her work as a teacher-playwright, this remained a top priority for Burroughs. As she noted in *When Truth Gets a Hearing*, Black people had generated enormous profits for white business owners since slavery and received little to no profit in return. During the Depression she doubled down on her belief that Black people should create wage-earning opportunities for themselves and their communities.

In 1934 Burroughs made her vision a reality when she transformed the NTS campus into a cooperative for the mutual benefit of herself, students, and unemployed Black people in the community surrounding the school. The cooperative, which lasted into the early 1940s, came right on time, considering that most Black women had been excluded from the 1933 National Industrial Recovery Act, 1935 National Labor Relations Act, 1935 Social Security Act, 1936 National Labor Relations Act, and the 1938 Fair Labor Standards Act, which all excluded agricultural and domestic workers.[3] Collectively, the acts provided employees with social security benefits, collective bargaining power, and the right to form unions and receive a minimum wage and time-and-a-half compensation for overtime work. Without these labor protections, most Black women in domestic service were left to fend for themselves. Within two years, Burroughs's experiment in self-help employed more than four hundred unemployed and underemployed Black people who became producer-owners of Cooperative Industries, an organization that served several thousand Black people in Washington, DC. The cooperative also provided practical work opportunities for students who wanted to make a living from farming.

As with previous moments in her life, Burroughs had to balance her achievements with personal hardships. While establishing the cooperative, Mother Bell and Burroughs's ride-or-die friend Maggie Lena Walker passed into history. Although their deaths undoubtedly impacted Burroughs personally, she was not left alone to provide essentials for her school and community. Before passing away, Maggie Lena Walker, through her bank, provided life insurance for NTS staff and health services for cooperative members that lasted for several years. Burroughs's aunts and cousins also came to the rescue with farming resources from rural Virginia that helped Burroughs support the cooperative and provide food for NTS students. By extending these crucial resources to the NTS and its cooperative, Walker and Burroughs's family members helped keep the doors of the NTS open during one of the most difficult periods Burroughs ever faced. Burroughs's creative and entrepreneurial projects, supported by friends and family, and driven by her extraordinary artistic and organizing work, helped further establish her as one of the most impactful Black labor leaders of the twentieth century.

NACW Women Driving Economic Change through the Arts

On May 17, 1929, artists, civil rights and religious leaders, and community members crowded into the popular Dunbar Theater in Philadelphia, Pennsylvania, eager to see Burroughs's *When Truth Gets a Hearing*. There were no empty seats in the house. NTS student actors, sponsored by Maggie Lena Walker, had already been traveling across the country to perform the play in Chicago, Richmond, New York City, California, and Washington, DC. In Philadelphia word spread quickly about these successful shows, and people greatly anticipated the performance there. Du Bois also helped advertise the Dunbar Theater show by announcing it in *The Crisis* for more than a year prior to the performance. Walker's and Du Bois's support came at a crucial time. Burroughs was recovering from throat surgery for the better half of the year and could not do the advertising and fundraising on her own.

Du Bois attended the performance to represent the national office of the National Association for the Advancement of Colored People and support Burroughs, who had recently joined the association's board of directors. Du Bois was so looking forward to attending the play that he sent Burroughs a telegram the day before the performance to request that she reserve two extra seats for his friends at the box office. After the performance, Du Bois told her, "Your ability to hold the mass of our people is extraordinary."[4] Burroughs responded that she had drawn inspiration for some of the lines from Du Bois's *Darkwater* for the play. As she put it, "I think your appeal for Negro womanhood in your 'Dark Water' is very strong and I hope you noticed that I had put a sentence from that splendid appeal into the mouth of the representative of Negro womanhood."[5] Burroughs's play was also supported by her friend and Harlem Renaissance writer Alice Dunbar-Nelson. Like Burroughs,

Dunbar-Nelson used creative writing to advocate for Black workers, as evidenced by "To the Negro Farmers of the United States," Dunbar-Nelson's loving tribute to sharecroppers.[6] After attending the Dunbar Theater performance of "When Truth Gets a Hearing," Dunbar-Nelson wrote this glowing review of the play:

> Nannie Burroughs's pageant, "When Truth Gets a Hearing," played to a record house at the Dunbar Theatre in Philadelphia on last Thursday night. It was mighty well done. The girls spoke clearly and delightfully. No mealy-mouth mumbling, but enunciation and articulation that was a delight to the ear. The acting was natural and graceful and some quite dramatic. And the singing was excellent. We could have wished that the audience were less enthusiastic, for often they voiced their approval so vigorously and whole-heartedly that some of the lines were lost, especially in the very well-done Labor Chorus when it gave Dett's Music in the Mines. The story of the progress of the race and all the good Race Hokum was so well presented that even the most saturated ones of it forgot to be bored and applauded vigorously the fresh viewpoint of the young women of Miss Burroughs' school.[7]

When Burroughs premiered her play at the Dunbar Theater, she and NTS students joined an illustrious list of Black playwrights and actors whose work had been showcased there. In the 1920s and 1930s, Black theater was flourishing in several cities, including Philadelphia, and a number of playwrights and artists associated with the overlapping eras of the New Negro Movement, Harlem Renaissance, and Black Little Theater Movement had presented their work at this esteemed and distinctive venue.[8] During its nearly thirty-year existence, several major Black artists and all-Black casts graced the Dunbar stage, including Lena Horne, Duke Ellington, and the Nicholas Brothers, while important works of Black theater were performed there, including *Shuffle Along* and Burroughs's *When Truth Gets a Hearing*.[9]

The Dunbar Theater was a Black-owned theater and jazz club established to provide a supportive venue for Black artists outside of the racist politics of Broadway theater and entertainment.[10] Like Zora Neal Hurston, Alice Dunbar-Nelson, Alaine Locke, and W. E. B. Du Bois, Burroughs was highly critical of formulaic plots and minstrelsy representations of Black people in Broadway shows, and the Dunbar Theater provided an

Figure 7.1. Student actors in *When Truth Gets a Hearing*. Nannie Helen Burroughs Papers, Prints and Photographs Division, Library of Congress.

important platform for artists pushing back against those stereotypical depictions. As Burroughs claimed, "Novelists and playwrights have never done Negroes justice. If they were to tell the story as it is or let Negroes play their part as they live it in everyday life, Negroes would actually run away with every show and leave guest audiences standing up and applauding wildly. But, instead of triumphs, when novelists and playwrights get through caricaturing Negroes, they play the leading role in 'The Imitation of Life.'"[11] Burroughs advanced her uncompromised vision by writing beyond the white gaze and representing Black people's histories and everyday experiences in what she believed were authentic and thereby relatable ways to Black people. Instead of aiming to feature her plays on Broadway stages, she selected Black-owned and experimental venues, including churches, auditoriums, schools, and small theaters, for her productions to ensure authenticity and accessibility to Black people across socioeconomic backgrounds.[12]

Like her former teachers Mary Church Terrell and Anna Julia Cooper, Burroughs found pedagogical freedom in creative writing as well as additional ways to build institutions and extend her organizations'

reach for the political and economic empowerment of Black people. Un-
bounded by the traditional structures of books and newspaper articles,
these National Association of Colored Women teacher-playwrights viv-
idly illustrated to large public audiences the kind of world they had been
organizing to make a reality since the founding meeting of the NACW
in the late nineteenth century. They wrote new theatrical works that
integrated examples of African American, African, and Caribbean histories of resistance into their plays as inspiration for Black resistance
against injustices in the world. Their plays were also extensions of their
classrooms. As teacher-playwrights, they educated the public about
US, European, Caribbean, and African histories that young people and
working adults never learned from standard school textbooks. Burroughs, Cooper, and Terrell developed plots, characters, and musical
arrangements to promote resilience, joy, and critical thinking as important guiding frameworks for expanding the Black Freedom Movement against systemic inequalities. Reparative justice, in the ways they
imagined it, usually prevailed at the end of their plays. Always working
for the common good, Burroughs and her former teachers used the proceeds from the plays to invest money in their schools, organizations,
and churches.

After starring as Harriet Beecher Stowe in W. E. B. Du Bois's *Star
of Ethiopia*, Mary Church Terrell wrote *The Phyllis Wheatley Pageant-
Play* in the 1930s to educate the public about Black women's resistance
during slavery through the story of Phyllis Wheatley and her family's activism against slavery. Terrell's play remained in circulation into the early
1940s, and part of the proceeds went to Burroughs's alma mater Dunbar
High School, formerly known as M Street School.[13] Anna Julia Cooper
wrote several plays over the course of two decades. Most notably, in 1940
she wrote *From Servitude to Service: Contributions from the Negro Peoples in American History*. In what could be read as a prelude to Nikole
Hannah-Jones's *1619 Project*, Cooper's pageant was set in 1619 James-
town, Virginia, and featured debates between abolitionists, slave traders,
and British loyalists about slavery and its long-term implications beyond emancipation. Her plays were performed by Dunbar High School
students at various churches around the city that had a long history of
supporting Black women organizers, including Nineteenth Street Bap-

tist Church. Cooper invested the proceeds from her play into churches, Dunbar High School, and Frelinghuysen University.[14]

Burroughs's body of plays preceded her mentors', revealing her deep and longtime passion for creative writing. Collectively, her plays took on labor exploitation, European colonialism, slavery, and women's work and patriarchy in the Black church. NTS actors usually performed *Where Is My Wandering Body Tonight?* on Mother's Day at the NTS for the surrounding Deanwood community and at churches. Taking inspiration from the temperance movement song "Where Is My Wandering Boy Tonight?," Burroughs wrote the play as a story about a domestic worker whose son decides to leave home and never talk to her again. Burroughs wrote the play to initiate community conversations about the devaluation of Black mothers' sacrifices, intellect, and work in their churches, families, and homes.[15] *Slabtown Convention* was mostly performed at Baptist churches to raise money for various funds, such as for construction and student scholarships. In the script, Burroughs centered her contentious experiences working with National Baptist Convention leaders and members of the Woman's Convention to inspire conversations about the politics of patriarchy and fissures among women and between women and men in Black churches. *When Truth Gets a Hearing* was typically performed in larger and more public venues across the country, and the proceeds from the showings went to the NTS as well as Black organizations including the National Association for the Advancement of Colored People and Carter G. Woodson's Association for the Study of Negro Life and History.[16]

While Burroughs committed the proceeds from her plays toward the immediate needs of the NTS and Black churches and organizations, she wanted the plays to become the financial gifts that kept on giving to Black communities beyond her lifetime. As she told Du Bois, "I feel that somebody could take this pageant [*When Truth Gets a Hearing*] and make it fit to be of real service to the race."[17] An astute businesswoman, Burroughs wrote director's notes for other women to direct her plays to protect the elements that had contributed to their success, including stage props, musical selection, diction, and lighting.

Knowing that future directors would put their own spin on the plays, Burroughs warned them not to make the plays didactic or overly comedic in ways that would bore audiences or reproduce stereotypes about Black people. As she explained, she skillfully infused humor, sarcasm, and wit into her scripts to draw the audience into thinking about heavy topics. Addressing future directors in her director's notes for *Slabtown Convention*, Burroughs wrote,

> THIS PLAY IS NOT A BURLESQUE. Performers spoil it when they try to "make up something" or add something funny. Slabtown, as written, is humorous enough, but it also has sense enough in it to challenge the most discriminating good performer as well as to delight an audience that wants something very different and at the same time teaches a quality of common sense much needed in Church life. . . . Do not play with "Slabtown." Play it. Let the audience get the point and do the laughing.[18]

Burroughs also instructed directors not to sacrifice the serious parts of the original scripts. In her notes for *Where Is My Wandering Boy To-night?*, she mandated that one of the characters deliver a speech in the middle of the play to ensure that audiences understood it was a production about the social, political, and economic struggles of Black mothers. Included in this passionate speech were these instructive lines:

> A long day in domestic service, working in a laundry or dry cleaning establishment brings the Negro woman the lowest income of any wage earner. . . . If she is qualified to teach, meeting the requirements as a white instructor, she receives a salary one-third to one-half that of the white woman who teaches the same subjects in the same city. The Negro mother rears her family under a terrible handicap. . . . The Negro woman sees the ability of her children suppressed by poverty and prejudice—a hangover from slavery.

Integrating her legislative knowledge and experience into the speech, Burroughs instructed the character to speak about the political disadvantages of Black mothers, from voter suppression in the South to infant mortality to laws that failed to address poverty in the Washington alleyway communities. According to Burroughs, despite all the economic, social, political, and religious adversities Black women faced, Black mothers were remarkably raising future generations of self-respecting, fearless, and gracious daughters and sons.[19]

As a strong proponent of Black entrepreneurship, Burroughs must have been proud to witness the financial rewards of her plays. Civil rights leader Adam Clayton Powell Sr. told his Harlem congregation of Abyssinian Baptist Church that all Baptist churches were indebted to Burroughs for her work. He declared, "As much as the churches have gained from Nannie Helen Burroughs's idea of Women's Day and from her famous play *Slabtown Convention*, every church ought to set aside one Sunday in the year to be known as Nannie Helen Burroughs Day and send this money, every dollar raised on that one day in the year, and endow and operate the school which she founded for women and girls in Washington, DC." That same day, Powell's congregation pooled resources and donated five hundred dollars to Burroughs's school.[20] *Slabtown Convention* has remained popular in the twenty-first century and is performed in churches to bring visibility to the undervalued work of women in the church and to raise funds for scholarships and building projects.[21] Although *Where Is My Wandering Boy Tonight?* is not performed as widely as *Slabtown Convention*, it remains one of the boldest stage productions about working-class Black mothers during the racial segregation era.

Burroughs's creative writing and organizing earned her the admiration of her friends and colleagues. At the request of the NACW, she authored and directed *Lifting as We Climb*, a play based on the history of the National Association of Colored Women, a story she had witnessed first-hand as a teenager at the founding meeting at Nineteenth Street Baptist Church.[22] Carter G. Woodson and the leadership committee of the Association for the Study of Negro Life and History appointed Burroughs as cochair of a national arts and education conference. In her leadership role, she brought together professors, high school teachers, and Harlem Renaissance artists such as Countee Cullen, Georgia Douglas Johnson, and Langston Hughes to discuss how they could collectively advance the study of Black art and history.[23] Taken together, Burroughs's theatrical works and arts-based organizing reveal how she was able to draw on a vast array of expertise, cutting across activism, history, and literature to inspire Black people to think about socioeconomic and political problems while showing what a better world could look like. In *When Truth Gets a Hearing*, she vibrantly illustrated Black economic empowerment and what needed to be done to bring that new world into fruition.

Imagining a Movement for Labor Justice across the African Diaspora

Like Burroughs's federal housing study, *When Truth Gets a Hearing* was a distinct contribution to labor movements. Throughout Burroughs's career as a labor leader, one of the themes that underpinned her work was achieving labor justice through Pan-Africanism. In her playwriting, Burroughs continued to turn to this theme to frame and structure a larger aesthetic vision and social action message for labor resistance.[24] Whereas Burroughs was critical of Black people in her other play *Slabtown Convention*, she laid the blame for Black people's oppression on white people and European colonialism in *When Truth Gets a Hearing*. *When Truth Gets a Hearing* urged Black people to harness inspiration from their African diasporic histories, their faith, and their African and Caribbean sisters and brothers who had defeated European colonialism to continue fighting for their own inalienable rights to life, liberty, and the pursuit of happiness in America. Justice was on their side because of the enormous moral gravity of their resistance to blatant exploitation.

The script centers the physical, intellectual, and cultural work of African Americans in a courtroom where the history of enslavement and European colonialism is put on trial. The main characters are the plaintiffs, witnesses, defendants, prosecutors, and a judge named Justice. White slaveholders and their descendants in the United States, the Caribbean, and Africa were the defendants in the character Justice's courtroom. Through a medley of witnesses who take the stand, Burroughs addresses the political and philosophical debates concerning labor, civil, and women's rights. These witnesses include Labor, Ex-Slave, Representative of the Negro Race, Womanhood, Opposition, Injustice, Public Opinion, History, Christianity, Truth, Fair Play, Business, Prejudice, Ignorance, and Error. Highlighting Burroughs's Pan-Africanist ideologies, Ethiopia, Haiti, and Liberia are characters who testify to the long history of oppression against Black people and their innate ability to rule themselves.[25] One of the play's central messages is that since slavery and its legacies were at the root of racial oppression, labor rights were at the heart of equal citizenship for Black people. Liberation, however, could not be achieved for African Americans until the United States reckoned fully with the economic disenfranchisement of African Americans during and after slavery.

For Burroughs, Black music was inherent to Black resilience and resistance. She integrated songs composed by NTS teachers and famous Black musicians and slavery-era spirituals to touch the hearts and minds of audience members. Burroughs wanted audiences not only to listen to the characters' lines but to *feel* the words and engage in social action. Burroughs made her spiritualized racial politics known at the beginning of *When Truth Gets a Hearing*. Before the actors entered the stage, she instructed the audience to stand and sing all three lengthy stanzas of "Lift Every Voice and Sing," commonly known as "the National Negro Anthem."[26] As a reviewer of a showing in Washington, DC, wrote: "The play was enriched by the singing of a number of carefully selected spirituals by a women's choir, which was particularly effective in the Labor Chorus. A quartette of deep full voices singing, 'Nobody Knows The Trouble I've Seen,' brought forth a storm of applause."[27] At the Dunbar Theater in Philadelphia, the Labor Chorus of NTS students sang a rich medley of songs, from "Steal Away to Jesus" to Black Canadian composer Robert Nathaniel Dett's "Music in the Mine" to the NTS's original composition "We Have Fought Every Race's Battles but Our Own."[28]

Just as she taught NTS students that learning the history of slavery was critical to recognizing the value of their work and themselves as workers, Burroughs presented to her audiences the immense contributions of enslaved Black people to the United States. The character Ex-Slave, for example, delivered an opening argument in the court case describing what she endured during slavery to explain why Black people's citizenship rights were long overdue. The character stated that not only did the US government need to grant them the promises of the Thirteenth, Fourteenth, and Fifteenth Amendments, but it also needed to compensate Black people for building America's economy and physical infrastructure before the Civil War. Ex-Slave testified that she had "worked for the upbuilding of America for 250 years" and "never received a cent for my labor." She continued, "I felled trees, tilled fields, protected homes, nursed the children of another race, made brick, built big houses for others and cabins for myself. . . . I wore the commonest clothes, ate the commonest food—was chased by bloodhounds, pursued by slave catchers."[29]

The play addressed these same themes through the other defendants. After Ex-Slave finished her testimony, Justice called Labor to the stand. Labor's testimony picked up where Ex-Slave's testimony ended. She detailed the connections between slavery and the continued exploitation of Black people after the Civil War:

> Within my sable hands I bear the implements of toil through the centuries. No spot in this land is free from the touch of my hand nor the might of my muscle. . . . I have tickled the chocolate soil of Louisiana, and sweet-tempered cane has responded to my blandishments. . . . I made every valley of the South a palm of God's hand, heaped with high cotton, corn, and tobacco. . . . Before the world had machinery to do the hard, heavy, back-breaking work, I was its most dependable hewer of wood and drawer of water. With the coming of machinery, the world that climbed on my strong shoulders, cast me aside.

It was therefore outrageous, Labor continued, that "the Negro is the lowest paid, the worst treated, the last hired, and the first fired" in the twentieth century economy. As she claimed, "Injustice has set up a system of wage robbery that forces the Negro to live below the standards of decency."[30]

Labor also argued that Black people had limited options for fighting for labor rights due to racism and sexism in labor unions. She testified, "I did the hard work which white men could not or would not do. . . . Injustice owes the Negro billions of dollars as the result of wage discrimination. She keeps the Negro out of labor unions so as to keep him in industrial servitude. She keeps him out of labor unions to use him as a mud sill–a doormat and a buffer in industry." Labor's testimony about Jane Crow unionism and wage theft was clearly taken from Burroughs's experiences of leading the National Association of Wage Earners and when the International Congress of Working Women rebuffed her attempts to organize with them on behalf of Black household workers. In Labor's last remarks, espousing Burroughs's self-help beliefs, Labor emphasized to Justice that she was not looking for charity because she "could not live on charity" and charity "crucifies my self-respect." She wanted "economic justice" because "no race has nay right to hinder, circumscribe nor prevent another race from making an honest living in any field of endeavor."[31]

For Burroughs, the play was clearly about labor justice for Black Americans, specifically Black women. When Womanhood walked into the courtroom, the NTS chorus sang "I'm So Glad." Through her character Burroughs gendered conversations about the importance of Black labor resistance and economic empowerment. "Justice," Womanhood asserted,

> let me tell you something about the economic problems of the womanhood of my race. Black women toil and toil hard. We have three million homes in the United States. Out of these homes over three million of us work out while only one-fifth of the women of the white race are forced to leave their children and go to work all day. These millions of our women are compelled to accept the most undesirable hours and lowest pay. We are working and fighting for our daily bread like men. . . . The Negro woman comes seeking the protection of the law and the recognition of her legal rights. She will do the rest.[32]

Burroughs's organizing for labor reform in household employment was undoubtedly reflected in Womanhood's statement.

Similar to other playwrights of the Black Little Theater Movement, Burroughs upheld Ethiopia in her play as a "Black heaven," or a model example of Black freedom. Ethiopia, she argued, began as Abyssinia, a massive empire that covered most of Central and East Africa. This rich cultural region, according to Burroughs and others who believed in Ethiopianism, was the birthplace of the Black race, Christianity, and the origin of the most advanced civilization in the world that preceded European colonialism. Ethiopianism began as a late nineteenth-century Black church movement to preserve African cultures and values throughout the diaspora; instill racial pride; and to promote a belief that African independence would lead to the fall of white supremacy throughout the West.[33] Expanding and extending this ideology into her work, Burroughs incorporated Ethiopia and the independence movements of Liberia and Haiti into *When Truth Gets a Hearing* as Black liberation models for African Americans.

Burroughs's decision for NTS actors to represent Ethiopia, Haiti, and Liberia paralleled her curriculum-building work at the NTS and in the International Council of Women of the Darker Races to educate young people about the resistance of people in Africa and the Caribbean. She admired the militancy and defiance of Haitians, Ethiopians, and Liberians in declaring their independence from France, Italy, and Britain, respectively, and she saw parallels between their continued fight against these colonial powers that sought to retake control of their countries and African Americans' continued struggle against Jim and Jane Crow. When Ethiopia took the stand, she declared, "Abyssinia [Ethiopia] is an illustration of how far [and] how long the Negro can keep on keeping on. We have the oldest organized government on the face of the earth. The line is absolutely unbroken from Solomon until the present ruler. Before the Christian era, or what you call the classical age, we developed a very high type of culture in North and Central Africa." Prejudice interrupted Ethiopia and said, "It's strange you did so much over there and when we brought representatives of your race over here, we had to appoint over-seers to make you work." Ethiopia responded, "Our civilization shows that Africans worked. He is not accustomed to being worked."

Burroughs's beliefs in the power of Black entrepreneurship and the importance of Black people working for and governing themselves ran prominently through the testimonies. Haiti and Liberia followed Ethiopia's testimony by noting the successes of their independence movements. Haiti told Justice during her testimony, "I gave to the world a Touissant L'Overture and a Dessalines. In my land, the Negro runs his own government." Representing the descendants of Black American settlers, Liberia asserted, "Justice, I am Liberia, a child of the American slave trade. When Opposition was raging against us in America, we fled to the land of our fathers and established a government of our own. . . . We would rather die trying to be free than to live in a slave pen. We are building our own schools, churches, and hospitals."[34]

Although Burroughs used the play to encourage African diasporic coalitions and convey a broader awareness about struggles and achievements in Africa and the Caribbean, she believed that African Americans needed to fight for what was rightfully theirs in the United States. She expressed this view specifically through the characters of Business and Representative of the Negro Race. As Business declared, African Americans needed to build on the remarkable progress they had made in America despite centuries of oppression. Alluding to Burroughs's long-time vision of transforming sharecropping and the historic business achievements of her friend Maggie Lena Walker, Business noted that African Americans were already "editing papers, publishing books, and getting ready to put Negro farming on a basis." She also boasted about the "strength of the St. Luke's Bank presided over by a Negro woman" and the "well managed" Black banks in Washington City, Philadelphia, and Chicago. The character Representative of the Negro Race later declared that while "the Negro does not like the way he is treated," he had "bought and paid for his citizenship rights," and was "going to stay here until Shiloh comes." Convinced by the moving pro-Black liberation testimonies from a range of characters in the United States and beyond, Justice announced at the end of the pageant, "Right and not *white* shall reign in this world; character and not color shall be exalted in this land; righteousness and not race shall rule in this world."[35]

After performing the play at the Dunbar Theater and at Baptist churches in Philadelphia, Burroughs took the production back to DC, furthering its message and financial rewards among African Americans. The NTS troupe performed the pageant in front of more than one thousand people at a fundraising event for the Association for the Study of Negro Life and History.[36] After performing for the association, Burroughs took the young troupe to New York City for a two-week residency.[37] At a time when Black Americans continued to suffer from disparities in government policy, business, and education, it is not difficult to imagine the extraordinary impact this play would have had on the NTS students who acted and sang in it. Through her play, Burroughs taught students acting and singing techniques while showing them how they could use art toward community action. Indeed, the success of *When Truth Gets a Hearing* underscored Burroughs's truly remarkable versatility and capacity to connect students with large community audiences to imagine and financially support institutions and organizations working to transform the world.

Building Curriculum to Chart Work Opportunities in Black Arts and Culture

In the overlapping New Negro Womanhood and Black Arts Movement eras of the 1920s, some Black women insisted on following their self-defined ambitions, refusing to work in domestic service for the majority of their lives or avoiding it altogether, even if it meant further economic instability or risking jail time. Some women chose to work in domestic service temporarily and only when it suited them, while others became psychics, numbers runners, and sex workers. Black women also took their chances at pursuing careers in the arts and became beauty culturalists, playwrights, actors, singers, chorus dancers, and poets.[38] Although Burroughs would not have promoted sex work or gambling, she kept up with Black women's shifting interests and demands. Inspired by overall generational changes and the Black Arts Movement, Burroughs expanded the NTS curriculum to chart new pathways for students interested in pursuing arts-based careers.

While touring with the NTS troupe, she worked with faculty to redesign the course offerings at the school to include more arts courses and to revamp the music courses. In 1929 she announced that they had "remodeled" the curriculum as the "social order was being made over," or as new avenues of employment were becoming available to women in domestic and arts occupations. In addition to developing more homemaking and household management courses, they developed new interior decorating, handicraft (practical arts), and music (vocal and instrumental) courses.[39] Burroughs made concerted efforts to recruit who she considered the best musicians to teach the courses, and she insisted on students learning music composed by Black musicians. In 1914 she invited Gregoria Fraser Goins, Afro-Dominican pianist and teacher at the Washington Conservatory of Music and School of Expression, to teach the fifteen students who were enrolled for music and to train other teachers on how to teach music. It is unknown how long Goins taught at the NTS, but she clearly believed in the merit of the program. She maintained communication with Burroughs and often donated money to the school.[40]

Just as Burroughs had done with her trade courses, she created internship opportunities for students interested in the arts by recruiting them to act in her plays. Through the plays, Burroughs and NTS faculty helped students "widen their vision" and "discover in themselves new possibilities."[41] A student named Carrie could not wait to tell people in her hometown in California about her learning experiences while taking arts courses at the NTS. She wrote, "I shall tell you something very interesting. Miss Burroughs put me in her play called 'When Truth Gets a Hearing.' We played in the Richmond City Auditorium, which is equivalent to the Philharmonic. The people went wild over the play. . . . The cast is going to present the play in Philadelphia and next in New York . . . So, as you can see, I am getting a bit of travel free." Carrie also shared details about the vibrant intellectual life on campus. She went on a field trip with her classmates to the Smithsonian Institution, saw "a wonderful exhibition of Negro art," and was looking forward to singing in Spanish at the inaugural NTS concert. The cherry on top for her was having the chance to meet and speak with Mary McLeod Bethune when she visited the campus.[42] These rich experiences that emanated from the intellectually nurturing and artistic environment that Burroughs and NTS faculty created helped students like Carrie see the world and herself in new and expansive ways.

Burroughs's arts curriculum was deeply felt by students and had game-changing influences in the film and music worlds. Through her playwriting and integration of an arts and culture curriculum to buttress the classical education at NTS, she helped inspire generations of Black women to reimagine what they could do with their lives and the impact they could have on their communities and the larger society. While there were racial and gender barriers in the arts, NTS students could look to alumni for ways they could craft careers for themselves without sacrificing their self-respect and politics. NTS alumna Ethel Moses, nicknamed "the Black Jean Harlow" of the film industry, was part of the incoming class of 1920.[43] Soon after graduating from the NTS, she became a popular singer, dancer, and actor in the film industry and the Harlem dance and music scene. Quickly developing a reputation in the United States and Canada, Moses was widely revered for her artistry, political activism, and beauty. She made her acting debut and rose to stardom in the industry after starring in Black filmmaker Oscar Micheaux's *Temptation* (1935), *Underworld* (1937), and *God's Step Children* (1938), and Irwin and Hazele Franklyn's *Gone Harlem* (1938).[44] Moses was a racial justice activist on- and off-screen. Her roles disrupted caricatures of Black women as either Mammy or Jezebel, and in 1939 she was escorted out of Madison Square Garden by police when she led a protest against a Nazi rally.[45]

Agnes Nebo von Ballmoos, the first Liberian ethnomusicologist, who graduated from the NTS junior college, provided a powerful example for younger generations of NTS students of how to craft unprecedented

Figure 7.2. A postcard advertising the film *Temptation*. Ethel Moses is featured on the right in a dark green dress.

careers in the arts. While Moses was making waves in the United States and Canada, von Ballmoos was paving a way for Black women in ethnomusicology in the United States and Africa. Rather than adhering to the status quo, von Ballmoos spent her career challenging notions that African folk songs were not "real" music or worthy of academic study and performance. After graduating from the NTS junior college, she earned a bachelor's degree from the Philadelphia Conservatory of Music and returned to Liberia to teach students folk songs at schools with Eurocentric curricula.[46]

Von Ballmoos returned to the United States when former First Lady Patricia Nixon awarded her a Fulbright Fellowship to pursue a master's degree in ethnomusicology at Indiana University.[47] Integrating her foundational training at the NTS and her graduate school education, von Ballmoos published arrangements of three Liberian folk songs. Her arrangements are housed at the Library of Congress and the Boston University Music Library and are still performed today in the United States, Liberia, and the United Kingdom. Von Ballmoos was joined in making music history by writer and civil rights activist Sue Bailey Thurman, who attended the NTS for her primary school education and the Spelman Seminary (now Spelman College) for college preparatory courses. Thurman became the first Black woman to earn a degree in music from Oberlin College.[48]

NTS alumni who did not pursue careers in music and acting were motivated by Burroughs's use of the arts for community organizing and fundraising. One of the most concrete examples of this was their establishment of Nannie Helen Burroughs Clubs during the 1920s and 1930s and in cities such as New York City; Mound Bayou, Mississippi; Toledo, Ohio; Baton Rouge, Louisiana; Decatur, Alabama; and Everett, Washington.[49] In the spirit of Burroughs's work, alumni founded Nannie Helen Burroughs Clubs to promote women's organizing through the arts, politics, and community initiatives, explicitly embracing the cultural and political empowerment the NTS had offered them.[50] In Toledo, Ohio, the Nannie Helen Burroughs Arts Craft Circle organized community luncheons and arts education programs for young people and seniors.[51] The New York City club organized theater parties, dances, and card tournaments in honor of women leaders and Black organizations. They also sang at fundraising programs in support of Black women's institutions such as the White Rose Mission Home, the first settlement home and travelers' aid society in New York City for Black women and girls.[52] Burroughs Clubs across the country organized musical events to raise money for the NTS and scholarships for students to attend Howard University. These clubs became such an integral part of the organizing networks and traditions of Black communities over the years that even women who had never attended the NTS joined them.[53]

Extending her own influence beyond her school, Burroughs sought to challenge racial and gender barriers in the arts by advocating for Black musicians. She was most vocal about her support for her younger Baptist "sister" Marian Anderson. Burroughs was outraged when the school board barred Anderson from performing at Central High after the Daughters of the American Revolution prohibited her from performing in Constitutional Hall. Burroughs declared,

> If a renowned colored concert artist is not good enough to sing in a public auditorium, simply because she is colored, then whites who propagate or condone such race discrimination and injustice are not good enough to teach youth or preach peace on earth, good will to men. Colored persons and the small group of civilized white persons who live in Washington are being forced to fight both the Revolutionary War and the Civil War all over again. . . . It is evident that Washington has an antiquated board

of education—a left-over from a day that is "Gone With The Wind." . . .
Until Washington becomes Exhibit A of good will, the nation should
stop spending money to send "ambassadors on good will sprees to other
countries."[54]

Burroughs's and other Black leaders' outcry led to First Lady Eleanor
Roosevelt's resignation from the Daughters of the American Revolution
in protest. Anderson's concert was rescheduled and took place at the
Lincoln Memorial with millions of people in attendance.

Burroughs's writings and curriculum building along with the careers
and community organizing of NTS alumni show that Burroughs's creative vision for driving community organizing and change in society
through the arts is one of the greatest legacies of her activism, stage productions, and pedagogy. While organizing students and Black communities through the arts, Burroughs always had her eyes set on pulling the
NTS and the surrounding community out of the Depression. She came
up with another practical and innovative idea that would not only save
her school but would help the people who lived closest to it survive for
many years to come.

Burroughs Launches a Cooperative at the NTS

While fundraising and expanding the school curriculum, Burroughs
joined the NTS with the global cooperative movement to promote Black
economic empowerment and provide essential resources for students,
staff, and community members. According to Jessica Nembhard, cooperatives are democratically controlled companies owned by the people
who use their services and share the profits. The producer-owners are
an autonomous association of people who design their cooperatives in
a variety of ways to best meet their social, cultural, and economic needs
and goals. As early as the nineteenth century, mutual aid organizations
throughout Asia and Europe established cooperatives for its most marginalized communities. It was not until the Depression era when the cooperative movement became popular in the United States. From large
cities to small rural towns, people pooled their resources to establish cooperatives that produced food, jobs, housing, electric energy, childcare,
and other essentials for their communities.[55]

In 1934 Burroughs assumed a leadership role in the national and global cooperative movements by becoming the president of the Northeast Self-Help Cooperative, later Cooperative Industries. She made history as one of few women in the world who led and managed a cooperative.[56] As president, Burroughs convinced more than two hundred people to join her cooperative in its early years. One local newspaper reporter noted that producer-owners of Cooperative Industries often made sacrifices to grow and sustain their neighborhood initiative. The reporter asserted, "Quietly, without fanfare, without publicity, the residents of a northeast-colored community, Deanwood, are building up what someday may be an ideal co-operative community. . . . At the outset most of the enterprises depended upon non-salaried volunteer workers, and members frequently exchanged services and goods in breaking the bones of poverty."[57] The community's commitment to the cooperative matched the dedication of the leader. Another local journalist captured Burroughs's significant role in organizing the co-op when she wrote, Burroughs's "unselfish devotion to the cooperative ideal, coupled with her ambition . . . runs through the story of Cooperative Industries, Inc., like a bright, strong thread holding together the pattern of a tapestry."[58]

Figure 7.3. NTS student working on the community farm. Nannie Helen Burroughs Papers, Prints and Photographs Division, Library of Congress.

Figure 7.4. Cooperative Industries members sewing dresses. Nannie Helen Burroughs Papers, Prints and Photographs Division, Library of Congress.

Figure 7.5. Burroughs with student and community workers at Sunlight Laundry, circa 1930s. Nannie Helen Burroughs Papers, Prints and Photographs Division, Library of Congress.

The installation of this cooperative at NTS had an immediate and long-term impact on the employment and health of students and the local community. Through the cooperative, Burroughs provided hundreds of jobs for Black women and men in Deanwood and other neighboring communities who were unemployed, underemployed, or refused to work any longer as domestic workers. Producer-owners and NTS students farmed and raised livestock on the NTS campus providing fresh and nutritious foods at a time when many families across the country had gone hungry and suffered from malnutrition. Workers of Cooperative Industries turned the classrooms into an assortment of businesses, including a community library, medical clinic, broom factory, community laundry, sewing unit, canning department, grocery store, and furniture (barrel-chair) manufacturing unit. The cooperative's manufacturing units were especially important to Burroughs's mission to dismantle racial and gender barriers in manufacturing jobs for Black women. The manufacturing and store units offered community members the experience of shopping for supplies and furniture at fair prices and without the humiliation of racial discrimination they often experienced at white-owned stores. Although Black people could shop in some white-owned stores in DC, shop owners often inflated the prices of their products when selling furniture to Black customers.

Burroughs also used the cooperative to break down barriers in the laundry trade for Black women. She applied several times for city grants to designate her laundry as a relief work center for unemployed women in the surrounding community. As she argued, there were no relief work opportunities in the neighborhoods near her school. Her laundry would be more accessible and conveniently located for people who could walk to work instead of spending their earnings on carfare to get to work.[59] Carter G. Woodson came to Burroughs's aid until she could convince the city to invest in the laundry. He found several local Black businessmen who were interested in leasing the laundry building until Burroughs received a grant to transform it into a work relief center.[60] Their rent payments to Burroughs went a long way in keeping the school afloat until she received government assistance. In 1934 Burroughs was most pleased when she was finally awarded a five-thousand-dollar grant from the Self-Help Division of the Federal Relief Employment Association to create jobs for unemployed residents of northeast DC to work at Sunlight Laundry on the NTS campus. As Burroughs claimed, "This is expected to supply a great need among Washington's less fortunate." Reaching out to all residents, she declared, "Men and Women from the community are employed."[61]

Burroughs believed that Sunlight Laundry was beneficial for the community and the NTS. Before the laundry's establishment, the NTS spent five hundred dollars a year sending students' laundry to commercial laundries. After facing financial challenges during the Depression, Burroughs was acutely aware of the benefits that would come from students doing their own laundry. Her thinking was that

> since sheets must be laundered, they should bring money in by the process instead of taking it out. If they had a big, modern laundry, the girls who desired to do so could learn the work as a trade, and by taking in outside work, those who needed to earn their school expenses could do so, at least in part, and the school could earn a profit on its investment—all instead of paying out $500 a year to somebody else for washing sheets.[62]

Without a doubt, she had certainly scored big when she established Sunlight Laundry.

Burroughs's cooperative gained local and national recognition throughout its existence. As the *Greenbelt Cooperator* reported, "this Negro cooperative earned the respect and admiration of the white and colored population for its plucky up-hill fight against almost insuperable odds. It has a record of splendid achievements since it was established nearly five years ago, under the leadership of Miss Burroughs." By 1936 the cooperative consisted of more than four hundred producer-owners who served hundreds of families in DC. News about Cooperative Industries spread to nearby states. In 1939 a group of housewives from Greenbelt, Maryland, visited the NTS to learn from Burroughs how to start a cooperative of their own. The *Greenbelt Cooperator* reported, the visitors "were impressed by the loyalty and common-sense manner in which deep-seated and difficult economic problems are being solved by members of Cooperative Industries, Inc., and it is evident that the program of self-education and self-help among these people is bearing fruit in better understanding between the white and colored race while battling the common evils of depression and poverty."[63]

The group of visitors likely heard about Cooperative Industries from producer-owners of a cooperative in Maryland who Burroughs worked with throughout the year. Considering that it took time for crops to grow, Burroughs and producer-owners in Maryland often shared harvests across their farms so that they would never run out of food. Willie J. Hardy, a former DC council member who had grown up in Marshall Heights, a community near the NTS, recalled how important Cooperative Industries and Burroughs's arrangement with the farm in Maryland was for her family and others in the community. Hardy's mother drove a truck to the farm in Maryland every week to plant and pick fruits and vegetables. In the evenings, she would return with a truck full of apples, potatoes, strawberries, and other foods. As Hardy recalled, "Somehow the word got out and everyone came to that area to pick up produce, but everyone knew that it was Nannie Helen Burroughs who made it possible that we could have so much food. I could remember being told to take sacks of food to different women's homes. I believe that because of that food that came out of that farm, which Nannie Helen Burroughs made possible, my parents together caused a lot of us not to go hungry."[64] Hardy's mother especially respected Burroughs for enabling her to provide food and clothing for her sixteen children through the cooperative.

Hardy was equally appreciative of the sewing department of the cooperative that filled another essential need, especially for young girls like her in the community. She recalled that many parents at the time could not afford dresses and slips for their daughters to wear to school. According to Hardy, Burroughs remedied this problem through the co-op sewing department. She recalled, "I remember them making dresses and slips, and I wore slips made by Burroughs out of flour sacks. And girls in public schools wore the same dresses, it might have been a different print, but it looked the same and that was exciting. No one talked about whether you were middle-class or got this dress from Nannie Helen Burroughs' school."[65]

Many Black women across socioeconomic class in the early twentieth century did not have access to fresh foods and adequate prenatal services and childcare in their communities. Through the cooperative, producer-owners addressed the health disparities and maternal mortality rates documented in the *Negro Housing* report produced by the federal committee that Burroughs had chaired. Member-owners opened a medical clinic that offered free and low-cost healthcare services to NTS students and community members. Always dedicated to meeting the needs of Black women, Burroughs opened a Maternal and Child Welfare Center as part of Cooperative Industries. The center provided nutritious meals as well as maternity and daycare services. The healthcare and education components of the cooperative were precursors to community health clinics established by the Black Panther Party and Black welfare activists in the 1970s.[66]

While the Cooperative Industries clinic was partially supported by a federal grant, the clinic would not have been possible without the financial support of Maggie Lena Walker.[67] Burroughs was aware of Walker's declining health and made a point of expressing her sincere gratitude for her friend's steadfast loyalty and support, telling her, "You are indeed and in truth a real soldier of the cross."[68] In a follow-up letter a few months later, Burroughs told her that she was glad to have a friend like her, especially during a period of financial trials and tribulations.[69] The grant Burroughs had secured to establish the cooperative was not enough to fund all its services or cover the doctor's salary at the clinic and the benefits of NTS staff who worked overtime to support the school and the cooperative. Before passing into history in 1934, Walker helped Burroughs establish a St. Luke coupon club to help defray NTS maintenance costs so that Burroughs could allocate more money to the cooperative. They both believed that people would participate in the program since it required them to donate coupons and not actual money. The coupon club was intended to supplement Burroughs's campaign of soliciting one million Octagon soap wrappers to submit to the Colgate Company, which would in turn give the NTS four thousand dollars for them.[70]

In the absence of adequate government funding, Burroughs's family provided critical support for her, and she provided earning opportunities for them. Her aunts and cousins provided labor and farming resources that helped the cooperative and NTS thrive throughout the 1930s. James Poindexter, Burroughs's first cousin on her mother's side of the family, was described as someone who gave many years of faithful service to the NTS.[71] He worked at the school during the harsh winter months, helping Burroughs shovel snow and coal and assisting her with winterizing the buildings for several years. He considered Burroughs his favorite cousin. As he once told her, "I talk about cousin Nannie all the time" in Virginia.[72] While James was always willing to help Burroughs, working at the NTS helped him contribute to his own household during a time of year when jobs were scarce in a small rural town like Orange. Fred Poindexter, James's brother, and Rachel Winston, Burroughs's maternal aunt, provided livestock for the NTS farm. James coordinated Burroughs's purchase of a horse that he brought to the NTS from Virginia. He also bought unused farm equipment from her when she needed easily accessible cash.[73] Aunt Rachel shipped eggs, pigs, turkeys, and chickens to the NTS that Burroughs purchased for the farm and to help provide supplemental income for her aunt.[74]

Burroughs had a big heart. Her family knew she would do as much as she could to help the family even when they could not give her something in return. They reached out to her for anything from employment assistance to when they were in trouble with the law. When Burroughs's maternal cousin Edna Crawford asked her for financial assistance due to unemployment, she told Burroughs that her mother had always said that Burroughs would never let her want for anything if she knew she was in need.[75] Burroughs's paternal uncle Charles Burroughs felt the same way. He was not too ashamed to ask his niece to bail him out of jail when he was incarcerated.[76] While helping family members, Burroughs managed Cooperative Industries through her relationships and shared resources with family, community members, and friends.

Managing the co-op was not enough for Burroughs. Eager to see all Black people establish cooperatives, she promoted the cooperative movement at the NTS and throughout Washington, DC. In fact, she circulated information about the cooperative movement like it was the gospel.[77] Burroughs put her own advice into practice. She developed co-op study courses at the NTS that were open to both students and community members and taught them how to start their own cooperatives. Inspired by their cooperative experiences, in the 1940s, NTS students named their school paper *Co-Op: Official National Trade and Professional School Paper*. Student editors featured stories about the many ways that faculty, staff, and Burroughs worked cooperatively to build the social, intellectual, and worker mission of the school. Burroughs's aim of establishing a cooperative that would lead women to pursue careers in a trade they actually enjoyed was reflected in an op-ed written by Edna

Young. After taking co-op sewing courses at the NTS, Young was convinced that she wanted to pursue a career in sewing. As she explained, "The interest I have in sewing is not only to cut and sew pieces of material, but to see the development of my work. It is really interesting to see complete garments develop from the pattern through the cutting and fitting to completion."[78] Due to Burroughs's persistence, curriculum, and educational campaigns, Cooperative Industries served hundreds of families and students into the early 1940s.

Burroughs made producing stage plays and managing a cooperative look easy, but the challenges were steep along the way—not only financially but personally. At some point in the 1930s, Burroughs underwent throat surgery and another surgical procedure to address what she described as a "personal thing." Downplaying her illness, Burroughs told reporters, "They took out everything but my crazy bone when they operated on me." Her undisclosed operation led to several months of treatment at New York City's Presbyterian Medical Center.[79] In addition to battling health issues, Burroughs lost three women she loved dearly. In 1934 Maggie Lena Walker passed away, and the following year Burroughs's maternal aunt Rachel Winston died. Then, on June 30, 1935, Mother Bell passed away on the NTS campus at around eighty-two years old. Losing three of the closest women to her must have impacted Burroughs emotionally. Always a caring daughter, Burroughs kept her mother close to her. She buried Mother Bell at the Lincoln Memorial Cemetery, just outside of Washington, DC, where she herself would be laid to rest several decades later.[80]

<hr />

Along with her spiritual faith, Burroughs could always rely on writing—her first love—to get her through the highs and lows of her life and career. When Burroughs was in her early twenties, she desired to become a full-time public speaker and writer. If there were more occupational options for educated Black women like Burroughs in the twentieth century, and if she could have taken a sabbatical like professors today, more than likely her dream would have come true. Still, by integrating her passion for writing and advancing Black political and economic empowerment, Burroughs launched a historic labor periodical, *The Worker*.

By the late 1920s, the paper had become defunct due to limited resources and finances. To make matters worse, some of the leaders of the
National Baptist Convention, USA, were relentless in their attacks on
Burroughs and the NTS. They continued withholding financial support
for the school, auditing the school's financial records, and disparaging
her name in church meetings. Burroughs had expected this hostility,
considering that she had battled male leaders who tried to stop her rise
to national leadership ever since she had established the Woman's Convention. What was most hurtful to her was that some members of the
Woman's Convention had joined the men in their plans to take over the
NTS and damage her reputation.

Burroughs had few options but to turn to Una Lawrence, a writer
for the Woman's Missionary Union, the women's auxiliary group of the
majority-white Southern Baptist Convention. Together Burroughs and
Lawrence revived *The Worker* and transformed it into an important
source of income for the NTS. Even when Lawrence left her position
as coeditor of the paper, Burroughs continued pushing her labor rights
mission through it. Due to her unyielding commitment to producing
literature as a tool for women's organizing against injustices, the paper
lived long beyond Burroughs herself, remaining in circulation into the
twenty-first century.[81]

Notes

1. Lawrence, notes from interview with NHB.

2. Sara Speaks, "Nannie H. Burroughs Stages Pageant," *Baltimore Afro-
American*, November 29, 1929.

3. Orleck, *Common Sense*, 151–53; Boris and Nadasen, "Domestic Workers
Organize!," 420.

4. W. E. B. Du Bois to NHB, May 17, 1929, W. E. B. Du Bois Papers.

5. NHB to W. E. B. Du Bois, May 21, 1929, W. E. B. Du Bois Papers.

6. Dunbar-Nelson, "To the Negro Farmers of the United States."

7. NHB, "Making Their Mark: By Their Fruits Ye Shall Know Them," 10.

8. The Dunbar Theater was part of a cadre of Black-owned theaters of the
Black Little Theater Movement. See Krasner, *A Beautiful Pageant*, 137.

9. Gates and Higginbotham, *Harlem Renaissance Lives*, 76, 219.

10. Hill and Hatch, *A History of African American Theatre*, 233; Anny Boddy,
"Phila. Has 'Something New under the Sun,'" *Philadelphia Tribune*, January 3, 1920.

11. NHB, untitled, n.d., NHB Vertical File, Moorland-Springarn Research Center, Howard University.

12. Krasner, *A Beautiful Pageant*, 211.

13. Mary Church Terrell, *Phyllis Wheatley Pageant-Play, 1932–1933*, Subject File–1962, Mary Church Terrell Papers, LOC.

14. Anna Julia Cooper, *From Servitude to Service: Contributions from the Negro Peoples in American History, A Pageant*, 1940, Plays and Programs Collection, Moorland-Springarn Research Center, Howard University.

15. NHB, *Where Is My Wandering Boy Tonight?*, n.d., Manuscripts Division, Moorland-Springarn Research Center, Howard University.

16. For example, *When Truth Gets a Hearing* was sponsored and performed by the National Association for the Advancement of Colored People in Birmingham, Alabama. See *The Voice of the People*, March 19, 1921. For coverage of a showing at an Association for the Study of Negro Life and History program, see "Bishop Advocates Study of Race: Dr. Woodson Presides," *Evening Star*, October 29, 1929.

17. NHB to W. E. B. Du Bois, May 21, 1929, W. E. B. Du Bois Papers.

18. NHB, Director's Notes on *Slabtown Convention*, NHB Vertical File, Moorland-Springarn Research Center, Howard University.

19. NHB, *Where Is My Wandering Boy Tonight?*

20. Alice Gantt, "Women's Day," n.d., NHB Vertical File, Moorland-Springarn Research Center, Howard University.

21. "'Slabtown' Celebrates Burroughs' Civic Service," *Johnson City Press*, June 24, 2020; "Zion Baptist Church Continues 150th Anniversary Celebration," *Afro News*, January 25, 2022; Delores Gullick, "'Slabtown Convention' Brings the House Down," *News Angus*, November 2001, 7.

22. *National Notes: Official Organ of the National Association of Colored Women* 30, no. 10 (July 1928): 4.

23. Carter G. Woodson to NHB, June 23, 1933, Box 32, Folder 19; NHB to Carter G. Woodson, June 27, 1933. Box 46, Folder 9, NHB Papers.

24. Burroughs wrote earlier versions of *When Truth Gets a Hearing* that date back to 1916. See Box 47, Folder 2, NHB Papers.

25. NHB, *When Truth Gets a Hearing* script, 1920s, Box 47, Folder 2, NHB Papers.

26. Burroughs's director notes, *When Truth Gets a Hearing* script, 1920, Box 47, Folder 2, NHB Papers.

27. Speaks, "Nannie H. Burroughs Stages Pageant."

28. NHB, *When Truth Gets a Hearing*.

29. NHB.

30. NHB.

31. NHB.

32. NHB.

33. Krasner, *A Beautiful Pageant*, 88.

34. NHB, *When Truth Gets a Hearing*.

35. NHB.

36. Speaks, "Nannie H. Burroughs Stages Pageant."

37. "Bishop Advocates Study of Race."

38. See Treva B. Lindsay's discussion of Black women playwrights and beauty culturalists in Washington, DC, *Colored No More*, 25–86, 111–37; Lashawn Harris's history of Black women numbers runners, sex workers, and psychics, *Sex Workers, Psychics, and Numbers Runners*; and Saidiya Hartman's discussion of Black women singers and occasional domestic workers, *Wayward Lives, Beautiful Experiments*, 77–79, 297–309, 340–43.

39. NHB, "Making Their Mark: By Their Fruits Ye Shall Know Them," 10.

40. NHB to Gregoria Frasier Goins, October 19, 1914, July 17, 1926, December 18, 1937, Box 36–2, Folder 29, Gregoria Frasier Goins Papers, Moorland-Springarn Research Center, Howard University.

41. Quoted from NHB, "Why Organize Our Young Women," 3.

42. Carrie, "An Open Letter: National Training Seminary, Lincoln Heights," *California Eagle*, June 28, 1929, 2.

43. Public announcement that Ethel Moses was attending the NTS. See "North Philadelphia Flashes," *Buffalo American*, November 18, 1920.

44. "Returns to Harlem," *Pittsburgh Courier*, April 4, 1936; "Cotton Club Girls," *Ebony*, April 1949; "Parsons Pretty Daughter Chooses Stage Career," *Pittsburgh Courier*, October 4, 1924.

45. Visser-Maessen, *Robert Parris Moses*, 14.

46. Student Registration Records, Box 151, Folder 10, NHB Papers; "Agnes Nebo Von Ballmoos, Our Late Directress," University of Liberia Chorus, http://www.ulachorus.org/founder.

47. "Agnes Nebo Von Ballmoos, Our Late Directress."

48. See Ballmoos, *The Role of Folksongs in Liberian Society*; Library of Congress, Copyright Office, "Catalog of Copyright Entries: Third Series," 1971, 293, 387, 1423; "Agnes Nebo Von Ballmoos, Our Late Directress"; Hill, *The Black Women Oral History Project*, 105.

49. *National Notes: Official Organ of the National Association of Colored Women* 30, no. 10 (June 1928): 5, 9; "Side Lights on Society," *New York Amsterdam News*, March 14, 1928; *National Notes: Official Organ of the National Association of Colored Women* 30, no. 11 (July 1928): 6, 12.

50. For example, see *National Notes: Official Organ of the National Association of Colored Women* 30, no. 11 (July 1928): 12.

51. William Marlowe, "Toledo," *Baltimore African American*, March 18, 1933.

52. "Side Lights on Society"; Frankye A. Dixon, "Music: Four Artists Appear on Program," *New York Amsterdam News*, June 5, 1929; "Society Notes," *New York Amsterdam News*, May 4, 1927.

53. "Club Chats," *New York Amsterdam News*, December 31, 1930; "Mrs. Ida S. Taylor, Founder of Rest Home," *Baltimore Afro-American*, January 13, 1979; Obituaries, "Jacqueline Lewis Snow," *Cincinnati Enquirer*, September 29, 2010; Kati Phillips, "YWCA Honors Women for Making a Difference," *Star-Gazette*, February 25, 2000; "Annie J. Bellue, 105, Devoted to Church," *Cincinnati Enquirer*, July 30, 1997.

54. "D.C. 75 Years behind Time—Miss Burroughs," *Afro-American*, March 4, 1939.

55. Nembhard, *Collective Courage*, 2–3.

56. Nembhard, 151–52.

57. "Better Buyers Pay a Visit to Unique Negro Cooperative," *Greenbelt Cooperator*, February 9, 1939.

58. Sylvia Weinberg, "Co-operation Theory Tested in Colonies: Greenbelt and Deanwood are Watched for Results of Social Value," *Sunday Star*, December 26, 1937.

59. Anson Phelps Stokes to NHB, July 6, 1934; Anson Phelps Stokes to Mrs. Elmwood, July 1, 1935, Box 28, Folder 7, NHB Papers.

60. NHB to Carter G. Woodson, May 20, 1932, Box 46, Folder 9, NHB Papers.

61. Malcolm S. Whitby, "Remarkable Results Gained in Interracial Field by Miss Burroughs, Baptist Leader," *Black Dispatch* (Oklahoma City), September 13, 1934; promotional pamphlet for Sunlight Laundry, Box 310, NHB Papers.

62. Hammond, *In the Vanguard of a Race*, 59.

63. "Better Buyers Pay a Visit."

64. Audio recording of NHB Papers dedication ceremony, September 23, 1976.

65. Audio recording of NHB Papers dedication ceremony, September 23, 1976.

66. See Annelise Orleck's discussion about Operation Life's clinic, *Storming Caesars Palace*, 211–90; For history of Black Panther Party as health activists, see Bassett, "Beyond Berets," 1741–43.

67. "New Faculty, New Ideas at Nannie Burroughs' School," *Pittsburgh Courier*, July 17, 1937.

68. NHB to Maggie Lena Walker, June 19, 1933, Maggie Lena Walker Collection.

69. NHB to Maggie Lena Walker, August 23, 1933, Maggie Lena Walker Collection.

70. McCluskey, *A Forgotten Sisterhood*, 112–13.

71. Downey, *A Tale of Three Women*, 17.

72. James was the son of Burroughs's maternal uncle Taliferro Poindexter. See James Poindexter to NHB, June 22, 1936, March 17, 1936, October 14, 1937, and n.d., Box 1, Folder 1, NHB Papers.

73. Fred was also the son of Burroughs's maternal uncle Taliferro Poindexter. See Fred Poindexter to NHB, May 21, 1936, April 19, 1943, Box 1, Folder 1, NHB Papers.

74. Rachel was Burroughs's mother's younger sister. Rachel Winston to NHB, July 8, 1938, Box 1, Folder 1, NHB Papers.

75. Edna was the granddaughter of Cordelia Mercer, Burroughs's mother's sister, with whom Burroughs and her mother had lived when they first moved to Washington, DC. Edna Crawford to NHB, May 21, 1933, Box 1, NHB Papers.

76. See Charles Burroughs to NHB, March 20, 1935, Box 1, Folder 1, NHB Papers.

77. See the following chapter for discussion about Burroughs's article about the cooperative movement in *The Worker*.

78. Edna Young, "Sewing Dept. at School Is Active," *Co-op News*, December 1942, Box 312, Folder 11, NHB Papers.

79. Margaret Lewis, "'They Can't Make Me Quit': School Founder Recuperating from Serious Operation," n.d., NHB Vertical File, Moorland-Springarn Research Center, Howard University.

80. For Jennie Bell's obituary, see "Deaths," *Evening Star*, July 1, 1935; and memorial page for Virginia "Jennie" Poindexter Burroughs Bell, *Find a Grave*, https://www.findagrave.com/memorial/235572844/virginia-bell.

81. The focus of the paper has changed since Burroughs was editor. The paper is controlled and circulated by the Progressive National Baptist Convention. See *The Worker*, PNBC, https://pnbc.org/publications/the-worker-magazine/.

CHAPTER 8

The Worker

A Literary Vehicle for Change, 1912–1961

Nannie Helen Burroughs believed in the power of literature to inspire organizing and change in society. In 1912 Burroughs launched *The Worker* from the NTS campus and produced the paper in the NTS Printing Department when it was established in 1916. The straight-to-the-point title of the periodical boldly proclaimed Burroughs's strong faith in workers for transforming an unjust world. The intellectual work of writing about disparities was not just a hobby or a pastime activity for her. It was God's work. A religious paper was therefore the perfect vehicle to advance labor reform for Black women workers. In an image of two Black women included in one of the early editions of *The Worker*—a writer coupled with a domestic worker who appeared in National Association of Wage Earners literature—Burroughs communicated that change required women's writings and manual labor (fig. 8.1). Thinking, writing—whether religious, political, or creative—and manual labor were on the same level of importance and went hand-in-hand.[1]

The very establishment of *The Worker* was a historic and personal achievement. Burroughs had editorial experience with papers of the Woman's Convention and National Baptist Convention, but she was rarely credited for her editorial work on the National Baptist Convention papers, which were under the direction of Lewis G. Jordon and other clergymen. Her paper was a declaration of her rise in national and international influence as a religious and labor leader. When Burroughs launched her paper, she joined a small cohort of women print shop owners in an entrepreneurial field dominated by white men.[2] As founder and

Figure 8.1. The front page of an early edition of *The Worker*. The images of a domestic worker and a writer convey Burroughs's philosophy that Black women writers and domestic workers were equally important to labor and civil rights movements. Manuscript Division, Library of Congress.

editor in chief of *The Worker*, Burroughs established the first international women's labor periodical of the twentieth century that was owned by a Black woman and housed at a school for Black women and girls. Before major labor periodicals such as *The Messenger* and the Communist Party USA's *Daily Worker*, there was *The Worker*. Unlike most labor periodicals of the twentieth century, Burroughs's paper centered women's writings and labor issues.[3]

Burroughs crafted *The Worker* into an international platform for women's religious philosophies and church organizing concerning racial, gender, and employment discrimination. Some of the editions were damaged in the NTS fire in 1926 and in 1940. Editions might also have been lost before the transportation of her school records to the Library of Congress. While only a few editions that Burroughs edited have been preserved, the surviving editions are a testament to how she advanced labor, women's, and civil rights movements through writing and publishing. Like the NTS, *The Worker* was Burroughs's lifelong project, and she kept it going until she became an ancestor in 1961. Her paper remained in print for several decades afterward.

During the early years of production, Burroughs marketed *The Worker* as an accessible periodical for people of all socioeconomic classes, inside and outside Baptist church circles. She designed *The Worker* as a conveniently sized paper that could be carried around and shared easily with others, and the annual subscription price was only twenty-five cents a year. The early editions of *The Worker* featured Burroughs's most radical ideas for effecting change. She authored articles condemning lynchings,

European colonialism, and employment discrimination. Her articles and mission had mass appeal. By the early 1920s, hundreds of people subscribed to the paper who lived in large bustling cities and small rural towns across the United States and parts of Africa, Latin America, Canada, and the Caribbean.[4]

Due to the Depression and Burroughs's limited finances, the paper became defunct by the late 1920s. Even while working to relaunch the NTS during the 1930s, Burroughs never gave up on *The Worker*. She saw her periodical as a promising source of revenue for the school and a vehicle to inspire women's organizing at a time when she believed the country was in dire need of their leadership. Burroughs's unyielding commitment to *The Worker* during a period of financial hardship and attacks on her school from National Baptist Convention, USA leaders left her with few options but to work with southern white Baptist women to bring her paper back to life. Burroughs invited Una Lawrence, member of the Woman's Missionary Union and editor for the Home Mission Board of the Southern Baptist Convention, to coedit *The Worker* with her.

While they faced racial tensions and health-related challenges during their partnership, Burroughs's and Lawrence's shared love for writing and literature sustained their working relationship for more than a decade.[5] In the process, they grew the readership of *The Worker* significantly and transformed the paper into a major revenue source for the NTS. They authored church materials on Black history and initiated interracial women's programs that had never been done in the history of the Baptist church. Ultimately, Burroughs was the one who was most committed to the paper and its founding labor and civil rights mission. By the mid-1940s, Lawrence had become interested in writing books and left her role as coeditor of the paper. Burroughs assumed her original position as editor in chief, which gave her more control over content. During the twilight years of her career, she boldly and uninhibitedly continued her initial mission of mobilizing Black women for racial and economic justice through the press.

Countering the White Press to Awaken Consciousness

Burroughs came onto the publishing scene with a fierce energy to express what she had not been able to write about as editor of Baptist newspapers. She was determined to counteract newspapers that printed misrepresentations of Black people and suppressed stories about the atrocities Black people experienced during and after slavery. As she declared, "The truth of the matter is that the Negro has suffered more from a silent, prejudiced, subsidized press than from any other sentiment-making force in the world. With the change of attitude on the part of the press, truth will get a hearing and the world will be introduced to that other group (nine-tenths) of Negroes that do not steal chickens, cut shines, loaf, nor commit outrages upon women."[6]

As president of a trailblazing school with editorial experience under her belt, Burroughs confidently articulated her most raw perspectives about race and labor in the early editions of *The Worker*. In 1915 she penned "What the Belgians Did to the Negro," a fierce criticism of Belgium and its colonization of the Congo that she featured on the paper's first page. Under the rule of Belgium's King Leopold II, Burroughs wrote, his "pals" and "pimps" forced more than twenty-five million Congolese to "gather ivory and rubber under compulsion of lash, bullet, fire, starvation, and without rest," while also burning down their homes. According to Burroughs, the devastation of colonialism was so detrimental to the Congolese that "if the blood from those who suffered and were murdered were collected in buckets, the containers would stretch four thousand miles." Burroughs encouraged the predominantly Black readership to learn more about the atrocities that Europeans had committed against Africans, especially at that time, a period of heightened European emigration to the United States. European colonialism in Africa, she argued, was a blueprint for Jim Crow in America. Aware of European immigrant violence and racism toward African Americans, she directed readers to pray that Belgian immigrants would not "turn again to smite us and lynch us in America."[7]

The 1918 edition of *The Worker* was arguably one of the paper's most political. Burroughs saw major disruptions in American political life, such as wars, economic recessions, and international political conferences, as rare opportunities to expose the federal government's complicity with racial segregation laws and employment discrimination. She dedicated most of the 1918 edition to challenging white people to live up to the promises of the US Constitution. As World War I was coming to an end, Burroughs demanded that the US government and everyday white Americans change their treatment of Black people. According to her, Black women and men had demonstrated their commitment to America by sacrificing their lives in the military and contributing their labor to the defense industry. It was long overdue that African Americans receive the same citizenship rights as white Americans.

In her article "That German Propaganda," Burroughs blasted white people for lynching Black men and accusing them of working as spies for Germany instead of praising them for their work in defending the United States. She asserted, "In Negro parlance, 'we ain't studyin' the Germans.' . . . These people who are so fearful of Negro loyalty are in fact, leaders of the 'American propaganda against true Democracy.'" Burroughs continued by arguing that Black Americans were in fact the most loyal citizens of the United States. As she put it, "When the records of the war are made up, we will find one hundred disloyal whites to every one disloyal Negro. Watch the prophecy. Being white is not a guarantee of loyalty. The Negro is getting quite tired of being suspected and convicted without evidence."[8]

Perceptions that Black men were disloyal led to unfounded rumors that they committed acts of violence toward white people. Burroughs reported that she hosted a two-day meeting on the NTS campus with a delegation of Black women from East Saint Louis who traveled to Washington, DC, to strategize how they would push Congress to pass antilynching legislation. The impetus for the meeting was a 1917 race riot initiated by white residents of Saint Louis who attacked Black communities after a Black man was accused of murdering a white man. According to Burroughs, prayer was women's spiritual work, necessary for addressing racial violence through legislation. Burroughs wrote that "women who were heartsick over the East St. Louis Riot . . . felt so helpless in the face of the known attitude of the Country when its citizens of Color are shot down and thrown into the river or roasted alive by patriotic(?) White citizens, as an expression of their contempt for law or order." Several of Burroughs's colleagues from Washington, DC, joined the East Saint Louis women at the NTS meeting in an act of solidarity. As Burroughs concluded, "Washington is just as willing to get behind them to pray and work for Legislation. . . . Let us Pray. Let us Work. Let us Believe."[9] Together, Burroughs, the East Saint Louis delegation, and women from Washington, DC, orga-

"The Worker"

Goes forth to labor for those who are being trained or definite and efficient service.

Published the 15th of each month by THE NATIONAL TRAINING SCHOOL FOR WOMEN AND GIRLS (INC.)
Miss Nannie H. Burroughs, President
Lincoln Heights, Washington, D. C.

Devoted to the moulding of sentiment in favor of special training for those who are to become housekeepers, homemakers, Christian workers, on the home and foreign fields; maids, domestic servants, stenographers, typewriters, musicians, dressmakers and milliners.

Entered as second class matter, April 15, 1912, at the Post Office, Washington, D. C., under the act of July 16, 1894.

Terms: 25 Cents A Year.

That German Propaganda

Any people who cannot tell you to save lives where they got it or what evil they have that there is a semblance of in it are talking about "The German propaganda among the Negroes." If it be that same group of people before the war, had nightmares over Jig-a-boo which they called "Social?" We have never known why are so fearful nor what the thing much feared looked like.

In frank, there are just about as many Germans or German sympathizers at work among the Negroes as there were "social equality" propagandists before the war and they are making about as much headway. In Negro parlance, "we ain't study'in Germans." The people who make war Jig-a-boos are a syndicated gang of half-hearted patriots who are making their living by telling war stories.

If Germany is depending on the American Negro to give her any kind of support in this war, she is laboring under a death-dealing delusion. The Negro is going to

see that she does it.

These people who are so fearful of Negro loyalty are in fact, leaders of "the American propaganda against true Democracy." This is the propaganda that America should fear. There are people in this Country, in high places, who would wage civil war rather than have this Government actually live up to the U. S. Constitution in dealing with all its citizens.

This talk of a "German Propaganda" is made by people who want to find an excuse for keeping the Negro out of good positions. When the records of the war are made up, we will find one hundred disloyal whites to every one disloyal Negro. Watch the prophecy. Being white is not a guarantee of loyalty. The Negro is getting quite tired of being suspected and convicted without evidence.

Leaders Who "But" at Prayers

Since the call to prayer following the St. Louis riot, two of our distinguished leaders have been heard several times to say in public addresses—"Prayer is alright —BUT," and what follows the BUT minimizes the power of prayer. There are no BUTS about prayer and its power.

The thousands who attended the meetings here have never stopped telling us how these trips to "The Mountain" early in the morning changed their spirit of vengeance into a spirit of forgiveness and a willingness to work with God and trust Him to right all wrongs. It is the state of mind evoked by prayer that counts.

We are bearing our burdens in this country with greater ease because there are some who will not fail to perform their religious duty and believe it the most important task. It nerves them for the battle with the world, the flesh and the devil. Do you remember that swashbuckling element who opposed Gustavus Adolphus and his pious Swedish Soldiers and affected to

on retiring knelt beside his bunk to say his prayers. His comrades made jeering remarks while he prayed, and asked him jeering questions when the prayer was done. One of them asked him why, if God heard his prayers, he came to be drafted? Another one asked him if he expected to pray the bullets away from him? Others said, "Aw, cut it out."

"The young man persisted calmly in his religious duty amid all these sneers. One day the captain of the company heard about this ribaldry and confirmed the report by listening one night. He promptly stopped it, and declared to the jeerers that he intended to recommend the promotion of the young man to be a sergeant in the company, thus making him an officer over his jeering comrades. The recommendation of the captain was accepted by a higher officer and that young man became an officer over his scoffers.

"That captain ought also to be promoted."

A leader who "cuts out" prayer or "Buts" at prayer is taking the people no where to do nothing. They have no power with God and less with man.

The Dust Cap a Badge of Dignity

It is surprising to find thousands of women who do not know the value of a dust cap and an apron or who think that these protectors of coiffure and of the housekeepers' livery are badges of servility.

The dust cap is the most valuable and most necessary part of the outfit of any woman who is responsible for any part of the house cleaning or cooking. The dust cap denotes pride. It shows that the woman values her hair and wants to protect it from dust. There is no greater enemy to the hair than dust. The dust cap is a badge of economy. Why allow the hair to get full of dust for the pleasure of paying to have this dust removed by a hair dresser or of taking the time that you might devote to something else to "launder it." Getting

Figure 8.2. January 1918 edition of *The Worker*. Courtesy of the Maggie L. Walker National Historic Site, National Park Service.

nized mass prayer meetings at Baptist churches in the city to demand antilynching legislation. Their meetings attracted as many as five thousand women to the city.[10] In addition to prayer, Burroughs asserted, eradicating racism required the government and churches to "purge America of its autocrats and enemies to Democracy."[11]

Inspiring Labor Education and Organizing

In the same 1918 issue of *The Worker*, Burroughs upheld manual laborers, not politicians, as the true heroes of US efforts in World War I. Putting women's and men's manual labors on the same level of importance, she argued that domestic workers, miners, and construction workers built the necessary infrastructure to sustain the country during the war. She explained,

> The man with shovel or hoe and the woman with spoon are two of the most valuable allies in this war situation. . . . To fail to impress them with the fact that without their unstinted support the country can never win this war is to neglect that part of the war work that is more important than selling Liberty bonds. . . . The millions who furnish fuel for furnaces, food for the Allies and those who build and keep our highways, hold the key to the situation. They are doing more than these millionaire businessmen.[12]

Considering that most men industrial workers were represented by unions that attested to the value of their labor, Burroughs published additional articles in the issue to convince readers that domestic work was patriotic work. She reported that she and Mary McLeod Bethune had co-organized a conference with President Woodrow Wilson's wife, Edith Wilson, to promote domestic science education. At the meeting, domestic workers and housewives learned cost-saving measures for supporting the war with inexpensive cooking and home maintenance resources and methods.[13]

In Burroughs's eyes, white people would not view domestic work as valuable work and raise the wages of domestic workers if Black women themselves did not see the occupation as respectable. In her article "The Servant—An Ally," Burroughs attempted to change Black women's views about the maid's uniform as a symbol of servility and oppression. In an effort to redefine Black women's perceptions about domestic work, Burroughs declared that uniforms were economical, ensured sanitary work conditions, and preserved domestic workers' dignity, health, and physical appearance. She wrote,

> The dust cap denotes pride. It shows that the woman values her hair and wants to protect it from dust . . . The dust cap is a badge of economy. Why allow the hair to get full of dust for the pleasure of paying to have this dust removed by a hairdresser or of taking the time you might devote to something else to 'launder it.' Getting the hair full of dust and washing it too

often, means a loss of natural oil which eventually means a loss of luster and then a loss of hair.

Like the domestic science lessons at her school, Burroughs emphasized taking pride in one's work while remaining attentive to their own health performing domestic work. According to her, "The dust cap is a sanitary protector. The hair falls. It falls into food. The cook should not season her food or garnish her dishes with an embellishment as expensive as human hair. Then too, falling hair is indicative of poor health. Food in which there is dandruff and hair is, therefore, seasoned with germs. . . . We need women in our homes wearing the livery typical of the dignified service that housekeeping is."[14]

While promoting pride in one's labor and health as methods for changing the everyday drudgery of domestic work, Burroughs used *The Worker* to inspire grassroots organizing for the larger project of changing racial and employment discrimination. In 1920 she published "A Trip South," an article in which she encouraged readers to learn from southern Black communities about how to organize against racial injustices. She detailed the travels she had taken throughout the South from January through February that year, meeting with local leaders about labor issues confronting their communities. Rather than traveling to the South to instruct Black people on how to better their lives, like some of her northern contemporaries, Burroughs wanted to "see, hear, understand, and consider thoughtfully and constructively what she saw, felt, and heard" about the race and labor question.[15]

The article made clear that Burroughs considered southern African Americans an important source of knowledge for labor resistance. As she wrote, "If anybody feels that the American Negro is not doing his own thinking in these days of readjustment, let him go with me on a trip down into the land of the Klan and he will come back with a new thought." She also wrote that Black people in the South were "thinking, planning, organizing, and getting ready for a long campaign against ignorance and injustice. . . . The South is trying his soul in the fire. The efficient will survive. The persecutors [read: whites] will die from a moral breakdown." In addition to organizing among southern African Americans, Burroughs was moved by her travels through rural towns where she saw women and men picking hundreds of pounds of cotton. Share-cropping, according to Burroughs, did not fully benefit white people. She asserted, "Their faces tell a sad story. It does not take a psychologist to see that the poor whites of the South are brutalizing their own souls. . . . Booker T. Washington warned them against such a moral undoing in his homely philosophy when he said, 'It is impossible for a man to keep another man down in the ditch unless he stays down there to hold him.'"[16]

In a subsequent article from 1922 titled "Colored Women Pass Up Tubs for Steam Laundries," Burroughs continued to highlight the grave urgency of organizing, particularly in the context of domestic workers, asserting that labor rights for domestic workers meant labor protections for all Black women workers.[17] Quoting findings from a US Department of Labor study, Burroughs reported that there was a declining percentage of Black laundresses who cleaned and steamed clothes in their homes. She urged local Black leaders to help protect the jobs of the "picturesque colored washerwoman," who was in danger of losing customers to steam laundries that primarily employed European immigrant women. As she passionately noted, Black women had been washing linens since slavery, and not all of them could work in commercial laundries because they had small children to take care of. Rather than simply competing with European immigrant women for jobs in commercial laundries, Black women needed to hold on to their home-based laundry jobs. After all, according to Burroughs, there were three advantages to home-based laundry work: 1) there were still customers who did not want their clothes washed with every "Tom, Dick, and Harry's," or a large group of other families' clothing; 2) many Black laundresses were skilled and paid special attention to expensive clothing, unlike workers at public laundries who washed and steamed in large bulk; and 3) Black laundresses' rates were cheaper than the rates of commercial laundries.

Burroughs insisted that Black leaders "push a campaign of education" to inform Black workers about capitalist and racist encroachments on their jobs and inform clientele about the benefits of having their clothes cleaned by laundresses. Otherwise, Black communities would suffer the consequences of losing an economic foundation for many Black households. As she put it, "We cannot afford to lose a single job. . . . Our leaders sat down and watched the passing of our whitewashing jobs, our shoe shining industry, our barber trade from the hands of Negro men, and now they are sitting down watching the passing of our laundry business into the hands of big corporations without realizing the economic and moral loss we will sustain thereby."[18] Considering Burroughs's close friendship with Carter G. Woodson, she might have influenced one of his seminal articles, "The Negro Washerwoman, a Vanishing Figure." In his article, he pleaded with Black people to do something about the "vanishing Negro washerwoman" who "continued at this hard labor" after slavery as the breadwinner of many Black families.[19] Burroughs acted on her frustration with what she considered Black people's indifferent attitudes to protecting jobs that Black women held since slavery. In the 1920s she established a public laundry at the NTS that was a precursor to the relief center laundry that she launched in the 1930s as part of Cooperative Industries.[20] While she advocated for home-based laundresses, she knew that Black people could not stop the wheels of industrialization. She had a two-pronged approach—asserting the importance of Black women's home-based laundry work and promoting industrial education among Black women to demand their place in commercial laundries.

Concerned about Black workers across socioeconomic class, Burroughs reported on statistics that pointed to racial inequalities in the labor market among white collar workers. Her article "Colored Women Pass Up Tubs for Steam Laundries" highlighted disparities among formally educated Black people. As she reported, "Regardless of the fact that Washington justly boasts of more educated Negroes than any other city in the world, in the tabulation of laundry occupations, the report shows that not a Negro is listed under Office Help. In the unskilled group, Negroes represent 85.1 percent as against 14.9 percent unskilled white. Here is food for thought and room for improvement." Highlighting this glaring statistic made clear to readers that employment discrimination was rampant across the board in the nation's capital. Similar to Burroughs's job experiences in the late nineteenth century, most educated Black people still could not obtain jobs that they were qualified for in the early twentieth century.[21]

Burroughs's politically religious writings resonated with an expansive readership. By the early 1920s, *The Worker* had several hundred subscribers, and Burroughs could no longer fulfill the orders through the print shop on her campus. To keep up with the demand, she outsourced printing of *The Worker* to a Black-owned print shop on U Street, or "Black Broadway," home to more than two hundred Black-owned businesses in Washington, DC. Burroughs's and her colleagues' bookkeeping provides detailed documentation attesting to the popularity and wide circulation of the paper. Subscribers to *The Worker* lived in large bustling cities from Los Angeles to Detroit and small rural towns from Cotton Plant, Arkansas, to Berlin, Georgia. While people in every state subscribed to the paper, the largest number of subscriptions were concentrated in the South.[22] The expansive and concentrated regional interest in *The Worker* reveals how the South remained an important touchstone for national Black women's labor and political organizing.

The Worker ledger from the year 1919 recorded subscriptions for all forty-eight states (table 8.1). The ledger contains a page for subscriptions in Cuba. Although there are no subscriptions listed in 1919, the page itself clarifies that Burroughs intended to reach and connect Black readers across the African diaspora. She was successful at gaining a few subscriptions a couple of years later in Haiti, Cuba, Jamaica, France, Guatemala, El Salvador, and Canada.[23] The international networks Burroughs acquired through her leadership role in the Woman's Convention enabled her to reach thousands of people inside and outside the United States.

While Burroughs was likely pleased to see the paper grow in popularity, she struggled to keep up with the financial costs of the expanding readership. She framed her request to increase the subscription fee in labor resistance language. In a blurb titled, "Another Strike: Have You Missed The Worker?," she announced to readers that *The Worker* had been on strike and had not been published in months due to an increase in production costs. She explained to subscribers, "It has been on 'Strike' for higher wages. Like most strikers, it wants to come back to work. We

Table 8.1. Subscriptions to *The Worker*, 1919

State	Subscribers
California	241
Connecticut	107
Cuba	0
Florida	585
Louisiana	376
Ohio	105
Pennsylvania	173
Texas	537
Utah	13

Note: Burroughs's listing of Cuba in the ledger shows that she intended to attract an international readership in the early years of the publication. See subscription ledgers in Boxes 333 and 71, NHB Papers.

decided to consult you about it. . . . Hundreds of our friends are urging us to let the little paper continue. They say they miss it."[24] Burroughs proposed to subscribers that she raise the annual subscription fee from twenty-five cents to fifty cents. Her strike and bargaining worked. With increased donations, Burroughs published another edition of the paper before the Depression hit. The continuation and expanded readership of the paper enabled her to use it as a platform to support the work and futures of other Black women and girls, most notably NTS students.

Creating Work Opportunities through Publishing

Burroughs leveraged *The Worker* to chart multiple avenues of employment for Black women and girls. She saw *The Worker* not only as a tool to inspire labor and political organizing but also as an internship opportunity for students that could lead to employment outside domestic service and sharecropping. Printing internships were nearly nonexistent for Black women and girls in the early twentieth century. Students who worked in the printing department at the NTS worked with Burroughs to prepare issues of *The Worker* for publication. They also filled printing orders from local community members. Burroughs paid students with the revenue from paper subscriptions, which helped students pay their tuition fees and send money back home to their families. In the process, students gained practical work experience in a trade where Black women were grossly underrepresented. Susie Green was inspired to open her own print shop after graduating from the NTS. Carter G. Woodson described Green as "an intelligent woman applying her education in a practical way, running a large-up-to-date print shop as well as others do" while "adding thereto a bit of art to which others do not generally give attention."[25] In the 1920s, Green was the sole Black woman owner of a print shop in DC. Burroughs initially met her on a speaking tour in Alabama. Ever since the age of seven, Green had worked to support her family. She was a farmer who supported her two brothers from selling vegetables she grew on her family's farm. As she recalled, "I grew vegetables and my two brothers sold them. My father died when I was 7. That's why I was doing the gardening. Miss Burroughs saw my garden and was impressed. She said if she ever got a small grant for gardening

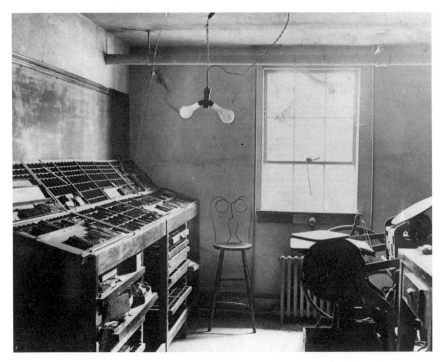

Figure 8.3. The print room on the NTS campus. Nannie Helen Burroughs Papers, Prints and Photographs Division, Library of Congress.

at her school in Washington she would send for me."[26] After establishing the horticulture and farming program, Burroughs made good on her promise and encouraged Green to enroll at the NTS.

When Green arrived in DC, Burroughs insisted she learn more than one trade to maximize her chances of securing employment after graduation. Burroughs detected Green's entrepreneurial aspirations from the pride she took in creating her own garden, and she insisted that Green study printing in addition to horticulture. Farming was Green's first love, and she was originally resistant to Burroughs's recommendation. But she decided to give it a shot, and doing so opened multiple career paths for her. After graduation, she worked at an insurance company and then bought her own print shop across the street from the popular Howard Theater in DC, making history as the only Black woman in the nation's capital who owned a print shop. Reflecting on her experience, Green said, "I think Miss Burroughs is one of the greatest women we've had. She was quite interested in preparing women to make a living in various fields. I think I would have made a good living at the market stall, but printing has been very rewarding. I've been very happy. The Lord works in mysterious ways. We never know why things happen but they do happen."[27]

Few things in life made Burroughs happier than when she could boast about her students' going into various fields of work. She believed that advertising their stories in *The Worker* was an effective promotion of the school and a guide for Black women and girls who were not enrolled in the NTS and desired better working conditions. While Burroughs bragged about students who became entrepreneurs like Susie Green, she also wrote about students who were making a way for themselves in household employment. She wrote an article about Beatrice Oger, an NTS alumna who had attained a live-in position in Philadelphia after graduating from the NTS domestic science program. Burroughs described Oger as a shy girl from southern Louisiana with a mixture of "Negro and French blood." She was not the most brilliant student, but she was admirably determined to learn what she could to obtain a living-wage job that would enable her to help her mother take care of her seven siblings.[28]

Coincidentally, Burroughs saw Oger while they were traveling on the same train heading to the City of Brotherly Love. When they saw each other, Oger thanked Burroughs for the domestic science education that she received at the NTS and told her that she talked so much about the school to her former employer "until she thought it was the only place on earth." It was Oger's obligation to family and sense of herself as a skilled worker that led her to quit a live-in job in DC and relocate for the new domestic service position in Philadelphia, which paid more and had better living conditions.[29] A few years later, Oger must have learned that an ideal domestic service job was hard to come by, no matter her expertise in domestic science. On September 26, 1924, after relocating to DC for another job, she joined Burroughs's National Association of Wage Earners. Burroughs's philosophical influences and the domestic science curriculum at the NTS, likely convinced Oger that joining a labor organization was important.[30]

Burroughs also published letters from former students who worked as missionaries and teachers in Africa. As a Pan-Africanist, Burroughs believed that teaching and social work were critical to addressing economic and racial disparities that resulted from colonialism. Highlighting former students' missionary work and letters was her way of inspiring readers to consider education and letter writing as other methods for organizing to improve the lives of African-descended people. Most students wrote to her from Liberia, a country where teaching and missionary jobs were most accessible to African Americans. Eager to rid the United States of free African Americans, the American Colonization Society financed the emigration of African Americans to the west coast of Africa, where they established the independent nation of Liberia in 1847. African American settlers welcomed the opportunity to escape racial violence and discrimination in the United States, even if it meant colonizing Africans' land in what became African American-controlled Liberia.

As the letters in *The Worker* reveal, missionary work had layered meanings for NTS students. It afforded NTS graduates like Clara Walker Blaine their desired opportunity to travel internationally and live in another country, which would have been unattainable or expensive for them had they not been missionaries. Soon after touching down in Dakar, Senegal, Blaine wrote, "I have seen the people in the marketplaces and about their huts. This is my first glimpse of the land to which I have wanted to come. The impressions will live forever in my mind."[31] For some students, missionary work was a gateway to building their own schools or accessing administrative and teaching positions at primary schools and colleges. For Black women in the United States, teaching positions and resources to build schools were very limited. Blaine begged Burroughs to visit her in Liberia so that she could see how well she had done there. She was happy to report to Burroughs that she had taught at a college, married, and became vice principal of a school. Clearly still missing and wanting to maintain connection with the supportive network at the NTS, Blaine asked about Burroughs's mother and the NTS staff.[32]

While some alumni expressed their proselytizing goals of converting Africans to Christianity, others felt a sense of racial kinship with African communities they worked and lived with. Burroughs and NTS history teachers taught students to take pride in their African ancestry and about the infrastructural havoc that European colonialism had on African communities. Graduates believed that the teaching and social work components of missionary work were ways that they could help their African sisters and brothers remedy systemic inequalities that resembled the injustices that African Americans experienced in America. As in the United States, schools for Black children in Africa were either underfunded or not funded at all, which left many teachers and administrators to fend for themselves to provide a quality education for their students.

Della Harris, an NTS alumna, told Burroughs that times of struggle at the NTS had prepared her for hardships in Monrovia, Liberia. She made Christmas dinner and presents for her students, similar to how Burroughs made use of her family's resources, the NTS farm, and donations to provide everyday and teaching resources for students. Detailing how she put her faith into action, Harris wrote, "We [were] almost despaired of being able to spread much cheer, as we had spent all our personal funds to keep the children in daily food, but you know me; I don't believe in giving up, so Mrs. Clark and I made some dolls for the small children, scoured the neighborhood for six miles round for eggs to make them cakes—with a success of three eggs." After receiving donations of butter, sugar, flour, roosters, and other essentials from local friends, Harris reported that her "anxiety had been richly rewarded." Despite the hardships, Harris said that she was "exceedingly happy" in her work and her only regret was that she had not moved to Liberia sooner than she did.[33]

Harris learned not only resourcefulness from the NTS but the importance of leadership training and developing relationships with local community members for advancing efforts to counteract inequalities through education. Harris's colleague wrote to Burroughs that village chiefs were pleased with her work and interactions with the community. Since she had begun teaching in the neighborhood school, the chiefs had become receptive to their daughters attending school. They requested that Harris teach their sons and daughters, and in return they would maintain the school buildings and grounds.[34] Harris's respected status in the community seemed to serve her ultimate goal of establishing a school in Liberia. The superintendent of the school system in Monrovia wrote to Burroughs that Harris was in fact an extraordinary teacher. As he put it, "Already she has won the hearts of the Liberian women. I want her to be to Liberian women what you (her teacher) are to the U.S.A. colored women."[35]

Aiming to follow in Burroughs's footsteps, Clarice Gooding, an NTS graduate who also taught in Liberia, told Burroughs she wanted to build her own school to help prepare students for political leadership positions. As she reported, "I have a little boy whose father said to me when he brought him to the Mission: 'Miss Gooding, this is my son. He must become President of Liberia, so I bring him to you for you to give him the first start. Take him and train him to become President.' Thus, you may say, we are not concerned about souls only, but the development of Liberia's future leaders."[36]

Christina Francois S. Guerrier, an NTS alumna from Haiti, returned to her home country to teach at a primary school soon after graduating from the NTS. She thought a lot about Burroughs's sacrifices and challenges while teaching in her own underresourced school in Jane Crow DC during the Depression. Guerrier wrote, "I read in some newspaper that the Americans are having hard times financially. . . . We are having a great struggle over here to live. . . . I think so much about you, the school, and my work here that my hair is actually gray. But I am trusting God." Like Clara Walker Blaine, Guerrier missed the network of people close to Burroughs who supported NTS students. Guerrier asked Burroughs to send her love to "Mother Bell" and Reverend Walter Brooks and all who knew her when she was at the NTS."[37]

After the fire on the NTS campus in 1926, Burroughs slowed production of *The Worker* to focus on her major fundraising campaign for the school and her leadership roles in several women's organizations. On top of juggling these important positions, she had to deal with the pressures of constantly defending her expenditures to leaders of the National Baptist Convention, USA, who accused her of mishandling school funds and attempted to claim full ownership and management of her school.

Burroughs leveraged her editorial reputation and connections with W. E. B. Du Bois to aid Reverend Walter H. Brooks in his defense of her school. In 1925 she urged Du Bois to publish in *The Crisis* an article that Brooks had written to demand that the convention refrain from acquiring more property. Burroughs and Brooks not only wanted to save the school, but they cared deeply about the convention and wanted to prevent it from going into a downward spiral. Burroughs told Du Bois that she wanted Brooks's article to appear in *The Crisis* because of its reach and respect for highlighting the contemporary implications of

Black history. She wanted Du Bois to publish the article before she and Brooks met with convention leaders about their attempts to take over her school. As she told Du Bois, "I am requesting that you let it come out in the May number. We are having an Executive Meeting in May, and we want to throw some light on this Baptist situation before the 'brethren' get together to 'scuss' it. . . . Do not disappoint me."[38] Du Bois did not disappoint. Brooks's timely article was printed in the May 1925 edition of *The Crisis*. In the article, he warned convention leaders that historical property disputes between Black Baptists led to internal disputes and divisions that distracted the convention from following God's purpose. As he put it, "The losses of the past should teach us wisdom for the future."[39]

Fellow editor and labor activist A. Philip Randolph used his paper *The Messenger* to publicly express his solidarity with Burroughs during her battle against the convention. Randolph and his editorial team announced:

> we wish to register our humble opinion that it would be a calamity to the National Training School were Miss Burroughs's position and control in the school, in any way, impaired. It is a matter of common knowledge that Miss Burroughs is the life and soul of the school. She is the school just as Henry Ford is the Ford Motor Company. . . . It is her genius that gave it birth and continuity. If she should leave it, it will die, perhaps, not physically, but surely spiritually. . . . Therefore, we rise to move that Miss Burroughs remain the regent queen of the National Training School. . . . Negro men ought to take off their hats in honor to such sacrificial spirits as Nannie Helen Burroughs, Mary McLeod Bethune, and Charlotte Hawkins Brown.[40]

For the next decade, Black leaders would continue using the press to loudly express their support for Burroughs during her battle with the convention. In the meantime, Burroughs turned to white Baptist women to revive *The Worker*, a paper that fed the spiritual needs, personal desires, and organizing goals she valued the most.

A Strategic Choice

Relaunching the paper was a daunting task. While Burroughs put on a brave face in front of adversaries and public audiences, she was vulnerable with her closest friends. She told Carter G. Woodson that she wanted him to prepare an advertisement of Sadie Daniel's *Women Builders* for publication in *The Worker* after Woodson had advocated for Burroughs to be included in Daniel's seminal book about women religious leaders. Burroughs, however, was overwhelmed by the constant challenges to her leadership and felt that she had not done enough to be featured in the book. As she confided, "I hope to accomplish something that will be enduring and constructive, but up to now I am woefully disgusted with what I have been able to accomplish for the women and girls of my race. Thank you for the fine encouragement that you always give me."[41] In addition to Woodson's unyielding support, Burroughs's decision to team up with Una Lawrence of the Woman's Missionary Union gave her the spark and financial resources she needed to accomplish more than she could have foreseen during her moment of despair. The financial support especially came in handy when buildings caught on fire at the NTS in 1926 and 1940 due to faulty wiring.

The religious foundations of the NTS and *The Worker* were important to Burroughs, and she needed to maintain their ties to the church. At the same time, she needed new allies outside the factions in the National Baptist Convention and the Woman's Convention. During the founding years of the Woman's Convention, she had established a relationship with Annie Armstrong, leader of the Woman's Missionary Union, and she had spoken in front of southern white Baptist women audiences to encourage them to join the Woman's Convention's fight against racial segregation. In 1902 Burroughs delivered a speech entitled "An Appeal to the Christian White Women of the Southland" in which she directly challenged white women in the audience to organize with Black women against racial segregation laws that made it illegal for whites and Blacks to sit alongside each other in train cars. Burroughs told them it was their moral responsibility to join their fight against racial discrimination. As she declared, "the law ignores the fact that beneath the black skin is a soul as immortal, a pride as exalted, an intellect as keen, a longing as intense as and aspirations as noble, as those which peep forth and manifest themselves in the proudest blue-eyed Anglo-Saxon man or woman." Afterward, Burroughs charged white women to join Black women and "put ourselves on record as the protectors and defenders of Christian womanhood, white or black."[42]

Burroughs returned to the Woman's Missionary Union to sell to Una Lawrence the idea of coediting *The Worker* as a way for women of the Baptist church to create an interracial women's movement to promote Christianity and end racial segregation. It did not take long to convince Lawrence that working together would be a worthwhile endeavor. Lawrence loved writing and literature and respected Burroughs, and she was one of the most receptive members of the Woman's Missionary Union to conversations about race. Commenting on Lawrence's unique attributes, Burroughs told her, "Where in the world could I find another white woman who has sense enough to get along with me. You are a marvelous person. You have sense and spirit; you are alert, you see, understand, and evaluate. You move forward. I like people who are that way." Her partnership with Lawrence was not without conflict, but their working relationship helped Burroughs protect her beloved school and periodical from shutting down.[43] Together, Burroughs and Lawrence organized the first interracial initiative for women of the Baptist church while significantly increasing subscriptions to *The Worker*, an important media source for women's organizing and funding for the NTS.

During Burroughs's and Lawrence's coeditorship of *The Worker*, the paper was a complex layout of Black and white women's conflicting and overlapping ideologies about missionary work and other forms of wage labor. There were articles authored by missionaries about the "heathens" of Africa and how difficult it was to convince the Seminoles in Florida to attend missionary schools and how poor white youth were susceptible to immoral habits and alcoholism because there were limited jobs and schools in Appalachia. There were also articles about the beauty of Africa and Black resistance and providing social and educational resources for underserved communities. Missionaries detailed providing school textbooks and kindergarten classes for Latin American immigrants and white miners in the hills of Kentucky, calling ambulances for the sick, running errands for disabled and elderly people, and attending to the "lonely." The articles and poems covering this wide array of women's work lived in the same periodical alongside each other and reflected Black and white women's diverse perspectives about race, religion, and women's work.

A key strategy Burroughs and Lawrence pursued to create a sustainable working relationship between white women and Black women across their distinct philosophies, backgrounds, and work experiences was to write articles for *The Worker* about how women of both races were best qualified to solve the race problem. Although she published articles that were palatable for white readers, Burroughs did not refrain from rocking the boat, nor did she abandon her racial and labor politics. According to her, educating white women about how systemic racism worked was essential to building a genuine and sturdy interracial women's movement. In her 1934 article "The American Standard of Living," she argued that one of the biggest failures of the National Recovery Act was the lack of government pressure on employers to pay Black and white workers equal wages. As she wrote, "The fallacious argument for a difference in pay of Negroes and whites is given in the familiar sentence that a 'Negro can live off less than a white man, and therefore does not need as high a wage. Of course, this is a falsehood.'"[44]

Disputing popular racist scientific claims that Black people were biologically inferior to white people, Burroughs continued, "There has been much talk about the inferiority of Negroes. But every serious student of anthropology, ethnology, psychology knows that there is no such thing as inherent racial inferiority. If Negroes do exhibit some differences that are inferior, it is because they have been forced to live on a lower standard because they have not been able to get adequate wages." Building more jails and enlarging police forces to incarcerate Black people rather than using national relief funds to change the institutions that caused their suffering left white people spiritually impoverished. As Burroughs concluded, "The society which robs them of adequate wages, however, does not escape suffering. . . . You can't hold a man in a ditch without getting some dirt on you."[45]

Burroughs used Negro Health Improvement Week, a national initiative launched by Booker T. Washington in 1915 to promote the importance of addressing health disparities to the advancement of Black economic empowerment, as an opportunity to further educate white readers about how unequal wages was a literal matter of life and death for Black people. In her 1935 article "Negro Health Week," she wrote, "In our 1934 lesson 'The Causes of High Death Rate Among Negroes' we said 'The white community is largely (not 'wholly' mind you, but largely) responsible.' We repeat the statement: 'The white community is *largely* responsible.'"[46] She pointed readers to excerpts from her 1932 *Negro Housing* report to explain how most Black people were prohibited from living in neighborhoods with sewage infrastructure, sanitary water, paved roads, and solidly constructed homes. Black people paid twice the amount of rent as white residents who lived in safer and more sanitary housing, though Black people earned far less than white people at the same jobs. After listing the recommendations proposed by the *Negro Housing* report for addressing this housing and labor crisis, Burroughs insisted that remedying the problem required legislative change and collaborative work between Black women and white allies.

Burroughs and Lawrence reinforced their call for interracial women's organizing in *The Worker* by sending representatives from the Woman's Convention and Woman's Missionary Union to participate in each other's meetings and strengthen communication between the organizations. In 1933, while representing the Woman's Convention at a union meeting in Virginia, Burroughs delivered her speech, "How White and Colored Women Can Cooperate in Building a Christian Civilization." She told the audience, "the women of the two races should unite in a common effort to defeat all common enemies to Christian growth. These enemies are ignorance, selfishness, indifference, antagonism or race prejudice." Highlighting the power of the written word and women's organizing, Burroughs continued, "In such an enterprise, we need literature, leadership and fellowship." To ease union members' discomfort or defensiveness about working with Black women and to convince them to donate money to the Woman's Convention, Burroughs assured the audience she was not blaming them for racism. In an overly generous gesture of goodwill, she said she was aware of white Christian women of the South, like people in the audience, who were kind to Black domestic workers and paid them living wages. Never fully compromising her racial pride, however, she gave examples of southern Black Baptist leaders, including her friends Mary McLeod Bethune and Margaret Murray Washington, whose writings and organizing she argued should serve as guiding lights for an interracial Baptist women's movement.

After delivering her speech, Woman's Missionary Union members donated $250 to start a Literature Department Endowment Fund in the Woman's Convention to help cover the costs of publishing *The Worker*.

The fund also supported salaries for Burroughs's longtime friend Ella Whitfield, secretary of the Literature Department, and NTS staff members who worked on the paper. As Woman's Convention and Woman's Missionary Union members continued attending each other's meetings, the union developed an interest in the NTS. Lawrence convinced the union to donate money for building repairs on the school's campus.

To deepen the collaborative work between the Woman's Missionary Union and Woman's Convention, Burroughs and Lawrence established interracial cooperative councils between white and Black Baptist women across the country. Their vision was to make these councils the grassroots organizing arms of *The Worker* to advance the religious and civil rights mission of the paper. They promoted Black history books and made plans to coauthor supplemental history materials to guide discussions in council meetings about the struggles and progress of Black people. Part of their thinking was that white women had further to go than Black women in seeing the opposite race as social equals because of their racial privilege. Black history literature would dispel stereotypes about Black people among union members and in the process Woman's Convention members would learn even more about their own history. According to Burroughs, Black people could never know enough about their own history.

Burroughs and Lawrence encouraged councils to read and discuss books authored by African American activists and labor scholars such as Lily Hardy Hammonds's *In the Vanguard of a Race* and Dr. George Haynes's *The Trend of the Races*.[47] In their respective missionary books, Hammonds and Haynes highlighted the theories, contributions, and lives of African Americans concerning religion, labor, music, scholarship, education, and politics since emancipation to provide "light of knowledge" to improve race relations.[48] Although they could not coauthor their own books due to time constraints, Burroughs and Lawrence began coauthoring a source book about Black Baptist History with selections from Carter G. Woodson's *The History of the Negro Church* for the cooperative councils.[49]

Burroughs and Lawrence also collected primary sources about the mothers of renowned Black male leaders to coauthor a book about reproductive labor as social activism. The book was Burroughs's idea, but time ran away from her and Lawrence before they could finish writing *Unsung Heroines among Negro Women*, a reference book about the mothers of Booker T. Washington, Paul Laurence Dunbar, George Washington Carver, Frederick Douglass, and Robert R. Moton. As Burroughs told Lawrence, she wanted to "pay richly deserved tribute to the mothers of the educated leaders of the first generation after slavery" who had done "all sorts of hard labor to send their sons and daughters to school" and "prepare[d] them for leadership among their people."[50] Although Burroughs did not have time to write a full-length book, she authored guides for women church members. Most notably, during her collaboration with Lawrence, she wrote *Negro Achievement from America's Tenth Men*, a guide for the interracial councils on how to plan a Black history program. The guide contained scripts for council members to recite details about the achievements of Black leaders including Booker T. Washington, Marian Anderson, Countee Cullen, and Alain Locke. She also included lesser-known famous women who had achieved unprecedented records in higher education, including Eunice Hunton, the first Black woman to earn a bachelor's and master's degree from Smith College within four years.[51]

While asserting herself as a race expert in women's church circles, Burroughs also used her pen and typewriter to position herself as an expert on race matters outside of the church. As she wrote for *The Worker*, Burroughs took on popular race leaders such as W. E. B. Du Bois. In her 1934 article in the *Baltimore Afro-American*, she declared that Du Bois had taken the wrong philosophical approach to solving the race problem when he asked readers of *The Crisis*: "How shall we conduct ourselves so that in the end human differences will not be emphasized at the expense of human advance?" She called the question an impertinent one and asserted that Black people need not hate white people, but they should not be concerned about how white people saw them. In the movement for racial justice, the Black community needed to let go of their "Uncle Toms," or Black people who were ashamed of their racial identity and aimed to please white people. Racial justice work, according to Burroughs, was a job for "colored people who are not ashamed nor afraid to be colored, who do not have the inferiority complex . . . the humblest person who has heart to hope, hands to labor, and a mind to think . . . who do[es] not think breaking into the white race is the way out; who believe[s] in the justice of God and the ultimate triumph of right."[52]

In another article, Burroughs criticized Du Bois's *Black Reconstruction*, calling it the imitation of Black life, or an inaccurate representation of Black people's experiences in the United States.[53] Burroughs's public challenge of her renowned colleague's political writings reflected her desire to write beyond the confines of church politics and to be taken seriously as a major thinker alongside Du Bois and other male leaders of the day. Either unfazed by Burroughs's critiques or taking heed to her call for recognition of her work and ideas, Du Bois asked Burroughs the following year to write an article for his pan-African encyclopedia project.[54] Appreciative of the invitation, Burroughs replied, "I seriously doubt whether I can write any matter worthy of encyclopedia. However, you may be assured of my interest and I will do all I can to help."[55] By the 1930s, Burroughs's hands were full with writing projects and behind-the-scenes work of managing her school and *The Worker* and organizing church women amid racial tensions.

Conflicts and Racial Tensions

Leading an interracial women's church movement was a tough project. While Burroughs and Lawrence made serious efforts to prevent racial conflict in the collaborative work between their organizations, Burroughs let Lawrence know when she saw blatant and subtle forms of racism when working with union members. After speaking at a union meeting in Jacksonville, Florida, she told Lawerence, "I noticed a tendency on the part of a few of them to stall or swallow when they got to 'Miss' or 'Mrs.,' particularly when speaking of colored women in the state. When I come across such cases I usually smile and say 'God bless them, they are trying; they have had a long way to come.'"[56] Burroughs was less patient when she faced backlash from some union members for her writings about systemic racism in *The Worker*. When Lawrence brought their criticisms to Burroughs's attention, she replied, "I shall always try to be patient and tolerant, but on the other hand, I shall have to speak the truth in kindness. I love your race a great deal more than they love mine. . . . Discussions of the problems [are] too vital for us to ignore and too real and universal for anybody to say that they don't know anything about them."[57]

Burroughs also pushed back when union members used racist language to describe their interactions with Woman's Convention members. When Kathleen Mallory, executive director of the union, visited a convention meeting in Jacksonville, Florida, she took notes on the physical appearances and diction of convention members. She compared Sarah Layten's light-complexioned skin to, in her words, Burroughs's "very dusky" skin tone. Mallory also commented on the accents of Bahamian guests at the meeting as well as the skin tone of a convention member that she identified as biracial. After apologizing for Mallory's notes, Lawrence confessed to Burroughs, "After your enlightenment of my own ignorance on the subjects of 'you people,' etc., I have been much more sensitive to possible causes of offense in our utter unconsciousness of such impossibility."[58]

Lawrence wanted Burroughs not to hold back in telling her what she thought about Mallory's use of the word "mulatto" and comparisons between the skin complexions of convention members. Burroughs replied, "Well, of all the veiled insinuations on the mulatto question, this beats it, from an intelligent woman and a Southerner who should never whisper the word. . . . Mrs. Craig is not a mulatto. She is light skinned with hair that is decidedly indifferent. My, my, my! This shows how badly we need contact." Burroughs insinuated that Lawrence ought to teach Mallory the error of her ways. As she put it, "My only hope is that she [Kathleen Mallory] doesn't make such blunders where our folks will get it."[59]

While dealing with racism in the Woman's Missionary Union, Burroughs faced intraracial conflict within her own convention. With cooperation from Sarah A. Layten, a cohort of male leaders in the convention redirected the Woman's Convention's funding to a seminary training school in Nashville, Tennessee. Burroughs confided in Lawrence that she was going to do "some very serious thinking" and "definite acting" about remaining corresponding secretary of the Woman's Convention because she did not "believe that God nor my friends want me to go on carrying a burden like this." She was most disappointed by Layten and other women who conspired with the men behind her back. As Burroughs told one of her friends in the Woman's Convention, "Why don't they come out in the open and repudiate me and the whole business with which I am officially connected. . . . Why tag along after our men and be used as tools and fools? An open fight is always interesting to me, if we are to fight at all, but this under-cover business is positively disgusting."[60]

Burroughs's allies went to the press and church pulpits to defend her against these serious efforts to remove her from her position in the Woman's Convention and the presidency of what was by then the National Trade and Professional School for Women and Girls. In 1939 Reverend Walter H. Brooks, Mary McLeod Bethune, and several other Baptist leaders organized an elaborate banquet "fit for the gods" in honor of Burroughs. They pledged one thousand dollars toward the school and promised regularly scheduled donations thereafter. To top it all off, they presented Burroughs with a purse with one hundred dollars inside.[61] An alumna of the school was compelled to write an op-ed in her former teacher's defense. Ruth Alexander Smith, graduate of the class of 1914 and chair of a Parent Teacher Association in Chicago, wrote,

> I have been reading the publicity given Miss Nannie Helen Burroughs and feel that some one of us who have graduated from that institution should add our disapproval of the present situation. . . . When the Baptists of the nation failed to send money for upkeep, Miss Burroughs not only gave her last dollar for food and coal for the comfort of the student body, but knew what outside organizations she could appeal to for further aid. When money for salaries was not forthcoming for teachers and janitors, I have seen her make the fires with her own hands to keep us warm, and [she] received little or no salary for her services during my stay there.[62]

The outpouring of support must have been encouraging to Burroughs. Expressing her renewed determination not to give up on the school, she told a reporter, "They can't make me quit."[63] With unrelenting support from her allies, Burroughs retained her positions as president and corresponding secretary and reached new leadership heights. In 1944 Shaw University recognized Burroughs for her intellectual and organizing work by awarding her an honorary doctorate. By the mid-1940s, Dr. Burroughs assumed full control of *The Worker* as sole editor. Lawrence gradually pulled away from her coeditor position while battling a sciatic nerve condition and after developing an interest in producing solo authored books. Lawrence also could have lost drive for completing her writing and organizing projects with Burroughs due to the interracial and intraracial conflicts.

After not hearing from Lawrence in months, Burroughs bluntly told her, "Lady, if you do not send that material [for *The Worker*] here *early next week*, I am going to get on my knees and tell the Lord about you. I am not going to pray for you—I am going to pray against you." She warned Lawrence that she will be "as hot as the weather" if "you don't stop writing books long enough to attend to some of our *United* business."[64] Despite Burroughs's disappointment, she maintained the large subscription base of *The Worker* and its revenue for the NTS. In 1948 Burroughs was elected president of the Woman's Convention, a key position that helped her continue to advance her broader ideas for Black economic progress while also providing administrative levers to provide more direct financial support to the school and *The Worker*.[65] Her role as president helped stabilize and expand the groundbreaking educational and labor projects that had been so central to her work.

Restoring the Original and Urgent Mission of *The Worker*

As Lawrence retreated from coediting *The Worker*, Burroughs took advantage of heightened sentiment across the country to publish articles about the importance of Black labor organizing. While establishing Cooperative Industries at her school, she published a 1937 article encouraging Black people to join the "economic renaissance for the masses" known as the cooperative movement. She assured readers that it did not take a lot of capital to establish a thriving cooperative. All it took was knowledge, respect for human values, and a strong work ethic. Burroughs asserted,

> Kagawa of Japan is helping us see the light. . . . The masses will someday discover their latent power. Then they will see the possibilities in a movement that is owned and directed by them as customers, with the profit going to themselves as owners. . . . Go to any meeting that is held in your community to discuss the Cooperative Movement. Get the A B C's of it. It is the only way out of this economic plight for the American Negro.

She explained, "The great army of white Americans are determined to make capital across, even if they have to sit down on it. (Sit Down Strikes). Negroes are not in on them and cannot therefore, sit down on it. Negroes are sitting down outside." According to Burroughs, Black people needed to redirect the one million dollars a day they invested in stores owned by white business owners and invest in themselves through cooperatives.[66]

No longer having to compromise on content for *The Worker* allowed Burroughs opportunities to write more articles about civil rights and workers' rights issues. She did not have the burden of making her articles palatable for white women in the church. In a 1937 article, she returned to championing labor reform in household employment. She reported to readers that she had attended a conference for industrial workers at which a social reformer declared to the audience that domestic service was a "blind alley occupation." Refuting what she considered a disparaging comment, Burroughs appealed to readers to see the value in household work and domestic workers. As she argued throughout her career, Black women needed to idealize the real before realizing the ideal. It was possible to work in domestic service and pursue other occupations. In the meantime, Burroughs continued, "'social 'reformers' like the one who spoke to industrial workers, should go somewhere, and learn some common sense."[67]

In the 1940s, Burroughs included more articles in *The Worker* that were critical of European colonialism in Africa. She published an article authored by Carol E. Dokes, a teacher and missionary from Montclair, New Jersey, who declared,

> one million African warriors served under European command either on the battlefields of France or Africa. . . . These men coming into contact with European civilization will learn all of its evils. They will learn what so-called Christian nations will do. . . . If they will listen to the Gospel story at all, they will probably say, 'Give me Christ without Christianity.' . . . In conclusion, shall we remember that prayer is of vital importance in all of our work.[68]

Dokes's article revealed how some Black women missionaries were critical of how Christianity was used to justify wars and European colonialism. On the contrary, Dokes and other Black women missionaries like her believed that Christianity was a belief system that could be used to counter oppressive conditions.

Burroughs herself returned to critiquing white Christians after Lawrence stepped down from her position as coeditor of the paper. When Burroughs became sole editor and president of the Woman's Convention, she established *The Worker* as the official organ of the Woman's Convention. Writing and envisioning organizing as an older and more established leader in the Baptist world, Burroughs authored articles that were not as radical as her writings from the 1910s and 1920s but were nevertheless aimed to galvanize Black women for labor and civil rights. As Bettye Collier-Thomas has documented, Burroughs used the paper in the 1950s not only to cover the work of missionary societies but to inform readers about *Brown v. Board of Education* and other legal decisions related to Black labor rights and the civil rights movement.

In the 1950s Burroughs used her position as president of the largest body of Black Baptist women to shore up women's spiritual faith and strength to co-organize the civil rights movement with her mentees Martin Luther King Jr. and Ralph David Abernathy. In a 1955 article, she instructed readers to lean on Christianity as a tool against oppression and white Christians who used religion in oppressive ways. She asserted,

> When we see the gross evils practiced against Negroes and so-called Christians keep their mouths shut, when we see the race Jim-crowed, robbed, cheated and left on the highway of life to die, we wonder how long will a just God withhold his wrath. But when we read history and think, we know that while God is taking a long time to move that He does move, and no man can stop Him. . . . Doubting gets us nowhere. Trusting God and working in spite of entrenched evil will get backward races out of the wilderness and out of the night.

In the same article, she reminded readers that working toward economic empowerment was just as important as working to change laws and institutions. As she put it, "Frederick Douglas[s] stated an eternal fact and pointed the only way up, when he said: 'A race which cannot save its earnings, which spends all it makes and goes in debt when it is sick, can never rise in the scale of civilization, no matter under what laws it may chance to be.'"[69]

Burroughs also supported civil rights movement leaders' efforts to become elected government officials. In her 1959 article "America—Half

Figure 8.4. President Burroughs speaks to a packed house on Woman's Day at a Baptist church. Prints and Photographs Division, Library of Congress.

Slave, Half Free," she argued that diversifying the federal government would strengthen and ensure democracy and the right to living wages. She asserted, "A democracy cannot become a reality with little men in control, who do not extend basic rights to everyone regardless of race, creed, or color. Everyone deserved the three basic fundamental rights: education, civil rights, and employment." Following up on her 1959 article, in her mockup notes for a 1960 edition of the paper, she noted: "The basic purpose of a democracy is to establish and promote a government of the people, by the people, and for the people. Not a government of white people. All must be given the same to learn and the same to earn."[70] While Burroughs always advocated for African Americans first, she believed that treating migrant workers with dignity and humanity was equally important to a democracy. After all, she had established her school to address the limited educational and job opportunities for Black migrant women and girls. Dorothy Richards, a white member of a Nannie Helen Burroughs Club in Ohio, recalled fond memories of co-authoring articles and supplementary study guides with Burroughs on issues confronting Black and Latin American migrant workers.[71]

As Burroughs restored the original mission of *The Worker* for labor rights, she continued her established practice of purchasing property to meet the needs of Black women workers. For decades she had criticized churches for not having a dedicated place for Black women missionaries to rest when they returned to the United States after traveling and working abroad. Missionary workers, she argued, were hard workers who gave their lives to serving other countries yet were prohibited from staying in comfortable hotels in their own country due to racial segregation laws. According to her, Black women missionary workers also did not have many places outside of churches to fellowship with each other. In the 1950s, she established and hosted a summer institute for Christian women workers at her school.[72] Just as she had done for Black women workers with her purchase of a headquarters for the National Association of Wage Earners and its related initiatives, Burroughs purchased a spacious building in Washington, DC, that she declared the National Headquarters for Missionary Committees of the Woman's Convention.[73] The headquarters contained comfortable beds and study, prayer, and fellowship rooms for Black women missionary workers. Burroughs also used the retreat building to host political meetings that addressed pressing issues confronting Black women and their communities in the United States and in Africa. In 1955 Burroughs hosted a Capitol Press Club meeting in the conference room of the retreat headquarters. She invited the media and several legislators to the meeting to hear and ask questions of William A. Ulman, assistant director of the Housing and Housing Finance Agency, who addressed Burroughs's and Woman's Convention members' questions about what the agency was doing to address the racial and class disparities inherent to the national housing problem.[74] Burroughs's organizing of the meeting, along with her call for housing legislation in a 1935 edition of *The Worker*, reflected her unyielding commitment to addressing the persistent housing crisis in Black communities.

Woman's Convention workers at the retreat continued Burroughs's advocacy for liberation movements in Africa beyond her lifetime. Retreat leaders authored study materials for Black women missionary workers to learn about and support independence movements across Africa. Retreat leaders drew maps of Africa that documented over time where Africans had won independence. The materials also included a charge to missionary workers to do what they could to help make a fully independent African continent a reality. As one study guide read, "The old colonial colors are fading fast and are being replaced by the bright hues of liberty. But the struggle is not yet over. It cannot be until every inch of African soil is cleansed of the taint of Colonialism. . . . This, therefore, is a challenge to Christian women everywhere." Sarah Willamson Coleman, retreat leader and author of the study guide, continued by urging missionary workers to travel to African countries to work as teachers and nurses at hospitals because little benefit would come from independence if people "continued to live on a bare subsistence level."[75] Coleman's study guide extended Burroughs's early work to advance Pan-Africanism through education and *The Worker*.

The Worker and the National Trade and Professional School for Women and Girls were the hallmarks of Burroughs's triumph over efforts to destroy her life's work. Writing articles for her groundbreaking paper kept her writing and her ideas alive after she became an ancestor in 1961. From her sickbed in 1960, Burroughs prepared a list of topics for one of the last editions of *The Worker* that she would edit. She reached out to other renowned Black leaders such as Benjamin E. Mays, president of Morehouse College, and urged them to contribute articles to *The Worker* about issues ranging from the sit down strikes of the Student Nonviolent Coordinating Committee to the Great Migration to the disproportionate work women were expected to do in the church in comparison to men. While the world and the country were changing around her, there was so much to solve that dated back to her early days of organizing.[76] She wanted to capture it all in this late edition of *The Worker*.

Perhaps sensing that she was nearing the end of her life, she hurriedly wrote mockup notes for a 1960 edition of *The Worker* in nearly illegible handwriting. Powerfully summarizing her key philosophies, she wrote that Black people and white people had lived in the same country, but Black people had lived in another world. Black people deserved the fundamental right to learn and earn. In her words, "These two basic rights spell first class citizenship in a democracy. Without these we will always be second-class citizens." She warned Black women readers of *The Worker*

Figure 8.5. An elderly Burroughs working at her desk on the NTS campus. Prints and Photographs Division, Library of Congress.

to take this moment of reckoning seriously and assume leadership positions in movements against injustices. She concluded with this charge: "Women, we must not drag our feet this year. Rome, or America, is actually burning."[77] After Burroughs passed into history on May 25, 1961, her colleague and former student Alice Smith became managing editor of *The Worker* in 1962 and kept its legacy alive for several decades afterward.

Notes

1. The domestic worker image appeared in an announcement about the National Association of Wage Earners headquarters. See National Association of Wage Earners, "A National Domestic Service Practice House," Box 3, Folder 42, Mark Solomon and Robert Kaufman Research Files.

2. In the 1910s, white men far outnumbered women as print shop owners. See US Bureau of the Census, "Color and Nativity of Gainful Workers," *Thirteenth Census of the United States, 1910*, 11 and 14; US Bureau of the Census, "Color and Nativity of Gainful Workers," *Fifteenth Census of the United States, 1930*, 328.

3. Randolph and Owens founded *The Messenger* in 1917; see Kersten, *A. Philip Randolph*, 17. The *Daily Worker* was established in 1924; see Davies, *Left of Karl Marx*, 246.

4. See subscription ledgers in Box 302, NHB Papers.

5. Lawrence discussed her illness in a letter to NHB; NHB to Una Lawrence, October 26, 1935, Box 1, Folder 27, Una Lawrence Collection. Burroughs told a reporter she wanted to keep her health condition confidential; Lewis, "'They Can't Make Me Quit.'"

6. William T. Amiger to NHB, January 1921, *The Worker* 9 (October 1920–March 1921): 1, Box 333, Folder 2, NHB Papers.

7. Collier-Thomas, *Jesus, Jobs, and Justice*, 389.

8. NHB, "That German Propaganda," *The Worker*, January 1918, Maggie Lena Walker Collection.

9. NHB, "Let Us Pray," *The Worker*, January 1918, Maggie Lena Walker Collection.

10. Murphy, *Jim Crow Capital*, 48.

11. NHB, "That German Propaganda."

12. NHB.

13. NHB, "The Servant—An Ally," *The Worker*, January 1918, Maggie Lena Walker Collection.

14. NHB, "The Dust Cap a Badge of Dignity," *The Worker*, January 1918, Maggie Lena Walker Collection.

15. NHB, "A Trip South," *The Worker* 9 (October 1920–March 1921): 1, Box 208, NHB papers.

16. NHB.

17. NHB, "Colored Women Pass Up Tubs for Steam Laundries," *The Worker* 10 (November 1922): 1, Box 308, NHB papers.

18. NHB.

19. Woodson, "The Negro Washerwoman," 269–77. For further discussion about Woodson's integration of African American women into his scholarship, see Dagbovie, "Black Women, Carter G. Woodson, and the Association," 21–41.

20. NHB, "Who Will Help Us to Help Ourselves," *The Worker* 10 (November 1922): 1, Box 308, NHB Papers.

21. NHB, "Colored Women Pass Up Tubs."

22. See early subscription ledgers in Box 302, NHB Papers.

23. Dunlap, "Washington's Sweetheart," 83.

24. NHB, "Another Strike: Have You Missed the Worker?," *The Worker* 9 (October 1920–March 1921): 1, Box 308, NHB Papers.

25. Woodson, "Instructors Teach Students Instead of Books."

26. "Our 'Miss Burroughs' Was a Very Special Person." 1–2.

27. "Our 'Miss Burroughs.'"

28. NHB, "What Giving a Little Girl a Change Did for Her," *The Worker* 10 (November 1922): 3, Box 308, NHB Papers.

29. NHB.

30. Beatrice's membership card is located in Box 308, Folder 1, NHB Papers.

31. Clarice Gooding to NHB, n.d., *The Worker* 9 (October 1920–March 1921): 1, Box 333, Folder 2, NHB Papers.

32. NHB, "National Training School Girls," 38.

33. Della Harris to NHB, January 1, 1921, January 26, 1921, *The Worker* 9 (October 1920–March 1921): 1, Box 333, Folder 2, NHB Papers.

34. William T. Amiger to NHB, January 1921, *The Worker* 9 (October 1920–March 1921): 1, Box 333, Folder 2, NHB Papers.

35. Pickens, *Nannie Helen Burroughs and the School of the 3 B's*, 24.

36. NHB, "National Training School Girls," 39–40.

37. NHB, 37–38.

38. NHB to W. E. B. Du Bois, March 19, 1925, W. E. B. Du Bois Papers.

39. Brooks, "Unification and Division among Colored Baptists," 20–22.

40. "Editorials," *The Messenger* 10, no. 4 (April 1928): 84.

41. NHB to Carter G. Woodson, December 28, 1931, Box 46, Folder 9, NHB Papers.

42. Penn and Bowen, *The United Negro*, 523.

43. NHB to Lawrence, October 27, 1936, Box 1, Folder 28, Una Lawrence Collection.

44. NHB, "The American Standard of Living," *The Worker* 1, no. 1 (January–March 1934): 26–28, Box 333, Folder 3, NHB Papers.

45. NHB, "The American Standard of Living," 26–28.

46. Brown, "National Negro Health Week Movement," 553; NHB, "Negro Health Week," *The Worker* 2, no. 6 (April–June 1935): 14–18, Box 333, Folder 3, NHB Papers.

47. Editorial Committee, "Editorial," *The Worker*, n.d., Box AR631, Southern Baptist Convention Historical Library and Archives.

48. Quoted from Haynes, *The Trend of the Races*, xi.

49. NHB to Una Lawrence, November 21, 1935, Box AR631, Southern Baptist Convention Historical Library and Archives.

50. NHB to Una Lawrence, July 2, 1934, Box 1, Folder 27, Una Lawrence Collection.

51. NHB, "Program Suggestions: Negro Achievement from America's Tenth Man," December 3, 1937, Box AR631, Southern Baptist Convention Historical Library and Archives.

52. NHB, "Burroughs Says Dr. W. E. B. Du Bois Is Impertinent," *Baltimore Afro-American*, May 12, 1934.

53. NHB, untitled, n.d., NHB Vertical File, Moorland-Springarn Research Center, Howard University.

54. Due to internal disputes and lack of philanthropic support the encyclopedia was not completed. Gates, "W. E. B. Du Bois and the Encyclopedia Africana," 203.

55. NHB to Du Bois, December 4, 1935, W. E. B. Du Bois Papers.

56. NHB to Una Lawrence, October 27, 1936, Box 1, Folder 28, Una Lawrence Collection.

57. NHB to Una Lawrence, June 29, 1935, Box 1, Folder 27, Una Lawrence Collection.

58. NHB to Una Lawrence, October 27, 1936.

59. NHB to Una Lawrence, October 27, 1936.

60. NHB to H. M. Gibbs, December 22, 1937, Box 1, Folder 29, Una Lawrence Collection.

61. "Baptists Pledge $1,000 to Miss Burroughs' School," *Chicago Defender*, February 24, 1939.

62. Ruth Alexander Smith, "1914 Graduate Tells of Miss Nannie Helen Burroughs' Many Sacrifices for School," *Pittsburgh Courier*, October 22, 1938.

63. Lewis, "'They Can't Make Me Quit.'"

64. NHB to Una Lawrence, August 18, 1939, Box 1, Folder 30, Una Lawrence Collection.

65. Easter, *Nannie Helen Burroughs*, 44.

66. NHB, "What Do You Know about the Cooperative Movement," *The Worker*, April–June 1937, 5.

67. NHB, "Editorials: The Domestic Worker," *The Worker*, July–September 1937, 3.

68. Carol E. Dokes, "Africa's Pleading Call," *The Worker*, circa 1940s, Box AR631, Southern Baptist Convention Historical Library and Archives.

69. "Do Not Doubt God," *The Worker*, July–September 1955, 20, 54–55, 94.

70. NHB, editorial notes for untitled article, *The Worker*, 1960, Box 47, Folder 11, NHB Papers.

71. "Annie J. Bellue, 105."

72. "Final Rites: Dr. Nannie Helen Burroughs."

73. The retreat building was located at 1022 Maryland Avenue in Northeast DC. "The Retreat For Foreign Missionaries and National Headquarters Missionary Committee Woman's Auxiliary National Baptist Convention, U.S.A., Inc.," Box 204–1, Folder 4, Sarah Williamson Coleman Papers.

74. "Hostess to the Press," April 12, 1955, *Atlanta Daily World*.

75. Sarah Williamson Coleman, "Africa Today: A Challenge of the Sixties to the Christian Church: A New Africa On An Old Continent," 4–5, Box 204–1, Folder 4, Sarah Williamson Coleman Papers.

76. NHB to Benjamin E. Mays, March 12, 1960, NHB Vertical File, Moorland-Springarn Research Center, Howard University.

77. NHB, editorial notes for untitled article.

Epilogue

Black Clubwomen in Labor History

Her school sat on the streets named after two white slaveholders and it's important that in 1976 we changed the names of those streets in honor of the daughter of a former slave.

> —Willie J. Hardy, representative of Deanwood, Washington, DC

When I was 10 years old, Julia Brooks, daughter of Reverend Walter Brooks, used to visit my mother every summer when she was attending school at Columbia University. She said, 'I want you to come to Washington.' . . . So, I came down and spent the whole summer with Reverend Walter Brooks and his daughter. . . . I was very young then, but she said, 'Let's go out to Nannie Helen Burroughs' school.' I do remember sitting on her porch and swinging on a swing and watching this very strong powerful woman because you see you had to feel her presence even as a young child.

> —Dorothy Porter Wesley, curator of the Moorland-
> Springarn Research Center, Howard University

What Miss Burroughs meant to me was that she was an example. Her faith drew you close to God. It inspired you. Her mottos: "Think—don't make excuses, make good. Don't explain. Your friends don't need it. Your enemies won't believe it. Do your job so well that no one can beat you at it. If you have what the world wants, they will make a beaten path to your door." . . . She tried to help you beat inequalities. All that I owe is to God first, Nannie Burroughs, and my alma mater.

> —Alice Smith, NTS alumna and staff member

I look up at her as not only a woman but a dynamic person. A woman who was a leader and a pioneer in the field of women's rights and sound womanhood in young girls.

—Charles H. Wesley, founding president of Central State University and former director of research and publications for the Association for the Study of Negro Life and History

As they said about Jesus, it was nice to touch the hem of his garment. And it was nice to touch the hem of hers. . . . She had a twinkle in her eye that you never would forget. To me, she was not a beautiful woman, but she had the most beautiful soul. It was like gold. It was running over with understanding and the desire to help all mankind regardless of race, class, or color. She believed in helping the underdog. She felt that the upper person could get along, but the person who was down she was going to help first and give them a sense that there was something to live for.

—Regina Chandler, Burroughs's coworker, Young Women's Christian Association and National Association of Colored Women, Washington, DC

Being director was a hard job to do because Burroughs would have all kinds of song books and we had to go through all of them to pick out a message. She didn't just pick out a song for the music. It must say something. And I dare[d] not say I was tired. I went home and told my people, "I can't work with that lady cause she was too positive." I just couldn't understand her, yet God fixed me so I stayed there right with her.

—Daisy Young, music director, Woman's Convention

I became her pastor in 1946. She was able to accept the ministry of a young man 27 years of age with grace and dignity. . . . We would sit together and talk for hours about Black people, the Baptist Convention, and its auxiliaries, especially the woman's auxiliary, sometimes related to her own personal finances and life. It was overwhelming to pray with someone who you felt overshadowed you in every dimension. . . . In her final days there was division in our conventions. As a matter of fact, it was split and when she died I suppose then it meant that I as the pastor had to bring together the factions of our split convention that loved her so much in order to pay tribute and homage to her great life. There on that occasion truly came together some of America's great religious figures and stood upon a single platform and paid homage to a life that had literally spent its life blessing black and white people but most particularly her own people.

—Jerry A. Moore, pastor of Nineteenth Street Baptist Church, Washington, DC, city council member

On the afternoon of September 23, 1976, people who knew and had worked with Burroughs celebrated the dedication of her papers to the Library of Congress.[1] Aurelia Downey, president of the Nannie Helen Burroughs School, officiated the special ceremony, and former students, Woman's Convention leaders, DC city council members, pastors, historians, and archivists spoke about the impact Burroughs had on them and their community work. Across their distinct relationships and interactions with Burroughs, everyone expressed that she was someone who left an unforgettable impression on them personally as well as in the larger realms of labor, education, community organizing, the movement for women's rights, and the study of African and African American history. The diversity of people who could talk about her in such rich detail speaks to her love for Black people and the extensive networks she developed to effect change in society. It was not enough for her just to know a lot of people. She saw everyone, woman and man, young and old, churchgoers and non-churchgoers, as essential to making her radical vision for wage-earning Black people a reality. Like other Black women educators of her time and afterward, Burroughs had a "greedy" or insatiable determination to create a new labor world that had been due to Black women and girls since emancipation. She never stopped organizing for a world that she knew required herculean efforts to make a reality. While managing and building the NTS, she worked feverishly across institutions and organizations to change national and global economies to create a world of limitless and unimaginable opportunities for Black women and girl wage earners.

The same year of the dedication ceremony, in 1976, the Association of the Study of African American Life and History placed a bronze marker in honor of Burroughs at what was the National Trade and Professional School for Women and Girls, which by that time had been converted into the Nannie Helen Burroughs School, a private elementary school for boys and girls. As Dorothy Pierson, former associate dean of social work at Howard University, said at the dedication ceremony, Burroughs, from her death until the bronze marker ceremony, had been "buried in the public record without notice."[2] The previous year, in 1975, Mayor Walter E. Washington and city council member Willie J. Hardy also made an effort to preserve Burroughs's memory and dedication to the District by renaming part of Minnesota Avenue Nannie Helen Burroughs Avenue. That same year, Mayor Washington declared May 10 as Nannie Burroughs Day. Burroughs and her school were back in the news again years later. In 1981 the Nannie Helen Burroughs School was declared the oldest Black-owned and operated school in Washington, DC. The school operates now as the Monroe Charter School, a coeducational and private day school. The Trades Hall, built in 1928, the chapel, and the Abraham Lincoln archway at the campus entrance are the only surviving structures of the National Trade and Professional School for Women and Girls. On July 17, 1991, Trades Hall was declared a National Historic Landmark by the US secretary of the interior.[3]

The great need for Burroughs's expansive vision and advocacy for comprehensive labor reform echoes loudly in the twenty-first century. In the absence of her school, fortunately, we have the bold writings, research, and teaching practices she left behind. Her work challenges how labor resistance itself has been defined and studied. Burroughs' and her NACW friends' histories reveal that voter organizing, writing to inspire community action, employing intersectional research methods, creating art to inspire community action, and developing syllabi and academic and religious programs that counteract structural and social inequalities are all part of labor resistance. Through teaching, research, and writing, Burroughs became a leading organizer, philosopher, and strategist on the dilemmas of race, gender, migration, and labor. She built an institution into a hub of multiple public-facing initiatives and organizations to transform the US economy and change how people thought about labor. It was her intellectual work that drove her transformative community organizing.

Figure E.1. Dorothy Porter Wesley and Charles Harris Wesley at the dedication ceremony for the Nannie Helen Burroughs Papers at the Library of Congress in 1976. Manuscript Division, Library of Congress.

Figure E.2. Alice Smith at the Nannie Helen Burroughs Papers dedication ceremony. Manuscript Division, Library of Congress.

Figure E.3. DC councilmember Willie J. Hardy and Aurelia Downey, president of the Nannie Helen Burroughs School, at the Nannie Helen Burroughs Papers dedication ceremony. Manuscript Division, Library of Congress.

Burroughs's history opens the door to further study of the intellectual and community work of other Black clubwomen during the Jane Crow era to establish an expansive labor movement. While their goals were similar, they represented a wide array of life histories that informed their pedagogies, writings, and institution-building practices. For example, unlike Burroughs, Mary McLeod Bethune was not opposed to making her school a co-ed institution in her work to improve the working conditions of Black women and girls. As president of a coeducational school, her teaching practices overlapped with and were distinct from the practices at Burroughs's school. Black clubwomen's array of politics and strategies provide several tools for developing pedagogies, curricula, policies, and labor union practices that truly address race, and all its intersecting inequalities. Their work also provides fruitful roadmaps for how to convert labor research into community and legislative action. As labor scholars and organizers, Burroughs and her NACW allies produced some of the first intersectional labor studies and they developed the theoretical frameworks for these groundbreaking studies in their organizations and schools.

Burroughs and her NACW colleagues had a clear and in-depth understanding of the deeply rooted history of labor disparities that remain with us today due to the ever-present impact of slavery on US institutions. Wage disparities between Black women and their white men and women counterparts remain in every labor sector. Economist Michelle Holder described with resounding clarity the direct line between slavery and these persistent wage inequalities. As she asserted, "Though African American women have historically had the highest labor force participation rate among major female demographic groups in the US, they face both the gender wage gap and the racial wage gap—a reinforcing confluence that I term the 'double gap.'"[4] The pandemic was a harsh reminder of the precarious lives of Black women in service and low-wage jobs, women who were at the center of Burroughs's philosophies and organizing work. Domestic workers, teachers, restaurant workers, and millions of other workers, who are primarily women of color and essential to the economy, either lost their jobs or suffered severely cut wages. Black women continue to be the primary caretakers of their families and represent the majority of workers in jobs with the worst financial safety nets and benefits.

Heightened organizing for living wages, workplace protections, voting rights, and women's rights have brought to the forefront deep, historically rooted racial, class, and gender inequities across economic, legal, and political institutions that contribute to the precarity of Black women workers. The far-right majority of the Supreme Court has provided fertile ground for the passage of local and state laws that roll back centuries of progress. Just about every regressive policy that has made its way through city councils and state houses has significantly chipped away at civil, women's, and workers' rights: from open carry laws that make it nearly impossible for teachers and public service workers to do their jobs, to abortion bans and restrictions that make the work of healthcare professionals impossible, to penalties for teachers and professors for teaching Black history, to gerrymandered maps that in the words of three judges in North Carolina are made with "surgical precision" to silence people from changing these laws and policies.[5]

After the murder of George Floyd and the historic election of Vice President Kamala Harris, an alumna of Howard University and member of Alpha Kappa Alpha Sorority, Inc., the country has looked at Black women's organizations and historically Black colleges and universities for guidance in addressing injustices. Fully appreciating and understanding the significance of Black schools and Black women's organizations means unpacking and employing the unprecedented theories and work that emanated from these sites of organizing. Teachers from historically Black institutions from the National Trade and Professional School for Women and Girls, Spelman College, and Bennett College to the National Association of Colored Women's Clubs and the National Association of Wage Earners offer important context and strategies for organizing against the curtailment of workers', civil, and women's rights.

A serious engagement with the Black clubwomen's labor movement requires widening the scope of how labor resistance is defined and which people are recognized as labor leaders. For example, the Black clubwomen's labor movement invites us to think about Alpha Kappa Alpha Sorority, Incorporated's mobile health clinics of the Mississippi Health Project as not solely a volunteer service but a Great Depression–era labor project for Black sharecroppers and their families in the Mississippi Delta who could not afford quality medical care due to their nonexistent wages. Worker advocacy was also embedded in the voting rights and educational movement agendas of leaders of Delta Sigma Theta Sorority, Inc. Shifting how leaders are revered helps ensure that the generative possibilities of Black women's labor organizing are not lost to history. Learning about Burroughs's and other women leaders' achievements may result in a tendency to relegate them to the realm of meritocratic representation, as exemplars of "Black excellence" or individual people who defeated tremendous odds. We benefit more from grappling with their intellectual and community work to determine what we can put into practice in our time.

Burroughs and other Black clubwomen's initiatives, studies, and philosophies should be included in the core curricula of programs in labor studies, women's and gender studies, policy and legal studies, and other related programs. Their strategies were effective in developing broad-based and collective action necessary for contemporary organizing. The National Association of Wage Earners, for example, emerged from Burroughs's vision for the NTS and provides a starting point for identifying overlapping labor issues that can lead to cross-racial and cross-occupational labor alliances today, without diluting discussions about race and gender. Similar to the early twentieth century, when African American women were migrating to US northeastern cities for domestic service jobs, working-class white, Black, and immigrant women of color are concentrated in the most underpaid and under-insured jobs in the United States. What if teachers protesting low wages and poor health coverage in Texas, West Virginia, Oklahoma, and Arizona formed alliances with Black mothers and teachers in cities such as Chicago, Detroit, and Atlanta who have been organizing against the deterioration of public schools in their neighborhoods for decades? What if teachers across the country supported fast food workers in the Fight for $15 movement? The National Association of Wage Earners' and Burroughs's coauthored petition to the International Congress of Working Women offers important historical context and study guides for interrogating ideologies of race, class, and gender that uphold divisions between workers and impede the formation of an even more expansive labor movement.

While there are many challenges confronting the country, there is also great promise for creating a bold agenda to dismantle systemic and intersectional inequalities that impact people's everyday working lives. In 2023 the AFL-CIO elected its first national woman president and the first national Black secretary in US history. In 2023 the AFL-CIO Georgia chapter elected its first Black woman president. Over the last sixteen years, eleven states have adopted the Domestic Worker Bill of Rights, legislation that ensures that domestic workers are included in common workplace laws.[6] As during the time when the NTS housed several labor initiatives, the US South has become a site of historic labor organizing. Black labor researchers from across the South have organized the Advancing Black Strategists Initiative in partnership with historically Black colleges and universities and Jobs with Justice. Amazon factory workers in Bessmer, Alabama, launched a voting campaign to establish a labor union, and the Georgia chapter of the National Domestic Workers Alliance became major political organizers instrumental in turning the state "periwinkle," in the words of US Congresswoman Nikema Williams, in 2020 and 2023.[7]

Burroughs's push to democratize education is now integral to the presidential administration's plans to eliminate student debt and eliminate for-profit schools that have created even more enormous debt for working-class and middle-class people. President Joe Biden and Vice President Kamala Harris have explicitly made labor rights and union organizing part of their national agenda. Pushing a standardized minimum wage of fifteen dollars per hour for federal jobs, the administration is using theoretical frameworks and language developed in women's and gender studies, sociology, and African American studies classrooms to integrate intersectional labor issues into national conversations.[8] President Biden has nominated several Black women with intersectional labor analyses to key economic leadership positions. Cecilia Rouse, for example, is the first Black chair of the White House economic council, and Janelle Jones, an alumna of Spelman College, was the first Black woman chief economist of the US Department of Labor.[9]

Just imagine what would be possible if we centered Black women's labor histories in our classrooms, scholarship, labor organizations, and in a national labor agenda supported with federal resources. Labor reform for Black women—people at the intersections of racial, class, gender, and citizenship inequalities—would mean labor protections and a better quality of life overall for the majority of working people.

Notes

1. All quotes at the beginning of this chapter are from the various speeches delivered at the dedication ceremony of the NHB Papers. See "Reminiscences of Dr. Nannie Helen Burroughs."

2. Vernon C. Thompson, "Honoring a 'Total Person': Nannie Helen Burroughs," *Washington Post*, July 8, 1976.

3. McCluskey, *A Forgotten Sisterhood*, 163; Murphy, Melton, and Ward, *Encyclopedia of African American Religions*, 135; Edward D. Sargent, "Nannie Helen Burroughs School: Keeping a High Profile," *Washington Post*, July 23, 1981; "The Monroe School: Educating Today for Tomorrow's Success," https://monroeschool.net/m/; "National Training School for Women and Girls," Historic Preservation Review Board: Historic Designation Case Nos. 17–09 and 21–13, April 28, 2022, 1.

4. Holder, "The 'Double Gap' and the Bottom Line," 4.

5. Joseph Ax, "North Carolina Court Strikes Down State Legislative Map as Unconstitutional Gerrymander," Reuters, September 3, 2019, https://www.reuters.com/article/us-north-carolina-gerrymandering-idUSKCN1VO2MD/.

6. Kenneth Quinnell, "Black History Month Profiles: Yvonne Brooks," AFL-CIO, February 23, 2023, https://aflcio.org/2023/2/23/black-history-month-profiles-yvonne-brooks; National Domestic Workers Alliance, "Domestic Worker Bill of Rights," https://www.domesticworkers.org/programs-and-campaigns/developing-policy-solutions/domestic-workers-bill-of-rights/; New Jersey Legislature, New Jersey Domestic Workers' Bill of Rights, https://www.njleg.state.nj.us/bill-search/2022/S723/bill-text?f=S1000&n=723_E1.

7. Jobs with Justice, "Advancing Black Strategists Initiative," https://www.jwj.org/our-work/absi; Alina Selyukh, "Amazon Workers in Alabama Vote for Second Time in Union Effort," National Public Radio, February 4, 2022, https://www.npr.org/2022/02/04/1077089349/amazon-union-vote-alabama.

8. Vice President Harris, for example, frequently refers to systemic racism and sexism in her public talks and writings. President Biden signed four executive orders to fix the racial wealth gap. See "Remarks by President Biden at Signing of an Executive Order on Racial Equity"; "Biden-Harris Administration Issues an Executive Order."

9. Jim Tankersley, "Senate Confirms Cecilia Rouse as the First Black Chair of White House Economic Council," *New York Times*, March 2, 2021, https://www.nytimes.com/2021/03/02/us/politics/cecilia-rouse-economic-council.html; Lydia DePillis, "How Janelle Jones's Story about Black Women and the Economy Caught On," *New York Times*, April 13, 2023.

ACKNOWLEDGMENTS

Writing a book about a historical figure as extraordinary as Burroughs takes up a significant amount of one's personal life and the lives of their loved ones. I appreciate my support network, who traveled on this journey with me and were patient with me when I talked about Burroughs for the millionth time. I am so very fortunate to have a mother who is an intellectually curious educator and a voracious reader who pushes the boundaries of my thinking and writing. My mother was the most ideal person imaginable to talk with every day about my ideas for the book. She insisted on raising me in southwest Atlanta, a part of the city where I learned the richness of Black history from all of the lectures, arts performances, and events that my mother took me to. She was also very clear that I needed instruction from Black women educators in the Atlanta Public School system. Her politics and pedagogies helped me see the importance of Burroughs. Truth be told, there is a piece of Burroughs in my mother and all the Black women educators my mother insisted I learn from. Even before I began writing the book, with every single gem I discovered in the archive, I called my mother. A conversation about one archival source or one idea often turned into fruitful multi-hour phone conversations between us. While some archives are accessible, others require several phone calls and emails to enter. When I encountered challenges along the way, my mother put the spine in my back to press forward and continue my work. Mom, I love you more than words can describe.

It takes a patient person to wake up early in the morning to lively conversations between my mom and me about everything from Burroughs to politics to *Real Housewives of Atlanta*. As when I was writing my first book, my husband, Dennis Cunningham, was thoughtful and supportive in many ways. He read drafts of my chapters, cooked meals during my long writing days, and picked up our cats (Dottie, Mira, and Cheddar) from my desk when they demanded attention by standing in front of the computer screen. Whenever Dennis and I visited a museum just for the heck of it, Dennis considered it his personal mission to help me locate even more archival sources about Burroughs, as though ten thousand files at the Library of Congress were not enough. He bought books and would look for Burroughs's face in exhibits and bookstores. When he could not find her, which was mostly the case, he would say, "Well, I could not find Nannie, but I bet this woman was connected to her. You might want to look her up." On our anniversary, he surprised me with an edited volume he had purchased from a museum that included Burroughs's friend's writings, and that was exactly what I needed as I was wrapping up the book. Dennis, I appreciate you more than you probably know.

My late father was an essential person in my family network. I missed him a lot along this journey. As a Detroit-born Baptist and proud Morehouse College man, he would have loved having conversations about Burroughs and her labor organizing in the Baptist church and at her school. I appreciate his dear Morehouse and fraternity brother Lester Bentley for stepping into his place and supporting my work and career. His check-ins meant a lot during this process.

Since the first time I set foot in the Library of Congress, my Spelman sister Alethea Predeoux has been an unrelenting advocate for my work on Burroughs. Before I had grants to support my research trips to Washington, DC, Alethea's house was my second home. She welcomed me into her home, cooked delicious meals, and always offered a listening ear when I needed to iron out ideas concerning the book. Our conversations and outings in DC that had nothing to do with Burroughs were equally energizing for my soul and work. As someone who has devoted her career to advocating for workers, Alethea has been instrumental to bringing my work to labor audiences. Before I wrote the first book chapter, she told her colleagues in labor unions about my project and circulated my op-eds about Burroughs in labor union circles. Alethea connected me specifically with labor leaders who are building on Burroughs's legacy. President Randi Weingarten, Candace Archer, and Damon Silvers, thanks so very much for supporting my work and seeing the importance of Burroughs's life.

My dear friend Nadia Brown has also been essential to my research and the circulation of my public writings about Burroughs. I am grateful for Nadia's support during the grant-writing process, which resulted in a substantial grant that provided necessary resources for my multiple trips to archives across Washington, DC. I enjoyed and learned a lot from working with Nadia and her colleague E.J. of the Monkey Cage on publishing my *Washington Post* op-eds about Burroughs and my public and National Endowment for the Humanities-funded project about a historic Black town in Texas. Their commitment to promoting Black historical research makes clear that women editors with progressive politics matter!

My Spelman sister and Rutgers colleague Sheri Davis-Faulkner came into my life in the nick of time. I greatly appreciate her inviting me to opportunities to put my research into practice through teaching and writing. She introduced me to the Public Voices of the South program of the Op-Ed project, which prepared me for writing op-eds. I am proud of our co-designed and co-taught race, gender, and labor course that is cross-listed between Spelman College, Rutgers University, and the Advancing Black Strategists Initiative. Our unprecedented course has brought together students, Black labor organizers, and Black women leaders in labor movements from across the country to study and discuss the history and future directions of Black women in labor. Teaching Burroughs's and clubwomen's labor organizing in this unique space helped sharpen my ideas for the book.

The intersectional and interdisciplinary frameworks that are foundational to all of my writing, research, and teaching came from my Burroughs-like professors at Spelman College. They represent what is becoming a rare generation of scholars who take teaching seriously. Due to their institution-building and curriculum-building work, generations of Spelman students and graduates have produced groundbreaking scholarship about Black women. From Beverly Guy-Sheftall and her Women's Research and Resource Center and the comparative women's studies major, to Gloria Wade Gayles and her Resonance and Spelman Independent Scholars programs, and to Cynthia Spence's Social Justice Fellows Program, I acquired the tools and publication experiences to build a life I love—researching, teaching, and writing about Black women's labor histories. These brilliant educators have continued supporting my work inside and outside of the classroom to this very day. I aspire to evolve into a senior scholar who is as intellectually sharp and generous as them. While writing the book, I came to know community leaders Dianne Randolph, Alma Clark, and Betty Kimble of Denton, Texas. We collaborated on a National Endowment for the Humanities public history project about Quakertown, a thriving and independent town established by formerly enslaved Black people after Juneteenth. My community collaborators and the people who established Quakertown helped fuel my passion for completing this book. Their lives reflect Burroughs's zeal for working toward Black political and economic freedom.

Christopher Lura's critical eye and thoughtful questions and edits helped me tremendously in transforming early drafts of chapters into a book manuscript. I enjoyed and appreciated traveling with him on this multi-year journey and I look forward to working with him again on future projects.

Eileen Boris and Annelise Orleck also laid a foundation for the study of women's labor history and are committed to supporting younger generations of scholars. I was fortunate that Eileen's and Annelise's comments were the bookends of the revision process for my book. I appreciate Eileen's detailed and thoughtful comments on the earliest iteration of my book manuscript. Her comments helped me make the important shift from writing Burroughs's biography to writing Burroughs's labor history. Thankfully, my early academic training from professors at Spelman and educators in the Atlanta Public School system helped me develop the thick skin and eyesight to see and hear Eileen's sage advice embedded in question marks and words typed in bold and capital letters in her comments. Annelise, who provided comments on the penultimate version of my manuscript, has the rare ability of describing her request for revisions in an artful and encouraging way. For example, she told me, "Mow the lawn so that readers can see the flowers more clearly." Who knew that such a lovely worded directive would require so much work? At the end of the day, the work was worth it. Her feedback gave me the room that I needed to illustrate the agile, creative, and multilevel organizing of Burroughs and her NACW co-organizers.

One of the most valuable lessons I have learned from women educators in my life is the importance of supporting younger generations of scholars through teaching, collaboration, and writing. I come from a tradition that taught me that publishing and conducting research in isolation is not enough. I greatly appreciate the American Philosophical Society and the African American Intellectual History Society for funding that made it possible for me to mirror Burroughs's commitment to mentorship. Funding from both organizations allowed me to hire a student research assistant. I was very fortunate to develop a long-term and ever-evolving working relationship with Veronica Popp, a former student who shares my zeal for documenting Burroughs's labor history. The research and writing process would not have been as enjoyable and generative without Veronica. Some of my fondest memories include co-authoring articles and making a trip to the Library of Congress together. I thought Veronica's idea to visit Burroughs's grave was a bit strange, but I am glad I went along with her suggestion. While visiting the cemetery, we received an unexpected yet helpful history lesson about Black Washingtonians. Veronica pushed my thinking about Burroughs and inspired me to keep writing as I dealt with the racial and gender politics of academia. I take great pleasure in witnessing Veronica harness her love for labor organizing and history by establishing her own projects that bring Black clubwomen's work into greater visibility.

People who do historical research know that archivists are golden to the research process. My deep gratitude to Patrick Kerwin of the Library of Congress's Manuscript Division cannot be overstated. I greatly appreciate his consistent responsiveness, insights, and archival excavation work throughout my book journey. On my first visit to the Library of Congress, Patrick asked me, "So . . . when are you going to write a book about Burroughs?" At first, Burroughs's massive nondigitized collection was overwhelming to me. I responded to Patrick by giving him a friendly yet noncommittal southern smile. Undeterred, Patrick kept asking the same question during my follow-up visits, and I eventually told him that I would write the book. Patrick's encouraging support throughout the research process was critical and invaluable. He provided expert advice and assistance during my on-site visits and whenever I emailed him with questions. He also sent me sources when I needed them in a pinch and located rare and nondigitized sources that I did not find in the finding aids. Thanks so very much, Patrick.

Burroughs's work was so expansive that she worked with many people from different walks of life to improve the working conditions of Black women and girls. Her work is thereby spread across several archival collections across the country. I worked with multiple archivists who helped make sources in these archives available to me. Most notably, I extend my sincere appreciation to Holly A. Smith of the Spelman College Archives, Taffey Hall of the Southern Baptist Historical Library and Archives, Sonja Woods of the Moorland-Springarn Research Center at Howard University, Cheryl Ferguson of Tuskegee University Archives, Ethan Bullard of the Maggie Lena Walker National Historic Site, and Liz Menendez of the Charlotte Hawkins Brown Museum.

In conclusion, I thank Robert J. Patterson for establishing the Second Book Institute at Georgetown University. So often associate professors, especially Black women, have difficulty writing their second books as they prepare for promotion. We are often expected to do more service than our white colleagues, and most universities allocate resources to tenure-earning faculty. When I first began writing the book, I was a program director of women's and gender studies at a service-intensive university, and I was the only Black woman in my department. I was also in the process of establishing a women's and gender studies BA program. Without the institute, it would have taken much longer for me to focus on my book project while doing service and administrative work. The Second Book Institute set me on an early path for securing a book contract and working with Al Bertrand, director of Georgetown University Press. At our first meeting, I did not have to convince Al that Burroughs and her story were significant. He understood from day one the power and importance of Black women's labor organizing history. During the writing and research process, Al was understanding when life and department commitments sometimes got in the way of initial deadlines, and I enjoyed working with Al throughout the book production process.

Simply put, it took a village to produce this book. Thanks so much, everyone!

BIBLIOGRAPHY

Burroughs traveled extensively to create a world of opportunity for Black women and girl wage-earners. This meant that I needed to travel to several archives to document her labor history. Burroughs's diligent research of the labor problem required that I delve into census records of the US Department of Labor to trace her thinking and methods for establishing curricula and institutions to reverse the glaring economic inequalities that impacted Black women and girls. The voluminous Burroughs papers at the Library of Congress contain over 10,000 mostly non-digitized writings and school records, but her story does not stop there. Burroughs's organizing was expansive and required that I consult unpublished primary sources across multiple collections at and beyond the Library of Congress. As a teacher who barely made a living wage but was a renowned leader, Burroughs worked inside of the overlapping networks of the Black elite, middle-class, and working-class. Her labor history and influences were thereby buried in collections at public libraries, research centers, and historic sites named in honor of well-known leaders such as W. E. B. Du Bois and Mordecai Johnson and leaders who were not household names such as Andrew Lee Gill and Wilhelmina Adams. As an organizer who did a lot of uncredited behind-the-scenes work, Burroughs's name was not always highlighted in the finding aids of her co-organizers' collections. Piecing together her story from these unsuspecting sources entailed tracing her work through the names of her organizations, clubs, and school—the true mark of an organizer and thinker who often put the work before herself.

Archives and Special Collections

Adams, Wilhelmina F. Papers. Schomburg Center for Research in Black Culture, New York.

Brown, Charlotte Hawkins. Archive. Charlotte Hawkins Brown Museum and State Historic Site, Gibsonville, NC.

Bureau of Vital Records. Virginia Department of Health, Richmond.

Burroughs, Nannie Helen. Files. People's Archive, District of Columbia Public Library, Washington, DC.

Burroughs, Nannie Helen. Papers. Manuscript Division, Library of Congress, Washington, DC.

Burroughs, Nannie Helen. Vertical File. Moorland-Springarn Research Center, Howard University, Washington, DC.

Burroughs, Nannie Helen. Vertical File. People's Archive, District of Columbia Public Library, Washington, DC.

Coleman, Sarah Williamson. Papers. Moorland-Springarn Research Center, Howard University, Washington, DC.

Cooper, Anna Julia. Papers. Moorland-Springarn Research Center, Howard University, Washington, DC.

Davis, John Warren. Papers. Moorland-Springarn Research Center, Howard University, Washington, DC.

Douglass, Frederick. Papers. Moorland-Springarn Research Center, Howard University, Washington, DC.

Du Bois, W. E. B. Papers. University of Massachusetts Amherst Libraries, Amherst.

Gill, Andrew Lee. Papers. Moorland-Springarn Research Center, Howard University, Washington, DC.

Goins, Gregoria Frasier. Papers. Moorland-Springarn Research Center, Howard University, Washington, DC.

Grimke, Francis J. Papers. Moorland-Springarn Research Center, Howard University, Washington, DC.

Howard University Collection. Moorland-Springarn Research Center, Howard University, Washington, DC.

Johnson, Mordecai. Papers. Moorland-Springarn Research Center, Howard University, Washington, DC.

King, Martin Luther, Jr. Papers. Howard Gotlieb Archival Research Center, Boston University, Boston.

Lawrence, Una. Collection. Southern Baptist Convention Historical Library and Archives, Nashville.

Manuscripts Division. Moorland-Springarn Research Center, Howard University Library.

Mays, Benjamin E. Papers. Moorland-Springarn Research Center, Howard University, Washington, DC.

McDuffie, Irvin and Elizabeth. Collection. Atlanta University Center Library, Robert W. Woodruff Library, Atlanta.

National Baptist Convention Records. Southern Baptist Convention Historical Library and Archives, Nashville.

National Negro Business League Records. Library of Congress, Washington, DC.

Orange County, Virginia. US Department of Census Records.

Phelps Stokes, Anson. Family Papers. Yale University Library, New Haven, CT.

Phelps-Stokes Fund Records. Schomburg Center for Research in Black Culture, New York.

Pickens, William. Papers. Schomburg Center for Research in Black Culture, New York.

Plays and Programs Collection. Moorland-Springarn Research Center, Howard University, Washington, DC.

Recorded Sound Research Center. Library of Congress, Washington, DC.

Solomon, Mark, and Robert Kaufman. Research Files on African Americans and Communism. Tamiment Library and Robert F. Wagner Archives, New York University, New York.

Terrell, Mary Church. Papers. Library of Congress, Washington, DC.

Terrell, Mary Church. Papers. Moorland-Springarn Research Center, Howard University, Washington, DC.

Walker, Maggie Lena. Collection. Maggie Lena Walker National Historic Site, Richmond, Virginia.

Washington, Booker T. Collection. Tuskegee University, Tuskegee.

Washington, Booker T. Papers. Manuscript Division, Library of Congress, Washington, DC.

Women's Bureau. US Department of Labor Census Records, Washington, DC.

Published Sources

Aiello, Thomas. *The Battle for the Souls of Black Folks*. Santa Barbara, CA: ABC-CLIO, 2016.

Anderson, James D. *The Education of Blacks in the South, 1860–1935*. Chapel Hill: University of North Carolina Press, 1988.

Aron, Cindy S. "'To Barter Their Souls for Gold': Female Clerks in Federal Government Offices, 1862–1890." *Journal of American History* 67, no. 4 (March 1981): 835–53.

Austin, Paula C. *Coming of Age in Jim Crow DC: Navigating the Politics of Everyday Life*. New York: New York University Press.

Bacote, Samuel William, ed. *Who's Who among the Colored Baptists of the United States*. Kansas City, MO: Franklin Hudson, 1913.

Bair, Sarah D. "Educating Black Girls in the Early 20th Century: The Pioneering Work of Nannie Helen Burroughs (1879–1961)." *Theory and Research in Social Education* 36, no. 1 (2008): 9–35.

Balch, Emily Greene. *Occupied Haiti: Being the Report of a Committee of Six Disinterested Americans Representing Organizations Exclusively American, Who Have Personally Studied Conditions in Haiti in 1926, Favor of the Restoration of the Independence of the Negro Republic.* New York: Writing Publishing Company, 1927.

Banks, Nina. "Black Women's Labor Market History Reveals Deep-Seated Race and Gender Discrimination." *Economic Policy Institute*, February 19, 2019. https://www.epi.org/blog/black-womens-labor-market-history-reveals-deep-seated-race-and-gender-discrimination/.

Bassett, Mary T. "Beyond Berets: The Black Panthers as Health Activists." *American Journal of Public Health* 106, no. 10 (October 2016): 1741–43. https://doi.org/10.2105/AJPH.2016.303412.

Bates, Beth Tompkins. *Pullman Porters and the Rise of Protest Politics in Black America, 1925–1945.* Chapel Hill: University of North Carolina Press, 2001.

"Biden-Harris Administration Issues an Executive Order to Raise the Minimum Wage to $15 for Federal Contractors." The White House, April 27, 2021. https://www.whitehouse.gov/briefing-room/statements-releases/2021/04/27/fact-sheet-biden-harris-administration-issues-an-executive-order-to-raise-the-minimum-wage-to-15-for-federal-contractors/.

Blount, Jackie M. "Spinsters, Bachelors, and Other Gender Transgressors in School Employment, 1850–1900." *Review of Educational Research* 70, no. 1 (2000): 83–101.

Borchert, James. *Alley Life in Washington.* Champaign: University of Illinois Press, 1980.

Boris, Eileen, and Cynthia R. Daniels, eds. *Homework: Historical and Contemporary Perspectives on Paid Labor at Home.* Chicago: University of Illinois Press, 1989.

Boris, Eileen, and Premilla Nadasen. "Domestic Workers Organize!" *Working USA: The Journal of Labor and Society* 11 (2008): 420.

Boyce Davies, Carole. *Left of Karl Marx: The Political Life of Black Communist Claudia Jones.* Durham, NC: Duke University Press, 2007.

Bratton, Lisa. "'Chloroform Your Uncle Toms!' Using Census Records to Correct the History of the Outspoken Nannie Helen Burroughs." *Journal of the Afro-American Historical and Genealogical Society* 35 (January 2018): 7–12.

Brooks, Evelyn. "Religion, Politics, and Gender: The Leadership of Nannie Helen Burroughs." *Journal of Religious Thought* 44, no. 2 (Winter/Spring 1988): 7–23.

Brooks, Walter H. "Unification and Division among Colored Baptists." *The Crisis* 30, no. 1 (May 1925): 20–22.

Brown, Meredith Cooper, and Nicole A. Taylor. "Nannie Helen Burroughs (1883–1961)." In *Unsung Legacies of Educators and Events in African American Education*, edited by Andrea D. Lewis and Nicole A. Taylor, 9–17. New York: Palgrave Macmillan, 2019.

Brown, Roscoe C. "The National Negro Health Week Movement." *Journal of Negro Education* 6, no. 3 (July 1937): 553.

Burroughs, Nannie Helen. "The Colored Woman and Her Relation to the Domestic Problem." In *The United Negro: His Problems and His Progress*, edited by Irvine Garland Penn and John Wesley Edward Bowen, 324–29. Atlanta: D. E. Luther, 1902.

———. *First Annual Report of the Executive Committee of the Woman's Convention-Auxiliary to the National Baptist Convention*, 1901.

———. "How the Sisters Are Hindered from Helping." In National Baptist Convention, *Journal of the Twentieth Annual Session of the National Baptist Convention, Held in Richmond, Virginia, September 12–17, 1900*, 196–97. Nashville: National Baptist Publishing Board, 1900.

———. "Industrial Education—Will It Solve the Negro Problem?" *Colored American Magazine*, March 1904.

———. "National League of Republican Colored Women." *National Notes: Official Organ of the National Association of Colored Women*, July 1928: 10.

———. Preface. In Atholene Peyton, *The Peytonia Cook Book*, 1–4. Louisville, KY, 1906.

———. "Votes for Women: A Symposium by Leading Thinkers of Colored Women." *The Crisis*, 1915.

———. "Why Organize Our Young Women." *National Association of Colored Women's Notes* 16, no. 5 (May 1913): 3.

Butler, Amy E. *Two Paths to Equality: Alice Paul and Ethel M. Smith in the ERA Debate, 1921–1920*. Albany: State University of New York, 2002.

Butler, Selena S. *The Chain-Gang System, Read before the National Association of Colored Women at Nashville, Tenn., September 16, 1897*. Tuskegee, AL: Normal School Steam Press, 1897.

Carson, Clayborne, Stewart Burns, Susan Carson, Dana Powell, and Peter Holloran, eds. *The Papers of Martin Luther King, Jr.* Vol. 3, *Birth of a New Age, December 1955–December 1956*. Berkeley: University of California Press, 1997.

Chateauvert, Melinda. *Marching Together: Women of the Brotherhood of Sleeping Car Porters*. Urbana: University of Illinois Press, 1998.

Clark-Lewis, Elizabeth. *Living In, Living Out: African American Domestics in Washington, D.C., 1910–1940*. Washington, DC: Smithsonian, 2010.

Collier-Thomas, Bettye. *Jesus, Jobs, and Justice: African American Women and Religion*. New York: Knopf, 2010.

"Conventions." *Half-Century Magazine*, September–October 1924, 8.

Cooper, Anna Julia. *A Voice from the South*. New York: Oxford University Press, [1892] 1982.

Corey, Charles Henry. *A History of the Richmond Theological Seminary: With Reminiscences of Thirty Years' Work among the Colored People of the South*. Richmond: J. W. Randolph, 1895.

Dagbovie, Pero Gaglo. "Black Women, Carter G. Woodson, and the Association for the Study of Negro Life and History, 1915–1950." *Journal of African American History* 88, no. 1 (2003): 21–41.

Daniel, Sadie Iola. *Women Builders*. Washington, DC: Associated Publishers, 1931.

"The Delta Sigma Theta Sorority." *The Mirror*, Howard University Yearbook, 1915.

Dill, Bonnie Thornton. *Across the Boundaries of Race and Class: An Exploration of Work and Family among Black Female Domestic Servants*. New York: Garland Press, 1994.

Dosset, Kate. *Bridging Race Divides: Black Nationalism, Feminism, and Integration in the United States*. Gainesville: University Press of Florida, 2009.

Downey, Aurelia. *A Tale of Three Women: God's Call and Their Response*. Brentwood, MD: International Graphics, 1993.

Downey, Sheilena. "Precursor to Women of Color Feminism: The International Council of Women of the Darker Races of the World and Their Internationalist Orientation." *Meridians: Feminism, Race, Transnationalism* 19, no. 2 (October 2020): 271–77.

Du Bois, W. E. B. *Efforts for Social Betterment Among Negro Americans: A Social Study Made By Atlanta University*. Atlanta: Atlanta University Press, 1909.

———. *The Philadelphia Negro: A Social Study*. Philadelphia: University of Pennsylvania Press, 1899.

Dunbar-Nelson, Alice. "To the Negro Farmers of the United States." In *The Portable Nineteenth-Century African American Women Writers*, edited by Hollis Robbins and Henry Louis Gates Jr., 375–76. New York: Penguin, 2017.

Dunlap, Tameka. "Washington's Sweetheart: Nannie Helen Burroughs." PhD diss., Howard University, 2008.

Easter, Opal V. *Nannie Helen Burroughs*. New York: Garland, 1995.

"Equal Salaries for Teachers." *The Crisis: A Record of the Darker Races* 47, no. 1 (January 1940): 10.

Faderman, Lillian J. "Surpassing the Love of Men Revisited." *Harvard Gay and Lesbian Review* 6, no. 2 (1999): 26.

Foner, Philip. *Organized Labor and the Black Worker, 1619–1981*. Chicago: Haymarket, 2017.

Frye, Jocelyn. "On the Frontlines at Work and at Home: The Disproportionate Economic Effects of the Coronavirus Pandemic on Women of Color." *Center for American Progress Report*, April 23, 2020.

Garrett-Scott, Shennette. *Banking on Freedom: Black Women in U.S. Finance before the New Deal*. New York: Columbia University Press, 2019.

Gates, Henry Louis, Jr. "W. E. B. Du Bois and the Encyclopedia Africana." *Annals of the American Academy of Political and Social Science* 568, no. 1 (March 2000): 203.

Gates, Henry Louis, Jr., and Evelyn Brooks Higginbotham, eds. *Harlem Renaissance Lives from the African American National Biography*. New York: Oxford University Press, 2009.

Giddings, Paula. *In Search of Sisterhood: Delta Sigma Theta and the Challenges of the Black Sorority Movement.* New York: Amistad, 1988.

Gilkes, Cheryl Townsend. *"If It Wasn't for the Women...": Black Women's Experience and Womanist Culture in Church and Community.* New York: Orbis, 2001.

Givens, Jarvis. *Fugitive Pedagogy: Carter G. Woodson and the Art of Black Teaching.* Cambridge, MA: Harvard University Press, 2021.

Graves, Kelisha, ed. *Nannie Helen Burroughs: A Documentary Portrait of an Early Civil Rights Pioneer, 1900–1959.* Notre Dame, IN: University of Notre Dame Press, 2022.

Gray, Derek, and George Derek Musgrove, eds. *The NAACP in Washington, D.C.: From Jim Crow to Home Rule.* Charleston, SC: The History Press, 2022.

Greene, Lorenzo J., and Carter G. Woodson. *The Negro Wage Earner.* Washington, DC: Association for the Study of Negro Life and History, 1930.

Guy-Sheftall, Beverly. *Daughters of Sorrow: Attitudes towards Black Women, 1880–1920.* New York: Carlson, 1990.

———, ed. *Words of Fire: An Anthology of African-American Feminist Thought.* New York: The New Press, 1995.

Haley, Sarah. *No Mercy Here: Gender, Punishment, and the Making of Jim Crow Modernity.* Chapel Hill: University of North Carolina Press, 2016.

Hammond, Lily Hardy. *In the Vanguard of a Race.* New York: Council of Women for Home Missions and Missionary Education Movement of the US and Canada, 1922.

Harley, Sharon. "Beyond the Classroom: The Organizational Lives of Black Female Educators in the District of Columbia, 1890–1930." *Journal of Negro Education* 51, no. 3 (1982): 254–65.

———. "Nannie Helen Burroughs: 'The Black Goddess of Liberty.'" *Journal of Negro History* 81, no. 1–4 (Winter–Fall 1996): 62–71.

Harris, LaShawn. *Sex Workers, Psychics, and Numbers Runners: Black Women in New York City's Underground Economy.* Urbana: University of Illinois Press, 2016.

Harris, Sheena. *Margaret Murray Washington: The Life and Times of a Career Clubwoman.* Knoxville: University of Tennessee Press, 2021.

Harrison, Earl L. *The Dream and the Dreamer: An Abbreviated Story of the Life of Nannie Helen Burroughs and the National Trade and Professional School for Women and Girls.* Washington, DC: Nannie Helen Burroughs Literature Foundation, 1956.

Hartman, Saidiya. *Wayward Lives, Beautiful Experiments: Intimate Histories of Social Upheaval.* New York: W. W. Norton, 2019.

Haynes, George Edmund. *The Trend of the Races.* New York: Council of Women for Home Missions and Missionary Education Movement of the US and Canada, 1922.

Higginbotham, Evelyn Brooks. *Righteous Discontent: The Women's Movement in the Black Baptist Church, 1880–1920.* Cambridge: Harvard University Press, 1993.

Hill, Errol G., and James V. Hatch, eds. *A History of African American Theatre.* New York: Cambridge University Press, 2003.

Hill, Ruth Edmonds, ed. *The Black Women Oral History Project: From the Arthur and Elizabeth Schlesinger Library on the History of Women in America, Radcliffe College.* London: Meckler, 1991.

Hine, Darlene Clark, Wilma King, and Linda Reed, eds. *We Specialize in the Wholly Impossible: A Reader in Black Women's History.* New York: New York University Press, 1995.

Hobson, E. C., and C. E. Hopkins. *A Report Concerning the Colored Women of the South.* Baltimore, MD: Trustees of the John F. Slater Fund, 1896. Available via the Library of Congress, https: //www.loc.gov/resource/lcrbmrp.t2201/ ?st=gallery.

Holder, Michelle. "The 'Double Gap' and the Bottom Line: African American Women's Wage Gap and Corporate Profits." *The Roosevelt Institute*, March 31, 2020.

Hoover, Herbert. Message to the Committee on Negro Housing of the White House Conference on Home Building and Home Ownership. In *The American Presidency Project*, edited by Gerhard Peters and John T. Woolley. https://www.presidency.ucsb.edu/documents/message-the-committee -negro-housing-the-white-house-conference-home-building-and-home.

Hornsby-Gutting, Angela. "'Woman's Work': Race, Foreign Missions, and Respectability in the National Training School for Women and Girls." *Journal of Women's History* 31, no. 1 (Spring 2019): 37–61.

Jackson, Shanita S. "To Struggle and Battle and Overcome: The Educational Thought of Nannie Helen Burroughs, 1865–1961." PhD diss., University of California, Berkeley, 2015.

Johnson, Charles S. *Negro Housing: Report of the Committee on Negro Housing, Nannie H. Burroughs, Chairman, Prepared for the Committee.* Washington, DC: National Capital Press: 1932.

———, ed. *Opportunity: Journal of Negro Life* 1 (1923).

———. *Opportunity: Journal of Negro Life* 2 (1924).

Johnson, Karen A. "On Classical versus Vocational Training: The Educational Ideas of Anna Julia Cooper and Nannie Helen Burroughs." In *Education as Freedom: African American Educational Thought and Activism*, edited by Noel Anderson and Haroon Kharem, 47–68. Lanham, MD: Lexington, 2009.

———. *Uplifting the Women and the Race: The Educational Philosophies and Social Activism of Anna Julia Cooper and Nannie Helen Burroughs.* New York: Routledge, 2000.

Jordan, Lewis Garnett. *Up the Ladder in Foreign Missions.* Nashville: National Baptist Publishing Board, 1939.

Kelley, Blair L. M. *Black Folk: The Roots of the Black Working Class*. New York: Liveright, 2023.

Kelley, Robin D. G. *Freedom Dreams: The Black Radical Imagination*. Boston: Beacon, 2003.

Kersten, Andrew Edmund. *A. Philip Randolph: A Life in the Vanguard*. New York: Rowman & Littlefield, 2015.

King, Martin Luther, Jr. *All Labor Has Dignity*. Edited by Michael Honey. Boston: Beacon, 2012.

King-Calnek, Judith E. "John Mercer Langston and the Shaping of African American Education in the Nineteenth Century," 27–47. In *Education As Freedom: African American Educational Thought and Activism*, edited by Noel Anderson and Haroon Kharem, 27–47. Lanham, MD: Lexington, 2009.

Krasner, David. *A Beautiful Pageant: African American Theatre, Drama, and Performance in the Harlem Renaissance, 1910–1927*. New York: Palgrave Macmillan, 2002.

La Follette, Belle Case. "The Color Line." *La Follette's Magazine* 5, no. 34 (August 23, 1913): 6–7.

LeConté, J. Dill, Mercedez Dunn, Mona Taylor Phillips, Nzali Scales, and Cynthia Neal Spence. "Learning, Teaching, Re-membering and Enacting Black Feminist Sociology at a Black Women's College: A Love Letter to One Another." In *Black Feminist Sociology: Perspectives and Praxis*, edited by Zakiya Luna and Whitney N. Laster Pirtle, 123–26. New York: Routledge, 2022.

Leslie, Lavonne, ed. *The History of the National Association of Colored Women's Clubs, Inc.: A Legacy of Service*. Bloomington: Xlibris, 2012.

Levine, Susan. *Labor's True Woman: Carpet Weavers, Industrialization, and Labor Reform in the Gilded Age*. Philadelphia: Temple University Press, 1984.

Lewis, Andrea D., and Nicole A. Taylor, eds. *Unsung Legacies of Educators and Events in African American Education*. Cham, Switzerland: Palgrave Macmillan, 2019.

Lindsey, Treva. *Colored No More: Reinventing Black Womanhood in Washington, DC*. Champaign: University of Illinois Press, 2017.

Locke, Alain, ed. *The New Negro: An Interpretation*. New York: Albert and Charles Boni, 1925.

May, Vivian M. *Anna Julia Cooper, Visionary Black Feminist: A Critical Introduction*. New York: Routledge, 2007.

McCluskey, Audrey Thomas. *A Forgotten Sisterhood: Pioneering Black Women Educators and Activists in the Jim Crow South*. New York: Rowman & Littlefield, 2014.

———. "Setting the Standard: Mary Church Terrell's Last Campaign for Social Justice." *Black Scholar* 29, no. 2–3 (1999): 47–53.

"Median Salaries of Teachers in Specified Classes of Schools in the United

States, 1930–1935." In *Handbook of Labor Statistics, 1936*. Washington, DC: US Government Printing Office, 1936.

Miller, Kelly. "Surplus Negro Women." In *Race Adjustment: Essays on the Negro in America*, 168–78. New York: Neale, 1908.

Moore, Jacqueline. *Leading the Race: The Transformation of the Black Elite in the Nation's Capital, 1880–1920*. Charlottesville: University of Virginia Press, 1999.

Moore, Linda S. "Women and the Emergence of the NAACP." *Journal of Social Work Education* 49 (2013): 476–89.

Murray, Alana D. *The Development of the Alternative Black Curriculum, 1890–1940*. New York: Palgrave Macmillan, 2018.

Murray, Pauli. "Jane Crow and the Law: Sex Discrimination and Title VII." *George Washington Review* 34, no. 2 (December 1965): 232–56.

Murphy, Larry G., J. Gordon Melton, and Gary L. Ward, eds. *Encyclopedia of African American Religions*. New York: Routledge, 2011.

Murphy, Mary-Elizabeth B. *Jim Crow Capital: Women and Black Freedom Struggles in Washington, D.C., 1920–1945*. Chapel Hill: University of North Carolina Press, 2018.

Nadasen, Premilla. *Household Workers Unite: The Untold Story of African American Women Who Built a Movement*. Boston: Beacon, 2015.

National Baptist Convention. *Journal of the Twentieth Annual Session of the National Baptist Convention, Held in Richmond, Virginia, September 12–17, 1900*. Nashville: National Baptist Publishing Board, 1900.

———. *Journal of the Twenty-Ninth Annual Session of the National Baptist Convention Held with the Baptist Churches, September 15–20, 1909*. Nashville: National Baptist Publishing Board, 1910.

———. *Journal of the Thirty-Sixth Session: Journal of the National Baptist Convention, Held with the Baptist Churches, Savannah, GA, September 6–11, 1917*. Nashville: National Baptist Publishing Board, 1917.

———. *Journal of the Fortieth Annual Session of the National Baptist Convention*. Nashville: National Baptist Publishing Board, 1920.

———. *Twentieth Annual Session of the Woman's Convention*. Nashville: National Baptist Publishing Board, 1920.

National Domestic Workers Alliance. "Domestic Workers Bill of Rights." https://www.domesticworkers.org/programs-and-campaigns/developing-policy-solutions/domestic-workers-bill-of-rights/.

National Negro Business League. *Annual Report of the Sixteenth Session and the Fifteenth Anniversary Convention Held at Boston, Massachusetts, August 18, 19, 20, 1915*. Nashville: African ME Sunday School Union, 1915.

———. *Report of the Tenth Annual Convention of the National Negro Business League Held In Louisville, Kentucky. August 18–20, 1909*. Nashville: AME Sunday School Union, 1909.

National Register of Historic Places. "Trades Hall." https://npgallery.nps.gov /NRHP/AssetDetail?assetID=3fb95ebb-5d12-48f2-80b5-5802d98bda9d.

Nembhard, Jessica. *Collective Courage: A History of African American Cooperative Economic Thought and Practice.* University Park: Pennsylvania State University Press, 2014.

Orleck, Annelise. *Common Sense and a Little Fire: Women and Working Class Politics in the United States, 1900–1965.* Chapel Hill: University of North Carolina Press, 1995.

———. *Storming Caesars Palace: How Black Mothers Fought Their Own War on Poverty.* Boston: Beacon, 2005.

Ovington, Mary White. *Half a Man: The Status of the Negro in New York.* New York: Longmans, Green, 1911.

Parker, Alison M. *Unceasing Militant: The Life of Mary Church Terrell.* Chapel Hill: University of North Carolina Press, 2020.

Penn, Irvine Garland, and John Wesley Edward Bowen, eds. *The United Negro: His Problems and His Progress.* Atlanta: D. E. Luther, 1902.

Peyton, Atholene. *The Peytonia Cook Book.* Louisville, KY, 1906.

Phillips-Cunningham, Danielle. *Putting Their Hands on Race: Irish Immigrant and Southern Black Domestic Workers.* New Brunswick, NJ: Rutgers University Press, 2019.

Phillips-Cunningham, Danielle, and Veronica Popp. "Labor Organizer Nannie Helen Burroughs and Her National Training School for Women and Girls." *Journal of Women, Gender, and Families of Color* 10, no. 1 (Spring 2022): 9–40.

Pickens, William. *Nannie Helen Burroughs and the School of the 3 B's.* New York: 1921.

Pilgrim, Danya M. "Masters of a Craft: Philadelphia's Black Public Waiters, 1820–1850." *Pennsylvania Magazine of History and Biography* 142, no. 3 (October 2018): 269–83.

Pitts, Steven C. "The National Black Worker Center Project: Grappling with the Power-Building Imperative." In *No One Size Fits All: Worker Organization, Policy, and Movement in a New Economic Age,* edited by Janice Fine, Linda Burnham, Kati Griffith, Minsun Ji, Victor Narro, and Steven Pitts, 115–38. Champaign: University of Illinois Press, 2018.

Pius, N. H. *An Outline of Baptist History: A Splendid Reference Work for Busy Workers, a Record of the Struggles and Triumphs of Baptist Pioneers.* Nashville: National Baptist Publishing Board, 1911.

Popp, Veronica, and Danielle Phillips-Cunningham, "Justice for All: The Womanist Labor Rhetoric of Nannie Helen Burroughs," *Peithos: Journal of the Coalition of Feminist Scholars in the History of Rhetoric and Composition* 23, no. 2 (Spring 2021).

Preston, Ashley Robertson. *Mary McLeod Bethune, the Pan-Africanist.* Gainesville: University of Florida Press, 2023.

Proceedings of the Women's Industrial Conference. Washington, DC: US Government Printing Office, 1923.

Pryde, Marion J. "My Personal and Family Reminiscences of Dr. Carter Goodwin Woodson." *Journal of Negro History* 76, no. 1–4 (Winter–Autumn 1991): 101–5.

Purkiss, Ava. *Fit Citizens: A History of Black Women's Exercise from Post-Reconstruction to Postwar America.* Chapel Hill: University of North Carolina Press, 2023.

Pursell, Caroll. *A Hammer in Their Hands: A Documentary History of Technology and the African-American Experience.* Cambridge: Massachusetts Institute of Technology, 2005.

"Remarks by President Biden at Signing of an Executive Order on Racial Equity." White House, January 26, 2021. https://www.whitehouse.gov/briefing-room /speeches-remarks/2021/01/26/remarks-by-president-biden-at-signing-of -an-executive-order-on-racial-equity/.

Richardson, Clement. "Lewis Garnett Jordan." In *The National Cyclopedia of the Race, Volume 1.* Montgomery, AL: National Publishing, 1919,

Rief, Michelle. "Thinking Locally, Acting Globally: The International Agenda of African American Clubwomen, 1880–1940." *Journal of African American History* 89, no. 3 (Summer 2004): 203–22.

Roberts, Blain. *Pageants, Parlors, and Pretty Women: Race and Beauty in the Twentieth-Century South.* Chapel Hill: University of North Carolina Press, 2014.

Roberts, W. Lewis. "Property Rights of Married Women in Kentucky." *Kentucky Law Journal* 11, no. 1 (1922): 1–4.

Robinson, Henry S. "Julia Mason Layton, 1859–1926," *Negro History Bulletin* 45, no. 1 (January–March 1982): 17–20.

Rouse, Jacqueline Anne. "Out of the Shadow of Tuskegee: Margaret Murray Washington, Social Activism, and Race Vindication." *Journal of Negro History* 81, no. 1–4 (Winter–Fall 1996): 31–46.

Ruble, Blair A. *Washington's U Street: A Biography.* Baltimore, MD: Johns Hopkins University Press, 2012.

Second Annual Report of the Minimum Wage Board of the District of Columbia: For the Year Ending December 31, 1919. Washington, DC: US Government Printing Office, 1920.

Smith, Susan L. *Sick and Tired of Being Sick and Tired: Black Women's Health Activism in America, 1890–1950.* Philadelphia: University of Pennsylvania Press, 1995.

Stein, Melissa N. *Measuring Manhood: Race and the Science of Masculinity, 1830–1934.* Minneapolis: University of Minnesota Press, 2015.

Stewart, R. R. S. "Designing a Campus for African-American Females: The National Training School for Women and Girls, 1907–1964, and the Making of a D.C. Neighborhood." *International Journal of Interdisciplinary Social Sciences* 5, no. 2 (2011): 139–82.

Stokes, Anson Phelps. *Negro Status and Race Relations in the United States, 1911–1946: The Thirty-Five Year Report of the Phelps-Stokes Fund.* New York: Phelps-Stokes Fund, 1948.

Taylor, Traki. "'Womanhood Glorified': Nannie Helen Burroughs and the National Training School for Woman and Girls, Inc., 1909–1961." *Journal of African-American History* 87 (Autumn 2002): 390–402.

Trotter, Joe William, Jr. *Workers on Arrival: Black Labor in the Making of America.* Oakland: University of California Press, 2019.

United States City Directories, 1822–1995. Washington, District of Columbia, City Directory, 1892.

United States City Directories, 1822–1995. Washington, District of Columbia, City Directory, 1886.

US Bureau of the Census. *Ninth Census of the United States, 1870.* Washington, DC: Government Printing Office, 1872.

US Bureau of the Census. *Tenth Census of the United States, 1880.* Washington, DC: Government Printing Office, 1883.

US Bureau of the Census. *Twelfth Census of the United States, 1900.* Washington, DC: Government Printing Office, 1902.

US Bureau of the Census. *Thirteenth Census of the United States, 1910.* Washington, DC: Government Printing Office, 1911.

US Bureau of the Census. *Fourteenth Census of the United States, 1920.* Washington, DC: Government Printing Office, 1922.

US Bureau of the Census. *Fifteenth Census of the United States, 1930.* Washington, DC: Government Printing Office, 1931.

US Department of Labor. *Monthly Labor Review, June 1921.* Washington, DC: US Government Printing Office, 1921.

US Department of Labor, Women in Industry Service. *First Annual Report of the Director of Women in Industry Service for the Fiscal Year Ended June 30, 1919.* Washington, DC: Government Printing Office, 1919.

von Ballmoos, Agnes Nebo. *The Role of Folksongs in Liberian Society.* Bloomington: Indiana University Press, 1975.

Vapnek, Lara. *Breadwinners: Working Women and Economic Independence, 1890–1920.* Urbana: University of Illinois Press, 2009.

———. "The 1919 International Congress of Working Women: Transnational Debates on the Woman Worker." *Journal of Women's History* 26, no. 1 (2014): 160–84.

Visser-Maessen, Laura. *Robert Parris Moses: A Life in Civil Rights and Leadership at the Grassroots.* Chapel Hill: University of North Carolina Press, 2016.

Walker, Susannah. "'Independent Livings' or 'No Bed of Roses': How Race and Class Shaped Beauty Culture as an Occupation for African American Women from the 1920s to the 1960s." *Journal of Women's History* 20, no. 3 (2008): 60–83.

Wallach, Jennifer. *Every Nation Has Its Dish.* Chapel Hill: University of North Carolina Press, 2019.

Washington, Sondra. *The Story of Nannie Helen Burroughs: We Specialize in the Wholly Impossible.* Birmingham: Women's Missionary Union, 2006.

Weiss, Ellen. *Robert R. Taylor and Tuskegee: An African American Architect Designs for Booker T. Washington.* Athens: University of Georgia Press, 2012.

Williams, Fannie Barrier. "The Club Movement among Colored Women of America." In *A New Negro for a New Century: An Accurate and Up-to-Date Record of the Upward Struggles of the Negro Race,* edited by Booker T. Washington, 378–428. Chicago: American Publishing House, 1900.

———. "The Problem of Employment for Negro Women." *Southern Workman* 32, no. 9 (September 1903): 432–37.

Wilson, Francille Rusan. *The Segregated Scholars: Black Social Scientists and the Creation of Black Labor Studies, 1890–1950.* Charlottesville: University of Virginia Press, 2006.

Wolcott, Victoria W. "'Bible, Bath and Broom': Nannie Helen Burroughs's National Training School and African-American Racial Uplift." *Journal of Women's History* 9, no. 1 (1997): 88–110.

Woodson, Carter G. "The Negro Washerwoman, a Vanishing Figure." *Journal of Negro History* 15, no. 3 (July 1930): 269–77.

Wooten, Charles W., and Barbara E. Kemmerer. "The Changing Genderization of Bookkeeping in the United States, 1870–1930." *Business History Review* 70, no. 2 (Winter 1996): 541–86.

Yellin, Eric S. *Racism in the Nation's Service: Government Workers and the Color Line in Woodrow Wilson's America.* Chapel Hill: University of North Carolina Press.

Zax, David. "The Scurlock Studio: Picture of Prosperity." *Smithsonian Magazine,* February 2010. https://www.smithsonianmag.com/travel/the-scurlock-studio-picture-of-prosperity-4869533/.

INDEX

ABOUT THE AUTHOR

Danielle Phillips-Cunningham is an associate professor in the Department of Labor Studies and Employment Relations at Rutgers University–New Brunswick. She is the recipient of the National Women's Studies Association's Sara A. Whaley Book Prize for *Putting Their Hands on Race: Irish Immigrant and Southern Black Domestic Workers* (Rutgers University Press, 2020). Her articles about Nannie Helen Burroughs and women's labor history more broadly have appeared in the *Washington Post*, the Library of Congress blog, and academic journals, including *Signs: Journal of Women and Culture in Society, Women's History Review*, and the *Journal of Women, Gender, and Families of Color*. Phillips-Cunningham is also a co–principal investigator of Quakertown Stories, a Texas African American public history and curriculum project funded by the National Endowment for the Humanities. Her coauthored op-eds with Quakertown descendants were published by the *Washington Post*.

343